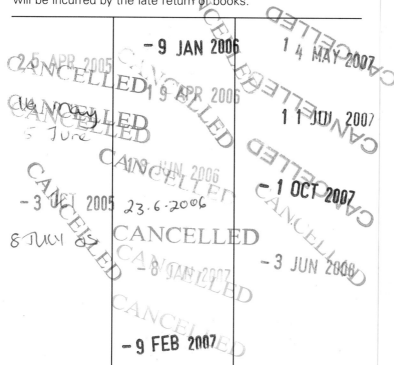

ICT and Language Learning: Integrating Pedagogy and Practice

Edited by Angela Chambers,
Jean E. Conacher and
Jeannette Littlemore

THE UNIVERSITY
OF BIRMINGHAM

UNIVERSITY PRESS

Copyright © Angela Chambers, Jean E. Conacher and Jeannette Littlemore, 2004

First published in the United Kingdom by The University of Birmingham Press, University of Birmingham, Edgbaston, Birmingham, BI5 2TT, UK.

ISBN 1-902459-50-4

British Library Cataloguing in Publication Data
A CIP catalogue entry for this book is available from the British Library

Printed in Great Britain

Contents

Acknowledgements ·

The editors would like to acknowledge the invaluable assistance of the following colleagues in the refereeing of the chapters included in this volume:

Terry Atkinson, University of Bristol
Prof. Dr phil. Uwe Bellmann, Hochschule für Technik, Wirtschaft und Kultur Leipzig
Dr Jean-Claude Bertin, Université du Havre
Françoise Blin, Dublin City University
Professor Graham Davies, Free-lance Educational Consultant
Professor Susan Hunston, University of Birmingham
Sake Jager, Rijksuniversiteit Groningen
Chris Kennedy, University of Birmingham
Dominic McEvoy, National Centre for Technology in Education, Ireland
Valère Meus, Universiteit Gent
Dr Liam Murray, University of Limerick
Dr Joseph Rézeau, Université de Rennes II
Mary Ruane, University College Dublin
Professor Dr Bernd Rüschoff , Universität Essen
Ray Satchell, University of Bristol
Dr Mathias Schulze, University of Waterloo
Dr Klaus Schwienhorst, Trinity College Dublin

The editors would like to acknowledge the funding provided by the European Commission for the TALLENT project, which provided the impetus for the writing of this book. They are also indebted to Brian O'Driscoll, Kirstie Raby and Clive Earls for their assistance in the final editing process, and to Gráinne Farren for the index.

Contributors

Richard Cauldwell is the proprietor of *speechinaction*. He is an author and publisher of electronic publications relating to the teaching of listening and pronunciation in the field of English as a Second/Foreign Language. His speciality is in exploiting recordings of spontaneous speech for academic, teacher-training, and classroom purposes. His 2002 publication, *Streaming Speech: Listening and Pronunciation for Advanced Learners of English*, was shortlisted for the 2003 BAAL Book Prize.

Angela Chambers is professor of applied languages and director of the Centre for Applied Language Studies at the University of Limerick, Ireland. She is editor, with Graham Davies, of *ICT and Language Learning: A European Perspective* (Lisse: Swets and Zeitlinger, 2001) and author of a number of articles on ICT and language learning. Her current research interests include corpora and concordancing, particularly the role of corpus analysis skills in developing writing skills.

Jean Conacher is senior lecturer in German and associate director of the Centre for Applied Language Studies at the University of Limerick, Ireland. She is author of a number of articles on the role of ICT in language learning. Her current research focuses on the interplay between learners, technologies and new language-learning environments.

Sake Jager is director of the Centre for ICT and Learning at the Faculty of Arts at the University of Groningen, the Netherlands. He has published several articles on the use of new technologies in language learning. His current research is on SLA and language-learning methodologies in computer-assisted language learning contexts.

Victoria Kelly is a PhD student at the University of Limerick, Ireland. Her thesis involves the analysis of a one-million-word corpus of contemporary written French and the subsequent development of language-learning applications for advanced learners of French. She is the author of two articles and one book chapter focusing on the use of corpora in language learning. Her current research interests include corpora and concordancing, with a particular interest in the use of corpora in language learning.

Jeannette Littlemore is a lecturer in English for Academic Purposes at the University of Birmingham, UK. She has taught and lectured in Spain, Japan and Belgium. She has written a number of articles on individual differences in second language acquisition, and on the role of ICT in language learning. Her current research interests include learner autonomy, figurative thought and language learning, the role of ICT in language learning, and individual differences in second language acquisition.

Freda Mishan is a post-doctoral fellow in the Department of Languages and Cultural Studies, University of Limerick, Ireland. Her research interests include the use of ICT, authentic texts and culture in language learning. She has contributed to English language courseware and has two articles in press in the area of ICT and authenticity in language learning. Her book, *Designing Authenticity into Language Learning Materials* (Bristol: Intellect), based on her PhD thesis, is forthcoming in 2004.

Siobhán Murphy is senior administrator at the University of Limerick Language Centre. Her previous position in the Language Resource Area involved working with IT in language teaching and learning.

Liam Murray lectures in French at the University of Limerick. He has been conducting research in CALL since 1989 beginning with hypertextual studies and continuing with courseware evaluation. He is the author of a number of articles on CALL evaluation and integration, and his current research interests also include machine and human language learning, automated summarisation techniques in language acquisition and text types.

David Oakey is a lecturer in English Language at the University of Birmingham. He has taught at schools and universities in Turkey and the UK. He currently gives classes in English for Academic Purposes (EAP) and runs an MA module in Computer-Assisted Language Learning. He has published on using computers to investigate multi-word items in academic discourse, and he is also interested in how the Internet can be used for teaching EAP.

Robert O'Dowd has taught English as a Foreign Language in various countries, including Hungary, Ireland, Spain and Germany. He recently completed his PhD on the development of intercultural competence in language learners through the use of networked technologies. He lectures in EFL at the University of León in Spain and also works on the development of classroom software for Cornselsen Publishing in Germany.

Bernd Rüschoff is chair and head of the Didactics Section of the English Department at Duisburg-Essen University, Germany. His research focuses on applied linguistics, second language acquisition and technology-enhanced language learning (TELL). He has been involved in a number of national and international research and development projects dealing with TELL, including projects supported by the European Union, and has contributed to a variety of Council of Europe activities. He has published widely in the above fields and acted as a consultant for both national and international institutions.

Peppi Taalas works as a researcher at the Centre for Applied Language Studies at the University of Jyväskylä, Finland. She is involved in the development of the Finnish virtual university and various staff development programmes. Her current research interests are learning interaction in virtual environments, change in learning and teaching cultures, teacher roles and attitudes in technology-enhanced language learning settings.

Thomas Vogel is the director for the Foreign Language Center at the Viadrina European University in Frankfurt (Oder), Germany. His research interests focus on second language acquisition, intercultural communication, teaching methodology, and IT in language teaching.

Introduction

Angela Chambers, Jean E. Conacher and Jeannette Littlemore

The increasing availability of computer-based applications for language learning has created a new environment for language learners and teachers, one which can be seen as either exciting and challenging, or alternatively confusing and threatening. On the one hand, there is a need for guidance on which tools have the greatest potential, while on the other, it is crucial that these tools are integrated into the language-learning process on a sound pedagogical foundation. This book aims to provide language teachers and trainers with a guide, in both practical and pedagogical contexts, to the effective integration of Information and Communications Technologies (ICT) into language teaching and learning, both inside and outside the classroom. It also aims to serve as an introduction to key areas in ICT for postgraduate students in applied linguistics and related disciplines, to introduce them to research and practice in new areas, and thus encourage further research and development in these areas.

It has long been recognised that there is a pressing need for research, both theoretical and empirical, to underpin developments in ICT and language learning, or, to put it more precisely, that practical developments should not be technology-driven, but rather theory- and pedagogy-driven (Little, 1998: 128). Indeed, alongside applied research projects, one finds a more or less continuous questioning of the very nature of computer-assisted language learning (CALL) and, in particular, of the nature of research in CALL (see, for example, Chapelle, 1989; Levy, 1997; Garrett, 1998; Davies, 2001). It is for these reasons that, despite the practical focus of this book, the contributors have ensured that each chapter situates the topic firmly in the context of the relevant research and pedagogy. A further common thread running through the volume is the recognition of the centrality of learner autonomy in language learning today (Holec, 1981; Little, 1991; Benson and Voller, 1997; Benson, 2001) and its theoretical and practical implications for self-directed language learning, in terms of individual responsibility for learning, informed decision-making, and the changing dynamic of the language-learning environment (see, for example,

Holec, 1988; Dam, 1994; van Lier, 1996; Sinclair *et al.*, 2000). In developing these arguments, recent studies have also begun to explore the very nature of language, and particularly literacy, in a global networked world, with an emphasis on the need to develop multiliteracies (Kasper, 2000), in particular electronic literacy, defined as 'knowing how to *select* and *use* tools for communication, construction, research and autonomous learning' (Shetzer, 1998; see also Warschauer, 1999). This volume aims to help both teacher and learner integrate the development of such electronic literacy into the broader linguistic and socio-cultural framework of the language-learning process.

The first three chapters focus on the contexts of language learning which have changed in fundamental ways as a result of theoretical, pedagogical, and technological developments in recent decades. In Chapter 1, **Conacher, Taalas and Vogel** review current understandings of language learning and learner autonomy, before examining the relationship of such understandings to the changing dynamics of both local and global learning environments. The authors explore how the greater integration of ICT into people's lives at a global level might be mirrored at the local language-learning level to support the development of multiliteracies. They conclude that now more than ever there is a need for pedagogically informed decision-making on the part of teachers and learners as to where, and how, existing and future forms of ICT best fit into the broader picture of the learner's world and language-learning needs.

Following on from this, **Jager** investigates the world of learning management systems, which aim to provide a rich, strongly integrated electronic learning environment where educational content can be delivered interactively within the context of a virtual classroom. Using an imaginary scenario, Jager begins by outlining how such a learning management system might be exploited in one specific language-learning context at university level. In his analysis of this scenario, the author explores both the positive and negative aspects of a wide range of institutional, pedagogical, and technical issues. While conceptually such learning management systems offer exciting new possibilities for framing the way in which language learning takes place, Jager sounds a note of caution. Software developers and language teachers, he argues, could learn much from the recent problems facing e-commerce. Only if Web-based language learning is rooted in sound pedagogical theory and practice will it have any chance of long-term success.

Drawing both on their collective experience of a variety of language resource centres (LRCs), here defined broadly to encompass anything from the corner of a library in a school or college to the virtual centres now emerging on the Internet, **Conacher and Murphy** examine both the theoretical and practical issues surrounding the establishment and evolution of language resource centres and explore the extent to which any language resource centre does in fact reflect the interplay of policy, pedagogical theory, and practice predominant in its local context. They begin with an account of the main types of language resource centres currently in existence, examining both their political and pedagogical rationale, before asking the question whether, despite their diversity, there are any factors common to successful LRCs which those wishing to establish such a centre might take into account. In their conclusion, they argue that any language resource centre with the right institutional support has the potential to play a pivotal role in the development of language-learning policy and practice at all levels within its host institution and beyond, and, in so doing, to feed into broader educational discussions on lifelong learning, flexible educational modes, and new learning environments.

In the remaining seven chapters, the focus lies on the integration of ICT in language teaching and learning. In turn, they cover those technological developments which, in the view of the editors and contributors, possess the greatest potential for enhancing the quality of language learning and teaching, which have been the subject of considerable innovation and advances in recent years, and which remain at the forefront of developments. The chapters not only combine theoretical discussions and practical examples, but also provide suggestions for further reading and future areas of empirical research.

In Chapter 4, **Murray** deals with evaluation criteria, an area of fundamental importance which has long been neglected, but is now increasingly receiving attention. Including the evaluation of CALL and WELL (Web-Enhanced Language Learning) software, the chapter is aimed at secondary and tertiary teachers of a second or foreign language who are intending, through choice or obligation, to investigate the possible uses and integration of these types of software into their respective curricula. With the rising tide of Web-based CALL materials of both a dedicated and coincidental nature, modern foreign language teachers increasingly need the appropriate evaluative tools to help them accept or reject these materials and give good reasons for doing so. Despite the recent criticisms of checklist criteria, the author argues in favour of the strict use of guidelines based on a solid theoretical background.

In Chapter 5, on the Internet, **Littlemore and Oakey** provide an overview of the ways in which the Internet can be used by learners to carry out meaningful, authentic tasks in the target language, the advantage of such authenticity being that it is likely to lead to increased levels of motivation and autonomy. They begin by looking at some of the main functions of the Internet, including e-mail, discussion lists, and chat rooms, and suggest ways in which these can be used to promote language learning. The chapter then focuses on the World Wide Web, and the authors comment on a number of sites explicitly devoted to language teaching. Finally, the chapter reviews three 'practical ideas' books that have recently appeared on the market, all suggesting ways in which

Web sites which are not specifically intended for language learners can be used to promote language learning. The authors discuss ways in which ideas from these books could be adapted to different language learning situations.

In Chapter 6, **Mishan** extends the potential of Web-based instruction to the authoring of Web sites by learners themselves, proposing a task-based framework in which language learners collaborate in the conception, creation, and maintenance of a Web site. The author first bases learner Web-authoring within the context of emerging accounts of work being done in this area, and indicates links to relevant research in second language acquisition. The learner Web-authoring task is then discussed in detail. This uses an iterative, three-stage framework which integrates reflective, evaluative, and language awareness-raising sessions, and subsumes essential conceptual and technical aspects of Web page creation. This is followed by an assessment of the language-learning potential of the methodology, using as criteria factors known to be essential to language acquisition such as motivation, confidence, and authentic language input and output. The conclusion looks to the potential for development of learner Web-authoring in view of the ever-increasing usability of Web-tools and the general shift in pedagogical orientation from teacher to student-directed learning.

In the seventh chapter, **O'Dowd** examines the ways in which intercultural e-mail exchanges can be used to promote language learning. Listing a variety of tasks that teachers can adapt for their own classes, he then identifies some of the key learning opportunities (both linguistic and cultural) that these activities are able to provide. After establishing a number of prerequisites necessary to ensure that intercultural e-mail exchanges achieve their maximum learning potential, he gives a detailed outline of an ideal procedure for setting up an e-mail exchange project. The chapter is illustrated with numerous examples taken from the author's own experience with intercultural e-mail exchanges. The appendices provide a useful list of sites that can be used to find potential partners, as well as a list of example projects.

In Chapter 8, on authenticity and authoring tools, **Rüschoff** points out that the advent of technology-enhanced learning materials requires a re-thinking of the methodological framework of language learning. Many assume that computer tools will facilitate the implementation of a methodology for language learning which focuses more than in the past on authenticity in contents, context, and task. The author argues that authoring tools are the perfect aid to assist teachers in their 'need to broaden their scope for creative pedagogical ini-tiatives' (Little *et al.*, 1989: 1). The chapter provides an overview of authoring tools for the creation of tutorial and exploratory exercises, as well as cognitive tools and text processing tools. With such tools, teachers can prepare tailor-made exercises for their classes, put together worksheets and create tasks which permit the learners to actively and often consciously explore the target language. Such tasks and learning projects will help to develop learners' language awareness and understanding of the structure and functionality of the target language. The potential of such tools when used by the teacher is described, together with examples of good practice. In addition, the chapter considers the possibility of placing authoring tools in the hands of the learner with the aim of enhancing the language learner's role as an experimenter and researcher in the classroom by means of authoring tasks.

In Chapter 9, **Chambers and Kelly** argue that the increasing availability of text corpora and of concordancing software provide an ideal environment for the development of learner autonomy. After providing information on the availability of large corpora and the possibility of creating small corpora, the authors review the many uses of both types of corpora, including the acquisition of vocabulary and grammar, the use of a corpus as an aid for the translator, the relevance of specialised corpora in Languages for Specific Purposes, and the potential of concordancing software for the study of literary and non-literary texts. Their conclusion assesses the implications of these developments for the changing roles of teacher and learner.

The topic of **Cauldwell's** Chapter 10 is the pedagogy of listening, an area which, he argues, has been hampered by the traditional association of reading and listening. Cauldwell emphasises that ICT, with its capacity to isolate key moments in recording, is uniquely placed to help students identify and cope with the essential characteristics of speech. With the help of ICT, he claims that it will be possible to revolutionise the way in which listening is taught and predicts a move away from general comprehension tasks, to tasks that specifically help learners to extract meaning from the 'acoustic blur'. The chapter provides examples of ICT-based listening exercises that can help learners appreciate the difference between real speech and the more artificial type of speech that their dictionaries and pronunciation guides might lead them to expect.

The majority of these chapters are drawn from the experience of researchers and course developers who have collaborated closely in a three-year LINGUA A funded project, entitled TALLENT (Teaching And Learning Languages Enhanced by New Technologies). The project involved the development and piloting of a course in ICT and language learning for language teachers and trainers, and revealed both the importance and the challenge of including within a short course not only technical training in the exploitation of the relevant technologies, but also reflection on the pedagogic principles underlying their use, and examples of the application of these principles. Indeed, one of the aims of this book is to provide the project partners with the opportunity to focus in greater detail on the integration of theory and practice than was possible in the limited time available in a short course. Equally, in order to provide a more comprehensive picture of the potential of ICT in language learning, the editors invited a small number of additional contributions. It is hoped that this volume will encourage those involved in language education, whether as teachers, trainers, or students, to see the potential not only for using these technologies in the learning and teaching process, but also, in following in the footsteps of the authors of the individual chapters, using their own experiences as the basis for further empirical research.

Finally, unless otherwise stated all the Web sites referred to in this book were downloaded in the week beginning 14 July 2003, and checked during the editing process (19–21 April 2004).

Bibliography

Benson, P. and P. Voller (eds.) (1997) *Autonomy and Independence in Language Learning.* London and New York: Longman.

Benson, P. (2001) *Teaching and Researching Autonomy in Language Learning.* London and New York: Longman.

Chapelle, C.A. (1989) 'CALL research in the 1980s: Setting the stage for the 1990s'. *CALL Digest,* 5.7, 7–9.

Dam, L. (1994) *From Theory to Classroom Practice.* Dublin: Authentik.

Davies, G. (2001) 'New technologies and language learning: A suitable subject for research?' In A. Chambers and G. Davies (eds.) *ICT and Language Learning: A European Perspective.* Lisse: Swets and Zeitlinger, 13–27.

Garrett, N. (1998) 'Where do research and practice meet? Developing a discipline'. *ReCALL,* 10.1, 7–12.

Holec, H. (1981) *Autonomy in Foreign Language Learning.* Oxford: Pergamon. (First published 1979, Strasbourg: Council of Europe).

Holec, H. (ed.) (1988) *Autonomy and Self-directed Learning: Present Fields of Application.* Strasbourg: Council of Europe.

Kasper, L.F. (2000) 'New technologies, new literacies: Focus discipline research and ESL learning communities'. *Language Learning and Technology,* 4.2, 105–28. Available http://llt.msu.edu/vol4num2/kasper/default.html

Levy, M. (1997) *CALL: Context and Conceptualization.* Oxford: Oxford University Press.

Little, D. (1991) *Learner Autonomy 1. Definitions, Issues and Problems.* Dublin: Authentik.

Little, D. (1998) 'Report on seminar on research in CALL, EUROCALL 97'. *ReCALL,* 10.1, 127–8.

Little, D., Devitt, S. and D. Singleton (1989) *Learning Foreign Languages from Authentic Texts: Theory and Practice.* Dublin: Authentik.

Shetzer, H. (1998) 'Strategies for promoting electronic literacy among students and instructors in IEPs'. Available
http://tc1.hccs.cc.tx.us/iweb/soochow/tesol98/electlit.html

Sinclair, B., McGrath, I. and T. Lamb (eds.) (2000) *Learner Autonomy, Teacher Autonomy: Future Directions*. London and New York: Longman.

van Lier, L. (1996) *Interaction in the Language Curriculum: Awareness, Autonomy and Authenticity*. London and New York: Longman.

Warschauer, M. (1999) *Electronic Literacies: Language, Culture and Power in Online Education*. Mahwah, NJ: Lawrence Erlbaum Associates.

CHANGING CONTEXTS

1 New language learning and teaching environments: How does ICT fit in?

Jean E. Conacher, Peppi Taalas and Thomas Vogel

1. Introduction

Many studies over the past twenty years have attempted to measure the impact of the introduction of new information and communication technologies (ICT) on the second language performance of learners (see, amongst others, Higgins, 1983; Lonergan, 1984; Pennington, 1989; Cobb, 1997; González-Bueno and Pérez, 2000). Such studies have traditionally regarded ICT essentially within Crooks's framework of computer-as-tutor, computer-as-pupil and computer-as-tool, with in each case, the computer and, more recently, broader interpretations of ICT, being placed at the disposal of the teacher and/or learner, to be exploited as effectively as possible in pursuit of a clearly specified goal (Crooks, 1994). Initial emphasis lay on quantitative studies, which testified to potentially increased rates of vocabulary acquisition, improved grammatical accuracy (Cheung and Harrison, 1992) and higher language grades as a result of the careful introduction of ICT into the learning programme. From these developed more sophisticated qualitative research approaches which attempted to explore the interface between ICT for language learning and various aspects of learner motivation and participation (Skinner and Austin, 1999), learning strategies, and learner types (Ulitsky, 2000). Almost simultaneously, studies emerged which explored the potential of ICT in promoting preferred learning approaches such as project-based learning (Debski, 2000) and self-directed learning (Motteram, 1997).

Common to many of these studies is a preoccupation with language learning as an activity which takes place in the classroom, or the self-access area, or the target country, environments which are somehow 'fenced off' from the wider experience of the language learner as an individual within a broader educational and societal culture, shaped both by local, national, and global events, and cultural understandings of reality. While as early as 1980, Breen and Candlin had pointed out that the classroom had its own equally valid authenticity, early studies of the role of ICT in language learning generally confined themselves to an analysis of content and task authenticity, rather than authenticity of experience. More recently, however, authors have begun to explore notions of multiliteracy whereby '[t]o be considered multiliterate, students today must acquire a battery of skills that will enable them to take advantage of the diverse modes of communication made possible by new technologies and to participate in global learning communities' (Kaspar, 2000: 106). The challenge for L2 learners is even greater:

> [They] must acquire linguistic competence in a new language and at the same time develop the cognitive and sociocultural skills necessary to gain access into the social, academic, and workforce environments of the 21st century. They must become functionally literate, able to speak, understand, read, and write [their L2], as well as use [this] to acquire, articulate and expand their knowledge. They must also become academically literate, able to read and understand [...] texts, analyze and respond to those texts through various modes of written and oral discourse, [...] Further, they must become critically literate, [... able] to evaluate the validity and reliability of informational sources [...] Finally, in our digital age of information, students must become electronically literate.
>
> (Kaspar, 2000: 106)

conclusion

The use of ICT in the language-learning process might, therefore, have an impact well beyond the language classroom, as students not only develop linguistic and sociocultural expertise through ICT, but also acquire ICT-related skills through the target language. On this basis, it could equip the individual to 'participate fully in all aspects of modern society' (Kaspar, 2000: 105) within a 'dynamic and ongoing process of perpetual transformation' (Neilson, 1989: 5).

If this interaction of ICT and language learning is to be fully explored, we need to consider how learners learn languages, how they understand and create the world around them, and how these understandings impact upon the teacher–learner relationship within the language-learning process. Only then can we begin to appreciate where, and how, different forms of ICT might fit into the wider picture of the individual learner's world and his/her language-learning experience. This chapter is, therefore, divided into three sections. Firstly, we examine the inter-relationship of second language acquisition theory and developments in ICT; secondly, we explore how current understandings, in particular in relation to autonomy in language learning are manifested in the dynamics of the learning environment and the relationship between teacher, learner, material, and media; finally, we offer suggestions as to how ICT might be integrated into new language-learning and language-teaching environments with the ultimate aim of combining increased linguistic and sociocultural competences with deepening functional, academic, critical, and electronic literacies.

2. The processes of language learning and ICT

It might be argued that developments in technology and language-learning methods have always been linked, not least since Gutenberg's invention of printing by moveable type in the 15th century led, first in Europe and then beyond, to the widespread distribution of text material and an increased emphasis on the written word. However, over the last hundred years this link has developed beyond the physical/product level, as researchers have sought to establish links between technology and learning at a psychological/process level. In many scientific fields there has been an increase in attention paid to the processes of the human mind, not least the processes that enable language acquisition. As technology has become more sophisticated, teachers and researchers have sought ways to tap these developments to support the language-learning process. The relationship between language learning and technology, however, has seldom been an easy one, and announcements heralding the latest technological solution to the challenges faced by language learners are often met with scepticism by language teachers and researchers alike. In this section, it will be argued that the key to integrating ICT into language learning in an informed and potentially successful way lies in our ability to learn from past experiences and current understandings of second language acquisition.

2.1. Learning from the past: One technology – one method

One example cited frequently today as proof of the failure of technology in language learning is the language laboratory, which was introduced into many schools throughout the 1960s and 1970s. Now, decades later, the language lab is sometimes reduced to being a storage room or simply another classroom, its technology only minimally upgraded since its installation. The high hopes which accompanied the introduction of the language laboratory dwindled away very quickly, as it became ever more obvious that the catch-all solution to quick and efficient language learning had not been found. Arguably, amongst the many reasons put forward in discussions on its lack of success, the most potent remains the criticism that the introduction of the language laboratory was promoted largely on adherence to a single methodology, the audiolingual method, which had developed from behaviourist psychological theory. Behaviourists such as Skinner and Watson viewed the language-learning process essentially as the imitation of correct utterances (Skinner, 1957); through such imitation, the structure of the language and target-like utterances would become automatic for the learner. Millions of learners with their headphones on and microphones placed firmly in front of their faces hoped that this process would somehow, and without much effort, miraculously lead to good results. Not only did their hopes remain unfulfilled, but research led by Noam Chomsky demonstrated that behaviourist theory was lacking: it could not account for the fact that learners could acquire the knowledge to create utterances which had not been presented to them in drills (Chomsky, 1975). The behaviourists had neglected perhaps one of the most important characteristics of human language: creativity. Not surprisingly, the demise of behaviourism as a theory of language learning dealt a heavy blow to the central role of the early language laboratories.

2.2. Learning from the present: Diverse technologies – diverse methods?

Fortunately, and this is the essential difference between the introduction of the language laboratory and the current debate on the use of Information and Communication Technologies in language learning and teaching, the integration of ICT into the learning environment is neither biased towards one specific theory of language learning nor dependent on a single methodology. Even a cursory glance at Web sites for language learning via the Internet alone highlights the fact that both teacher and learner are confronted with a smorgasbord of the different methodologies of the last 100 years, from grammar-translation to project-based teaching (Vogel, 2001: 135–6), with almost every method based on a different theory of language learning, while a similar glance at the CD-ROMs available for self-instructed learning reveals the existence of almost equal diversity in instructional styles and methods.

The reasons for this diversity are not clear-cut. On the one hand, it might perhaps be traced back to an over-emphasis on experimentation in technological design; until very recently, the development of Web sites and CD-ROMs was largely technology-driven, with little knowledge of, or concern for, the processes of language learning in evidence. As a result, sophisticated technical design may mask exercises based on the traditional behaviourist theory which remains little in evidence in other learning media today. On the other hand, as more language educationalists have become involved in Web and CD materials design, they have argued the case for understanding better the cognitive processes involved in language learning and incorporating this understanding into linking pedagogical and technological developments. Thus, attempts are beginning to be made in matching more holistic approaches to language learning with greater variety in language-learning software.

2.3. Learning from research in second language acquisition

In addition to learning from the practical experience of teachers and learners using technology in their language teaching and learning, it is fruitful to revisit the ways in which past researchers have viewed the cognitive processes referred to above, so that we can understand how technology might best be exploited in the language-learning process.

2.3.1. NATURAL ORDER OF LANGUAGE ACQUISITION

The most important findings of the last 30 years of research into second language acquisition (SLA) argue that SLA is a natural process with many broad similarities to first language acquisition, in that the individual learner creatively processes linguistic input and creates a systematic interlanguage, i.e. a learner language with its own rules and systematicity. This interlanguage follows a natural sequence of stages characterised by typical errors. These errors, it is argued, can be found in all learners learning a particular language as a second or foreign language, and are quite often similar to those found in first language acquisition (for an exploration of SLA research, see Ellis, 1994). This natural route of learning can be found in grammatical development and in phonological and lexical acquisition, and is independent of the acquisitional context. Errors can, therefore, be observed in both naturalistic and classroom second language learning. Research on the classroom as an acquisitional setting has shown that even the most sophisticated methods or explanations will not alter this particular route, nor prevent those typical errors which characterise the route to final correct language production (Bahns and Vogel, 2001). Consequently, it can be argued with some confidence that if we assume that ICT has a role to play in the cognitive teaching of grammar in order to avoid typical grammatical mistakes, we will inevitably fail. Research indicates that neither context factors nor the psychological make-up of individual learners have any impact on the systematicity of interlanguage development. Perhaps the answer lies not in what students learn, but how, and how well.

2.3.2. SPEED OF PROGRESSION AND ATTAINMENT LEVELS

In contrast to what research findings tell us about the lack of impact of context on the natural order of language acquisition, current thinking suggests strongly that both rate of learning (the speed with which the learner goes through the different stages of his or her interlanguage) and ultimate attainment level do very much depend on the acquisitional context and certain psychological learner characteristics. It is in these areas that the parameters of acquisitional contexts can differ qualitatively and where ICT potentially has an important role to play. Referring to the work of Wong Fillmore (1985) and Ellis (1985), McLaughlin (1987: 155) argues that the most important contextual features determining success in language learning are good input (selected for content with the learner's social needs in mind), learner awareness of their own needs, learner attitude towards the target language, motivation, and the existence of certain personality or cognitive style characteristics, such as the willingness to take risks, pattern-recognition abilities, tolerance of ambiguity, and skill in social interactions.

Thus, the quality of any acquisitional context depends on the extent to which it can influence both motivation for learning and the attitude of students towards the target language, while also providing opportunities for interactive learning. This raises the question as to how such research findings can be put into practice, and what role technologies might play within the language-learning context.

2.4. Linking SLA research, teaching practice and the language-learning context

One of the greatest challenges for applied language researchers is to discover successful ways of having their research findings incorporated into everyday language teaching. Indeed, over the years many attempts have been made to establish stronger links between research and practice. Within this section, we outline two examples, the second of which in particular explores to what extent teachers have developed understandings on the basis of SLA research, even if they are not yet fully in a position to put these into practice.

2.4.1. DEVELOPING TEACHING GUIDELINES

Every year sees new guidelines being introduced on some aspect of language learning, but that is not to say that we cannot learn from more long-standing examples. More than twenty years ago, for example, on the basis of findings in SLA research, Dulay *et al.* (1982: 263–9) established strikingly concrete overarching guidelines for teachers which remain equally relevant today in their emphasis on exposing students to natural communication, creating a supportive, relaxed atmosphere, and using current and relevant language in activities emphasising social interaction. In recognising the importance of input, learner-centredness (see also Nunan, 1988; Tudor, 1996), and affect (see also Dörnyei, 2001; Oxford, 1996), these guidelines provide a direct route from the more traditional classroom to a new learning environment which demonstrates greater adherence to the principles of real and relevant communication.

2.4.2. TRAINING COURSES

Training courses provide an important point of interaction for applied language researchers and language teachers and shed light on the challenge of putting principles such as those outlined above into practice. While language teachers may not always be in a position to keep continuously up to date with research findings, they often base their classroom methods on theories of language learning which are drawn from their own experience and might be termed 'intuitive'. As a result, they often have a very clear insight into both the merits and deficiencies of the learning context within which they perform. One example of this latter phenomenon emerged during the first pilot course of the TALLENT project, which was run in Limerick (Ireland) in July 2000, when a needs analysis questionnaire was administered to the participating teachers at the outset of the course.

Responses:
- *There is a lack of opportunity for the pupils to speak in teacher-directed activities.*
- *My students have no chance to speak or listen to a native speaker.*
- *Nobody writes any more.*
- *Young people don't like reading.*
- *It is very difficult to keep them talking in English.*
- *I find it quite difficult sometimes to encourage learner autonomy.*
- *Culture does not play an important role in my teaching, I confess.*
- *There are not enough lessons.*
- *I ignore a little bit my students' personalities.*

Figure 1: Teacher responses to TALLENT Questionnaire, administered by Vogel, July 2000 (for details of questionnaire, see
http://www.solki.jyu.fi/tallent/econtent.htm#needs).

One question asked teachers to highlight problems in their own language classrooms. Encouragingly, the responses typically provided (see Figure 1) reveal a good awareness of many broader issues under discussion in research on SLA and language-learning methodology. These responses arise, of course, from specific learning contexts (respondents worked in a range of EU countries, in diverse educational sectors), yet across the board the teachers subconsciously highlight as problem areas those which, as we have seen, researchers also indicate can have an important impact on the success or failure of the language-learning process (meaningful and realistic social interaction, motivation and input, individualisation).

The issue of meaningful and realistic social interaction is crucial, because all too often in the classroom students actually end up communicating in the target language in order to practise it, not to exchange information or engage in genuine conversation. In classrooms where everyone comes from the same linguistic and cultural background, students (and teachers) are usually well aware that they could communicate much better and more efficiently in their mother tongue. As a result, students are not motivated to communicate, as the situation in the language classroom seems too artificial. They are not at ease with a communicative situation, in which the main focus is on language learning, rather than the exchange of real information. Equally, restricted input (in some educational contexts limited to teacher and student utterances and to the textbook, occasionally accompanied by video and audio tapes) provides neither sufficient diversity of material for the learner to process, the opportunity to accommodate different learning styles, nor the sort of immediate cultural experience which helps students develop a positive attitude to the language. Finally, teachers are conscious that they often lack the time to cater for the individual psychological needs of students. They are not able to develop individual learning plans for autonomous learning with their students, regardless of how desirable they may consider this to be.

It is clear that many of these teachers' subconscious concerns are centred around the tension of combining a broad, often cost-effective, approach to language teaching with an appreciation of the needs of individual learners within particular learning contexts. This concern reflects an awareness of the potential link between the wealth of research supporting the value of greater learner autonomy within the language-learning process and the possibilities afforded by developments in ICT. In the section which follows, therefore, we explore the relationship between language learning, learner autonomy, and the learning environment, before examining, in Section 4, how ICT might be exploited in more effective ways within emerging language-learning and language-teaching environments.

3. Language learning, autonomy, and the learning environment

Interest in autonomy in language learning is not new, but since the end of the 1980s it has gained in importance in many countries, for political, economic, and pedagogical reasons (for a comprehensive discussion of autonomy, see Benson, 2001). This section examines how varied interpretations of autonomy can be applied to an exploration of different aspects of the language-learning environment and what role a deeper understanding of autonomy might have to play in the development of a more diverse and dynamic, learning-centred framework supported by the use of ICT.

3.1. Interpretations of autonomy in language learning

In 1990, Little developed a keystone definition of autonomy as 'a capacity for detachment, critical reflection, decision-making, and independent action. The various freedoms that autonomy implies are always conditional and constrained, never absolute' (Little, 1990: 7).

Some years later, Benson summarised the development of research into autonomy, and distinguished between three interpretations (technical, psychological, and political) of the concept of autonomy in language learning. Technical interpretations concentrate upon the framework within which language learning takes place; psychological interpretations on the transformation within the individual learner; political interpretations on the learner's power over the processes and content of their learning (Benson, 1997: 18–19). These interpretations are not mutually exclusive, and, indeed, Benson argues that most writers 'adopt a position representing a mixture of elements from each of the three' (Benson, 1997: 19). In his chapter, Benson goes on to demonstrate how positivism, (knowledge as reflection of objective reality), constructivism (knowledge as construction of meaning), and critical theory (knowledge as con-textualised interpretation of constructed reality) can be mapped roughly on to these three interpretations of autonomy (Benson,1997: 20–22). Understanding language learning is therefore both about understanding the cognitive processes by which we acquire language, and about developing a greater awareness of the context within which this learning takes place. Only by doing this, will we be better placed to understand the potential impact of introducing a new element such as ICT to the equation and to predict with greater certainty how its successful implementation can be secured.

3.2. Learner autonomy and the learning environment

In exploring the issue of learning environments, it is particularly useful to look at the types of conditions and constraints to which Little (1990: 7) alludes. Interestingly, Benson's categories of technical, psychological, and political interpretations may also prove a useful starting-point to examine in more detail how we understand learning environments in the broadest sense.

3.2.1. TECHNICAL AND PHYSICAL ASPECTS OF THE LEARNING ENVIRONMENT

While Benson argues that 'in "technical" versions of autonomy, the concept is defined simply as the act of learning a language outside the framework of an educational institution and without the intervention of a teacher' (Benson, 1997: 19), this is perhaps to define the term 'technical' too narrowly. In fact, researchers who approach autonomy from a technical point of view are largely concerned in the broadest sense with identifying the physical characteristics of the learning environment: for example, whether learning takes place primarily within a country where the target language is spoken or not, within the curricular and assessment structures of a formal educational establishment or not, within the classroom, a self-access learning centre, the workplace, or the home, with or without the support of a (native or non-native speaker) teacher, with the support of textbook, or video, or ICT, or a combination of media.

On this basis, the researcher's interest lies in describing the range of variables which can be identified, and in analysing the impact of changing one of those variables on a specific indicator, such as rate of learning or attested achievement in learning (see, for example, Müller, 1987). Perhaps what permeates this and other studies (for example, Warschauer, 1999) is the importance of identifying and understanding which aspects of any specific physical environment are fixed constraints (which neither the teacher nor learner has the authority to change), which aspects are theoretically modifiable, and which can be modified in practice. It is interesting to note that, in looking back at his own work, Warschauer acknowledges his own growing awareness of this:

> The first study I did on computer-mediated interaction made use of a controlled experiment (Warschauer, 1996). Although I felt that the study had value, I also felt that the experimental method of the study served to exclude the very contextual factors that were most important. I began to seek other approaches that were based on understanding learning in context rather than attempting to shut out context, and I eventually found a home in ethnography.
>
> (Warschauer, 1999: 189)

Warschauer demonstrates how both researchers and teachers can learn much from the lessons learned in earlier research work. In particular, teachers, who may see themselves as less concerned with controlled experimental research than with ensuring that their students can communicate effectively in the language they are learning, and who look to ICT to help them in this, can none the less benefit greatly from Warschauer's comments by looking closely at the contextual factors which have a bearing on the students whose learning they are planning to support through the use of ICT.

The first step, therefore, for any teacher considering introducing a new form of ICT into the learning environment is to map out the existing context. Potentially, the greatest challenge is presented by those forms of ICT which seem to offer the most learning potential (multimedia forms such as videoconferencing or Web learning), yet require the greatest level of technical expertise on the part of the teacher and/or learners. Assuming, however, that even teachers experienced in the use of ICT elsewhere might choose a simpler form to integrate into their students' language learning, it is possible to illustrate the value of mapping the language context with a more basic example. In this section, therefore, we will explore the situation of a language teacher who is planning to ask his/her students to enhance the school Web site by designing a suite of multilingual informational Web pages (see Chapter 6 for more on Web page design). In so doing, we consider some aspects of the learning context the teacher might need to take into account and how this might impact upon the potential success of such a project.

First of all, as with any other learning task, the teacher needs to think not only about the purpose of the activity, but also to identify the skills the activity is supposed to develop, and how the activity is linked to the overall goals set at the beginning of the course. So, the teacher might begin by defining (or revisiting) the overall course goal. This might be, for example, consolidating L2 writing skills, enhancing intercultural awareness, or providing an introduction to basic issues of translation and localisation.

Once this overall goal is clear, the activity (enhancing the school Web site) needs to be considered more closely, if it is to be designed and presented to the pupils meaningfully. Most importantly, what are the pedagogical considerations to be taken into account? Is the activity intended to, for example, encourage pupils to think about what might be of interest to visitors from other cultures, help pupils acquire the language needed to describe their school to speakers of other languages, or teach pupils how to design a Web page so they can go on to create their own individual multilingual homepage at a later date?

Such considerations can only be taken meaningfully if broader contextual issues are addressed; for example, are there fears that the prescribed syllabus will not be adequately covered if time is taken up with such project work? Will there be resentment that these pupils are receiving extra attention or support not available to all pupils within the cohort or the school? Finally, if the desired aim is to improve writing skills, for instance, can the existing assessment structures take account of this, and if not, to what extent can they be modified in agreement with the school authorities?

However, if the only contextual issues to be considered are pedagogical and curricular ones, the success of any such new venture is far from guaranteed. Teachers also need to examine closely the technical feasibility of the proposed activity and the impact of institutional policies. For example, what computers are available within the school, where are they located, are they available during the designated class-times, or will alternative arrangements have to be made? Does the school have a computer policy? Will pupils have direct access to the school Web page, or will the pages be created locally and transferred by a designated Web ? Is there an agreed house style for Web pages which might restrict what pupils can put onto the site? Will the teacher have the support of his/her department, or will there be concerns that this activity is a waste of time, a distraction which takes up time better spent on more traditional activities?

To highlight these questions is not to suggest that introducing ICT into language learning is not worth the effort, but rather that going into the process with an active awareness of the wider context can contribute significantly to the potential success of the undertaking. All too many teachers' accounts of their experiences introducing ICT highlight contextual aspects which greatly impacted on the project and which, with a bit of forward thinking, could have been avoided, or at least calculated into the equation (a wide-ranging discussion on this topic is to be found in the case studies presented in Warschauer, 1999).

3.2.2. Psychological aspects of the learning environment

Benson's second category in research on autonomy is that of the psychological approach, which again proves useful in examining how we understand learning environments in the broadest sense. For Benson, the psychological approach is characterised by an interest in the transformation which takes place within the individual learner as autonomy develops. Thus, it is argued that, while the physical characteristics of any learning environment may be more conducive to the development of autonomy), every learner within any learning environment has within them a more or less developed capacity for autonomy (in Little's terms). For example, we might contrast the opportunity to work within a self-access centre, using a range of media, towards goals set by individual learners (the success of which activity is judged by the learners themselves) against working within a highly structured syllabus, with a set textbook, towards specific externally set and assessed examinations

What does this mean for the language teacher wishing to explore the possibility of introducing ICT to the language-learning process? Above all, it means recognising the individuality of each language learner and considering the implications that this has in terms of the learner's current ability to make full use of the proposed technology, or to select the most suitable technology for their needs. As has already been argued, while technology will not have any major impact on the *order* in which a language is learned, research does suggest that for some learners it can contribute to an increase in the *rate* at which they learn, and their subsequent ability to *retain* what they have learned. (Groot, 2000). In combining a greater understanding of research into second language acquisition with a more in-depth knowledge of the styles and strategies adopted by their learners, the motivations behind their learning (perhaps most of all the recognition that these may be vastly different from the teachers' motivations for the learners), and the learners' attitudes towards the target language and culture, the teacher can develop a far more complex map of the psychological learning environment of the learner as an individual and as a member of a group. Much teaching, particularly within formal educational structures governed by principles of standardisation and cost-effectiveness, has in contrast concentrated to date on teaching the syllabus to a largely amorphous group of students who must fit their learning patterns to the established curricular path if they are to succeed.

3.2.3. POLITICAL ASPECTS OF THE LEARNING ENVIRONMENT

Benson's final category highlights the concentration of much research on autonomy on the political nature of language learning. This is potentially the most radical issue in relation to the introduction of ICT into the language classroom, and, therefore, the aspect of the learning environment most likely to constrain and determine which technologies are introduced, the extent to which they are integrated into the broader learning process, and the ultimate shape of the learning environment which is developed. Quite simply, the political issue raises questions of the learners' power over the processes and content of their own learning, and permeates all layers of the physical and psychological aspects of language learning. Viewing the learning environment as a political arena involves understanding that the structures within which we operate as teachers and researchers define for us and our learners what roles we play. In challenging those structures by introducing a medium as powerful as ICT to the equation, we open up the opportunity to hand over more control, but also responsibility, to the learner. Sometimes this happens with little opposition, in that we may offer the opportunity for learners to work at their own pace in the computer laboratory on familiar activities which they have met before in different forms and media. This is a common starting point for many teachers introducing ICT to their language teaching, as it allows all the participants to move forward together on largely familiar territory. What happens, however, when the leap is greater? Well-meaning efforts to transfer decision-making responsibilities from the teacher to the learner may equally well be interpreted by the learner and/or the educational establishment concerned as an abdication of responsibility on the part of the teacher. Yet, once learners have gained an understanding of the power involved in making decisions about their own learning, how can, or should, a teacher or institution hold them in check? And even though much responsibility has been passed from the teacher to the learner, to what extent does the nature of the learning materials selected re-establish a fixed and comfortable learning path for the learner as a consequence of the very way in which they have been developed?

Finally, as Little suggests, autonomy is not absolute. It is 'conditional and constrained [...] As social beings our independence is always balanced by dependence, our essential condition is one of interdependence' (Little, 1990: 7).

It is from a position of helping themselves and their students to understand the contextual nature of this interdependence that teachers can most effectively make decisions regarding the establishment of an optimal environment for successful learning to take place. In the final section of this chapter, we examine how ICT might be integrated meaningfully into such an environment.

4. Autonomy, SDL, and learning platforms – re-structuring the learning experience

A year after his above-mentioned publication on the topic, Little expanded his notion of autonomy, emphasising that 'it presupposes, but also entails, that the learner will develop a particular kind of psychological relation to the process and content of his learning' (Little, 1991: 4). This implies that individual learners need room and space to accommodate fully their *individual* style, approach, and rhythm in relation to the learning tasks at hand. Holec, in his emphasis on 'self-directed learning' (SDL), proposes a transfer of decision-making from teacher to learner to enable this accommodation to take place (Holec, 1981; 1988). Furthermore, in line with the interpretation of humans as social beings advocated by Little and others, Lave and Wenger (1991) and Resnick *et al.* (1991) argue that a successful learning process is social in nature. Researchers into language learning and communication have often found it useful to consider the participants in the process as actors playing roles. From this perspective, as the learning environment is modified, the learner and teacher roles need to be reconsidered and re-established flexibly to support diversified interaction, not only between the teacher and the learner, but also between the learners themselves (see for instance Kuure *et al.*, 2001a).

4.1. Moving away from traditional teaching

If we accept the premises that, in many parts of the world today, teaching frequently seeks to support learner autonomy and learner awareness, and that learning, or knowledge construction, takes place in interaction with other learners, we soon realise that traditional face-to-face teaching falls short in providing an optimal learning environment for this kind of learning (Legenhausen, 1999). Its often fixed linear structure leaves little room for the necessary 'side-steps' that make possible an extension to the core teaching where the various individual and group-learning processes can evolve and flourish. In a traditional learning setting (for example, a teacher teaching a group of students in a classroom within a 45-minute time slot), a student or a group of students can very seldom guide the teaching structure to include the kinds of elements and approaches that best accommodate their own needs at that particular moment.

4.2. Towards a new language-learning environment

What then is the kind of learning setting where these needs can be taken into consideration and addressed? What is the optimal learning environment? Of course, this will vary from one learning context to another, but, in global terms, this may well constitute a combination of face-to-face teaching and a variety of student-directed activities, through e-mail, chatrooms, Web sites, and so on (the next chapter discusses in more detail how these features can be brought together in dedicated learning platforms, but also points to potential conflict with the promotion of learner autonomy). Even in a less structured form, however, this type of combination has the advantage that it allows conventional teaching to branch out in many different directions according to the learners' interests and learning styles, without this branching out implying the use of a haphazard flurry of materials and activities. As ever in language teaching, clear goals and pedagogic thought are very much required. Hutchinson and Waters propose a move beyond a learner-centred approach to a 'learning-centred' one, whereby the aim lies in 'maximising the potential of the learning situation' (Hutchinson and Waters, 1987: 77). Thus, in relation to reading, for example, they draw on Stevick's belief that memorisation is aided by creating rich images (Stevick 1982), and argue:

> If an image gets into the brain through a number of different pathways – by hearing, reading, writing and speaking – that image is likely to be a richer image than if it gets in through only one pathway. The image will thereby be much stronger and much more easily accessible, since it will have more connections into the network. The fact that the learner will eventually use the knowledge gained only for reading is largely irrelevant. What is of most concern is how the learner can learn that knowledge most effectively. If the effectiveness of the process can be enriched by the use of other skills, then that is what should be done. (Hutchinson and Waters, 1987: 75)

4.3. Developing a model for a new language-learning and -teaching environment

On a broader scale, therefore, we can argue that placing the learner and learning at the centre of the learning process allows a common thread to be established within the learning environment, whereby teaching sequences, most commonly in the form of a course or a series of courses, also incorporate a variety of modes of teaching and learning. In this section we present a model of a new language-learning and -teaching environment which aims to demonstrate how an individual student's learning path might be identified, described and accommodated within a language-learning continuum that seeks both to acknowledge the complexities of the learner's background, language experience and learning goals, and to encourage learners to assume more responsibility for their language learning.

4.3.1. THE LEARNING CONTINUUM

Figure 2 is a graphic representation of a learning continuum which interprets Course X as an ongoing process whereby learners are engaged fully in the learning content within a diversified set of working and communication modes. This particular design presupposes the use of a learning platform as an extension to the face-to-face situations, although this could be substituted with a looser framework.

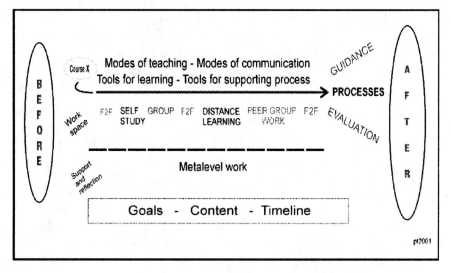

Figure 2: Learning process as the focal point of teaching.

The real challenge for the teacher lies in developing an ongoing understanding of the various processes that take place, whether on an individual or group basis, and how these processes can best be maintained and supported throughout the course. For the learner, too, there is, of course, the challenge of understanding that, inevitably, with this new 'freedom' comes a new responsibility for one's own action. From the outset, the teaching and learning goals need to be tied in with skills development, which again is tied into the activities and tasks in which the learners are engaged. This particular aspect is especially important in language learning since, as we have suggested above, the various skills can, and need to, be practised in many different ways during the course.

4.3.2. DIVERSE WORKING MODES

The working modes in the model change depending on which phase of work is being undertaken, and the learners engage in peer and group work to share some of the ideas they have formulated in the earlier phases. Some of these formulations and thinking processes are certainly private, but negotiation of meaning does take place among the different groups of learners (see, for instance, Rogoff, 1990), and the rhythm and working mode changes as the course progresses, with the various tasks being carried out partly individually and partly in groups. The peer groups can be employed for evaluation purposes or as the real audience for the work the learners have carried out. The face-to-face (F2F) sessions with the teacher remain a valuable element in the continuum. The work done, while being physically in one place, should have a social and reflective function concentrating on things that cannot or should not be carried out at a distance. The face-to-face meetings can also serve as an on-demand support element by dealing with issues that seem common in all groups at one specific time thus helping the learners carry on with their work more effectively. But very importantly the face-to-face meetings are needed to maintain the 'suspense' in the course by giving it concrete check-points, benefiting from the work the learners have done outside the classroom, and by giving the learners (who are otherwise often working alone or in small groups) a social space and sense of community they clearly appreciate and need.

4.3.3. DIVERSE PARTICIPATION

With the help of the different modes of communication it is also possible to invite external groups or individuals to participate in sections of the course. With e-mail the learners can, for example, contact outside experts for help and advice. The virtual section of the classroom, that is the learning platform itself, can easily be opened up to outside members, so broadening, for instance, the linguistic base in the home group or engaging with other interested parties to share the expertise of the group (see, for instance, Scardamalia and Bereiter, 1994 on distributed expertise and joint knowledge construction). These different communication modes can also have clear, built-in language-learning aims where learners are faced with different, largely authentic communication situations where they need to be able to use the language as a tool for finding the appropriate form of usage in order to reach a common understanding among the participants.

4.3.4. DIVERSE ACTIVITIES AND TASKS

The content and processes within this course are woven into a chain of activities and learning tasks which are designed to guide the learners towards the key areas of the content substance whilst at the same time allowing for divergence in both approach and interpretation. These tasks should include an element of problem-solving which encourages the learners to seek for unpredictable solutions and answers that in turn encourage interaction among the participants. Nevertheless, not every task can be open-ended nor aim to generate a diversity of answers. Especially in language learning, some tasks still need to be quite closed in order to build those linguistic skills which can form a ladder to higher-level activities and language usage. The most creative tasks, however, should support the learners' individual style and freedom to play around, and improvise, with language and communication.

4.3.5. PROVIDING SUPPORT FOR LEARNING: THE 'METALEVEL' SPACE

Coping with this freedom and variety requires much from both teacher and learner, and there are expectations of both that may be difficult to meet. The 'metalevel' space within the model (see Figure 2) is devised to help cope with this challenge. It is an integral part of the working space, but with a different focus and function. While the actual working 'area' (which includes both the face-to-face teaching and any other official meeting points of that specific course) is concerned mainly with the content itself, the metalevel space is a supporting arena for that work to be carried out successfully in its different stages and modes. This arena lies mostly within the electronic learning platform since it is a flexible, on-demand type of tool where issues are raised whenever there is a need. These issues can, and should, of course, be discussed further in the face-to-face situations.

The kind of topics that are discussed on the metalevel can be both non-content and content-related, but the main purpose of this space is to raise, as the name implies, metalevel questions and issues. Since the learners are to be the creators of their own learning processes and there are inevitable gaps in their abilities to become so, the metalevel work is intended to support the building and understanding of these abilities and skills by drawing attention to issues that are primarily to do with metacognitive skills. In addition to these skills, this is where the learner's awareness can be directed towards the key issues in learning a language or understanding oneself as a language learner. Furthermore, within this area the learners can voice their concerns and doubts about this type of learning, and importantly, they have the opportunity to exchange viewpoints with their co-learners and teachers in a way in which they would not usually be able to do. The metalevel area expands also to cover discussions around evaluation (see Kuure *et al.*, 2001b).

4.3.6. EVALUATION WITHIN NEW ENVIRONMENTS

In a new learning setting, it is clear that a conventional, largely outcome-oriented evaluation cannot be adopted to assess these types of processes. New forms of more process-oriented evaluation are required to complement, if not to replace, the existing evaluation practices. An electronic learning platform can also lend itself to the creation of, for instance, learning diaries or electronic portfolios. Warschauer (1999) indicates that the latter solution may prove more fruitful. The learners can and should be involved in planning and carrying out evaluation which is closely linked to the aims and objectives they have set for their own learning at the beginning of a course. The ability to set goals and assess the success of meeting these is a so-called transferable skill that any kind of modern teaching should aim to develop.

5. Conclusion

The term 'new learning environments' is often used as a synonym for computer-based learning, but while the computer in its many manifestations and growing versatility is likely to occupy an increasingly important place within language learning, it is the processes which take place within individual learners and between learner, teacher and materials which remain central to the success of learning. What is clear is that the days are over (if they ever existed) when we can consider the interaction of teachers and learners in the classroom as the single most important factor in our students' progress. Each of our students joins a course at a particular stage in their learning continuum. They bring a unique (language) learning history, individual personality, and skill-set which allows them to interact with other learners, teachers and resources (be they materials, native speakers of the target language, a particular learning technology) in a unique way. It is this interaction, the information transfer and communication which evolves, which encourages language learning and the development of the multiliteracies that Kaspar argues are a requirement for participation in 'global learning communities' (Kaspar, 2000: 106). As language teachers, our responsibility lies surely in drawing on our knowledge both of how language learning takes place and of how the ongoing process of reflection, decision-making, and evaluation can enrich that experience, if we are to help our students integrate and exploit the myriad of technological learning support systems which are now available to them. The role of language teachers may well be changing, but the challenge of helping students learn meaningfully and effectively remains the same.

Bibliography

Bahns, J. and T. Vogel (2001) 'Begründungen von fachdidaktischen Vorschlägen zur Grammatikarbeit im Fremdsprachenunterricht: Eine wissenschaftskritische Sicht'. In W. Börner and K. Vogel (eds.) *Grammatik Lehren und Lernen. Didaktisch-methodische und Unterrichtspraktische Aspekte.* Bochum: AKS-Verlag, 208–21.

Benson, P. (1997) 'Philosophy and politics of autonomy'. In P. Benson and P. Voller (eds.) *Autonomy and Independence*, 18–34.

Benson, P. (2001) *Teaching and Researching Autonomy in Language Learning.* London and New York: Longman.

Benson, P. and P. Voller (eds.) (1997) *Autonomy and Independence in Language Learning.* London and New York: Longman.

Breen, M.P. and C. N. Candlin (1980) 'The essentials of a communicative curriculum in language teaching'. *Applied Linguistics*, 1.2, 89–112.

Cheung, A. and C. Harrison (1992) 'Microcomputer adventure games and second language acquisition: a study of Hong Kong tertiary students'. In M. C. Pennington and V. Stevens (eds.) *Computers in Applied Linguistics*, 155–78.

Chomsky, N. (1975) *Reflections on Language.* New York: Pantheon.

Cobb, T. (1997) 'Is there any measurable learning from hands-on concordancing?' *System*, 25.3, 301–15.

Crooks, C. (1994) *Computers and the Collaborative Experience of Learning.* London: Routledge. (Cited in M. Warschauer and R. Kern (eds.) (2000) *Network-based Language Teaching: Concepts and Practice.* Cambridge: Cambridge University Press: 7).

Debski, R. (ed. and introd.) (2000) *Project-oriented CALL: Implementation and Evaluation. Computer Assisted Language Learning*, 13.4–5. (Special issue on project-based CALL).

Dörnyei, Z. (2001) *Motivational Strategies in the Language Classroom.* Cambridge: Cambridge University Press.

Dulay, H., M. Burt and S. Krashen (1982) *Language Two.* New York: Oxford University Press.

Ellis, R. (1985) *Understanding Second Language Acquisition.* Oxford: Oxford University Press.

Ellis, R. (1994) *The Study of Second Language Acquisition.* Oxford: Oxford University Press.

González-Bueno, M. and L.C. Pérez (2000) 'Electronic mail in foreign language writing: A study of grammatical and lexical accuracy, and quantity of language'. *Foreign Language Annals*, 33.2, 189–98.

Groot, P.J.M. (2000) 'Computer assisted second language vocabulary acquisition'. *Language Learning and Technology*, 4.1, 60–81.

Higgins, J. (1983) 'Can computers teach?' *CALICO Journal*, 1.2, 4–6.

Holec, H. (1981) *Autonomy in Foreign Language Learning*. Oxford: Pergamon. (First published 1979, Strasbourg: Council of Europe).

Holec, H. (ed.) (1988) *Autonomy and Self-directed Learning: Present Fields of Application*. Strasbourg: Council of Europe.

Hutchinson, T. and A. Waters (1987) *English for Specific Purposes. A Learning-centred Approach*. Cambridge: Cambridge University Press.

Kaspar, L.F. (2000) 'New technologies, new literacies: focus discipline research and ESL learning communities'. *Language Learning and Technology*, 4.2, 105–28.

Kuure, L., M. Saarenkunnas and P. Taalas (2001a) 'Negotiating a new culture of doing learning? A study of interaction in a Web Learning Environment with special focus on teacher approaches'. *APPLES* (http://www.solki.jyu.fi/apples).

Kuure, L., Saarenkunnas, M.and P. Taalas (2001b) 'Inside and outside of Webwork: Utilizing Web projects as resources for collaborative language study and learning'. In W. Fowler and J. Hasebrook (eds.) *Proceedings of WebNet 2001*. World Conference on the WWW and Internet, Orlando, Florida; October 23–27, 2001. Norfolk, VA.: Association for the Advancement of Computing in Education, 1201–6. [Book and CD-ROM]

Lave, J. and E. Wenger (1991) *Situated Learning. Legitimate Peripheral Participation*. Cambridge: Cambridge University Press.

Legenhausen, L. (1999) 'Traditional and autonomous learners compared: The impact of classroom culture on communicative attitudes and behaviour'. In C. Edelhoff and R. Weskamp (eds.) *Autonomes Fremdsprachenlernen*. Munich: Max Hueber, 166–82.

Little, D. (1990) 'Autonomy in language learning'. In I. Gathercole (ed.) *Autonomy in Language Learning*. London: CILT, 7–15.

Little, D. (1991) *Learner Autonomy 1: Definitions, Issues, and Problems*. Dublin: Authentik.

Lonergan, J. (1984) *Video in Language Teaching*. Cambridge: Cambridge University Press.

McLaughlin, B. (1987) *Theories of Second Language Learning*. London: Edward Arnold.

Motteram, G. (1997) 'Learner autonomy and the web'. In V. Dargueley *et al.* (eds.) *Educational Technology in Language Learning: Theoretical Considerations and Practical Applications*. Lyons: INSA , 17–24.

Müller, K. (1987) 'Zur Rolle des native speaker beim Fremdsprachenerwerb'. *Die neueren Sprachen*, 86.5, 383–407.

Neilson, L. (1989) *Literacy and Living: The Literate Lives of Three Adults.* Portsmouth, NH: Heinemann/Boynton-Cook.

Nunan, D. (1988) *The Learner-centred Curriculum.* Cambridge: Cambridge University Press.

Oxford, R.L. (ed.) (1996) *Language Learning Motivation: Pathways to the New Century.* Hawai'i: Second Language Teaching and Curriculum Center.

Pennington, M.C. (1989) 'Applications of computers in the development of speaking and listening proficiency'. In M.C. Pennington (ed.) *Teaching Languages With Computers: The State of the Art.* La Jolla, CA: Athelstan, 99–121.

Pennington, M.C. and V. Stevens (eds.) (1992) *Computers in Applied Linguistics.* Clevedon: Multilingual Matters.

Resnick, L.B., J.M. Levine and S.D. Teasley (eds.) (1991). *Perspectives on Socially Shared Cognition.* Washington, DC: American Psychological Association.

Rogoff, B. (1990) *Apprenticeship in Thinking.* New York: Oxford University Press.

Scardamalia, M and C. Bereiter (1994) 'Computer support for knowledge-building communities'. *The Journal of Learning Sciences,* 3, 265–83.

Skinner, B. and R. Austin (1999) 'Computer conferencing – does it motivate EFL students?' *ELT Journal,* 53.4, 270–79.

Skinner, B.F. (1957) *Verbal Behavior.* New York: Appleton-Century-Crofts.

Stevick, E. (1982) *Teaching and Learning Languages.* Cambridge: Cambridge University Press.

Tudor, I. (1996) *Learner-centredness as Language Education.* Cambridge: Cambridge University Press.

Ulitsky, H. (2000) 'Language learner strategies with technology'. *Journal of Educational Computing Research, 22.3,* 285–322.

Vogel, T. (2001) 'Learning out of control: Some thoughts on the World Wide Web in learning and teaching foreign languages'. In A. Chambers and G. Davies (eds.) *ICT and Language Learning: A European Perspective.* Lisse: Swets and Zeitlinger, 133–45.

Warschauer, M. (1996) 'Comparing face-to-face and electronic communication in the second language classroom'. *CALICO Journal,* 13. 2–3, 7–26.

Warschauer, M. (1999) *Electronic Literacies. Language, Culture, and Power in Online Education.* Mahwah, NJ: Lawrence Erlbaum Associates.

Wong Fillmore, L. (1985) 'Second language learning in children: A proposed model'. In R. Eshch, and J. Provinzano (eds.) *Issues in English Language Development.* Rosslyn VA: National Clearinghouse for Bilingual Education, 33–44.

Web sites

APPLES applied language studies journal:
http://www.solki.jyu.fi/apples/ [Downloaded 28 August 2003]
TALLENT needs analysis questionnaire:
http://www.solki.jyu.fi/tallent/econtent.htm#needs [Downloaded 28 August 2003]

2 Learning management systems for language learning

Sake Jager

1. Introduction

In the history of CALL, technological innovation has always provided opportunities for language learning. First and foremost among recent technologies is the Internet, particularly the World Wide Web, which has quickly made its way into the CALL community, since it seems particularly well-suited for using authentic, situated language material, fostering communication, and raising cultural awareness. As a result, CALL practitioners everywhere are starting to use the Web for language learning, usually in addition to face-to-face learning.

Exploiting the Web to its full potential, however, goes far beyond creating Web pages. It involves integrating resources already available on the Web, making use of synchronous and asynchronous communication, and providing other forms of interaction. In the past couple of years, there has been a steady increase in the use of learning management systems (also known as digital learning environments, electronic learning environments, online learning systems, course management systems, or e-learning systems), which provide a broad range of functions in one integrated package. This includes programs like *WebCT*, *Blackboard, Intralearn, Learning Space*, and many others (for more information, see the Web sites section at the end of this chapter). Put simply, these systems are general-purpose vehicles for delivering educational content and enabling virtual-classroom interaction. The systems offer the users a rich set of features, but require little or no programming effort on their part. Although not specifically designed for language teaching and learning, such systems may be put to good use in language-learning contexts too, albeit with certain restrictions.

In this chapter we shall assess the suitability of these online learning environments for language learning in more detail. Although the emphasis will be on practical aspects, the potential of the technology will be described from a methodological perspective. This involves presenting some general background on learning in today's information society and referring to more specific research on language learning on the Web. By outlining how these packages may be used for language learning, this chapter should provide guidance to both newcomers to CALL and those with experience in the use of more traditional, non Web-based forms of CALL. The strengths and weaknesses of learning management systems will also be discussed from an organisational perspective, which is why the chapter might also be of interest to administrators, managers, and directors of studies at institutions where languages are taught.

2. Research background

Understanding the potential of the Web for learning requires a brief introduction to some concepts of e-learning. Originally coined by industry in the wake of e-business and e-commerce, e-learning is gradually gaining acceptance as a general term for learning in which the Web has a key role to play. The Web is not simply regarded as an enabling technology to facilitate new methods of learning, but also as a restructuring technology transforming society. It is equated with revolutions such as the invention of print and the introduction of the telephone, radio and television (Rosenberg, 2001). The central argument is that we have moved into an information society, which calls for radical changes in education. Workers today have to process more information in a shorter period of time. Differences between blue-collar workers and white-collar workers are beginning to disappear. A large part of the workforce has to be trained as knowledge workers, capable of navigating large amounts of information. Because of rapid changes in technology and information, learning should be conceived as a continual process. Work is combined with learning, just as learning is increasingly combined with work. Urdan and Weggen claim that the 'fastest growing group attending higher education institutions are working, part-time students older than 25' (2000: 4). For reasons of cost-effectiveness, learning should be relevant to task and take into account prior knowledge and skills. This calls for flexible time schemes and individual study paths. Above all, learning should be motivating and challenging, if only to prevent staff from moving to competitors in the market at a time when skilled workers are hard to find. They conclude that learning should be brought to people, rather than bringing people to learning (Urdan and Weggen, 2000: 2–7).

Researchers on language learning or CALL generally acknowledge the possibilities of the Web for language learning (see, for example, Felix, 1998 and 1999; Debski, 2000; Warschauer, 2000 and 2001; Hogan-Brun and Laux, 2001), but there is also a strong feeling that the true potential of the Web remains largely unexplored. Felix (1999), who has published widely on the actual use of the Web for language learning, notices how the well-established, but by no means undisputed, practice of grammar-based teaching continues to be an important activity on the Web. She argues in favour of more 'student-centred learning, reflected in meaningful task-based activities, which exploits the new medium's unique potential for authentic learning experiences' (Felix, 1999: 86). Authenticity in this sense is well beyond the simulated practice typical of a lot of CD- ROM-based language learning. Warschauer (2001) suggests that we should have our students 'perform real-life tasks and solve real-life problems in a community of peers and mentors'. He notes that we have moved from 'Structural CALL' in the 1970s and 1980s, through 'Communicative CALL' in the 1980s and 1990s to 'Integrative CALL' in the twenty-first century, which he describes as follows:

> In contrast, integrative CALL is based on a socio-cognitive view of language learning. From this viewpoint, learning language involves apprenticing into new discourse communities. The purpose of interaction is to help students learn to enter new communities and familiarise themselves with new genres and discourses. From this point of view, the content of the interaction and the nature of the community are extremely important. It is not enough to engage in communication for communication's sake.
>
> (Warschauer, 2001)

In fact, providing authentic task-based learning is one the central principles of e-learning in general. In an excellent discussion of the impact of modern information society on the teaching of English, Warschauer (2000) makes it clear how relevant the current transformation of society is for the teaching of English. It will affect teachers, learners, how we read and write English, indeed what we mean by English, so profoundly that a new pedagogy is required. Aside from the elements discussed above, this also involves the 'guidance of a teacher or mentor to critically analyse the content, coherence, organisation, pragmatics, syntax and lexis of communication' (Warschauer, 2000: 528). The shift of the teacher's role from provider of knowledge to facilitator of learning is widely acknowledged today. One of the consequences for language learning is that it puts a premium on communication between teacher and student.

Researchers arguing in favour of task-based authentic learning, (see, for example, Felix, 1998 and 1999; Warschauer, 2000 and 2001; Hogan-Brun and Laux, 2001) agree that this type of learning is best scaffolded by having students set up individual or group projects, in which they seek to exploit the Web for social, career-oriented, and intercultural exchange. Debski (2000) reports on a faculty-wide initiative at the University of Melbourne to set up this type of learning. Although the project turned out successfully in the end ('Project-oriented learning with technology now has an established place in the curricula of seven language programs', Debski, 2000: 331), it is also evident that helping both teachers and students become accustomed to new technology and innovating pedagogy at the same time were major challenges.

As evidenced by the massive amount of language material available on the Web, quite often language teaching is not informed by any particular theory about learning or language acquisition. Teachers tend to take a more eclectic approach and seem to be particularly interested in making available to students whatever they deem useful for a particular learning situation. If anything, elements associated with more structural approaches to language learning, such as vocabulary and grammar, continue to be used even if the general perspective of a course is communicative, or integrative (in Warschauer's sense, discussed above).

In the next section, we shall discuss to what extent learning management systems are compatible with current practice and theory in Web-based CALL and whether they may serve as enabling technologies to carry the field forward in pedagogically innovative directions.

3. Learning management systems for CALL

There are a great many learning management systems available. One of the best sites for discovering which systems can be bought or used free of charge, and what functionality they provide, is Edutools (http://www.edutools.info/course/index.jsp). Although the differences between the systems may be considerable in some respects, they have a lot of functions in common. Since it is impossible to discuss the use of each of these systems for language learning, our primary frame of reference will be *Blackboard*, a system that is fast becoming the most popular for use in education. In doing so, the chapter will draw on experiences at the University of Groningen, where *Blackboard* has recently been introduced as a university-wide system for online learning and teaching. Unless otherwise stated, however, many of the points raised will also apply to other learning management programs not discussed here.

Following the major categories defined by Ko and Rossen's *Teaching Online* (2001), an excellent practical introduction to using the Internet for teaching and learning, the main features of learning management systems may be defined as follows:

Presentation Areas: Presentation areas are usually clearly set apart from other areas by separate buttons or links. They usually consist of sections for announcements, information about a particular course, and a space for course materials, such as *PowerPoint* slides, lecture notes, etc. Multimedia may be included in the presentation areas;

Discussion Forums: This area is set aside for threaded discussions, which may usually be initiated by both teacher and students;

E-Mail: E-mail functions are normally course-related, making it easy for teachers to send messages to students, and for students to send messages to each other and to the teacher(s). The messages may contain the usual attachments;

Chat and Whiteboard: The chat and whiteboard together constitute a virtual classroom in which real-time discussion on certain topics, including illustrations, charts, Web pages, etc. can be conducted. Chat sessions may be stored for later reference;

Group Activity Areas: The group areas contain specific functions such as the exchange of documents within a group, separate group discussion areas, group-based e-mail, and chat and whiteboard functions;

Web Resource and Linking Areas: These areas allow for all kinds of relevant resources available on the Web to be accessed from one specific location in the online course;

Assessment: Most systems provide assessment facilities consisting of quizzes, student tracking, and online grade books. The quizzes, which may be composed of multiple choice, true/false, and short answer questions, are mainly useful for self-assessment. They may include multimedia components (pictures, sound, video). Tracking options allow teachers to study which areas have been visited by which students at which time and/or for how long. They may be useful for optimising course content or giving individual advice to students. Finally, the online grade book may be used to register student marks for exercises, including tasks conducted away from the learning system.

The extent to which these packages can be used to implement the pedagogical approaches for using the Web outlined above will be demonstrated in the scenario presented below. It expands on an idea for using online job searching services, as presented in Hogan-Brun and Laux (2001).

4. Scenario: The Rijksuniversiteit Groningen

An English teacher at the University of Groningen is teaching a Business English class for a group of students in Communication Studies. She makes use of *Blackboard,* which has recently been introduced as the standard learning management system for the entire university. Her students already know the system because it is also used by teachers in the Department of Communication Studies. The English teacher has taken part in two half-day training sessions to learn the basics of using *Blackboard.* When she starts planning the course, her university has already put the course online, including the names of students who have registered for the course and the course description, which has been copied from the university's course catalogue. Students do not yet have access to the course, because the teacher has not yet made it publicly available.

The teacher begins by adding more specific information about the objectives of the course, for which *Blackboard* has a presentation area, namely 'Course Information'. A category for this type of information is also available, so she selects 'Objectives' as the title for describing what the course aims to do. She makes it clear that this is a project-oriented course, which tries to make students work with authentic language in business-related settings. Entering the information is simply a matter of filling in a pre-defined form and confirming her choice by clicking the 'Submit' button. This way of adding information to the course is much the same for each part of the course. Our teacher uses the same 'Course Information' area to enter other details about the course, such as requirements about attendance and participation, meeting times, office hours, grading policies, etc. Information is included on the two-hour weekly sessions for the entire group, participation in which is obligatory for all students, and on deadlines of work to be handed in.

She then goes on to provide specifics about the kinds of projects that students are expected to set up. She decides to use the 'Course Documents' area for this type of information. She sets up separate folders for each suggested topic. One such folder has been created for the topic 'Finding a job'. It describes the requirements of the topic in detail, pointing out that Web sites for this topic can be found in the 'Web sites' section of the course, for which she has used a folder structure similar to that in the 'Course Documents' section. It turned out that referring to Web sites in the 'Course Documents' section was more difficult to do, because it required knowing some HTML to enter in the relevant URLs in the running text.

A key element for this topic is the use of authentic job-searching services, several of which can be found in the 'Web sites' section of her course. She particularly likes *Monster*, an online job agency working worldwide and decides to include the UK Web site (http://www.monster.co.uk/) in her list of sites. She wants students to use this site or other sites for a number of activities related to finding employment: finding a job, writing a curriculum vitae (CV), writing a letter of application and attending job interviews. Only the last task has been set up as a classroom activity: most of the other activities are conducted online. She prefers to use the classroom primarily for face-to-face contact involving spoken communication in the target language. The teacher complements the career information that is available on the job-searching sites with more specific information about language use, employment and culture.

Students are expected to work in pairs in several parts of the project, so the teacher decides to set up groups for this particular project. Her teaching assistant creates several small groups consisting of two students and the teacher (to facilitate her role as observer of the group work), and one large group consisting of all the students and herself. For each group, the assistant activates file exchange, e-mail, group discussion, and virtual classroom.

Our English teacher devises other tasks for the Business English class, including one in which students create a Web site for marketing a new product they have 'developed' as part of the course, basically following the steps outlined above. She then makes the course available to students.

At the beginning of term, students logging into the University's *Blackboard* system notice that a new course has been made available, the Business English course for which they had registered half a year ago. There is an announcement from the teacher asking them to look through the available material and providing instructions on preparation for the first class meeting to be held later that week.

The 'Finding a job' topic is scheduled for Weeks 6–8, or rather classroom activities related to this topic take place in this particular period. Some students have started working on the assignments earlier. They have been asked to find online advertisements for jobs that match their own particular interests and qualifications (after graduation in Communication Studies). Relevant advertisements (three for each student) are to be made available to the entire class in the discussion forum set aside for this project, together with a brief explanation as to why they would be interested in filling the vacancies concerned. An additional task is to keep track of unfamiliar vocabulary as the number of advertisements grows, by compiling a list of unknown words and expressions. This list is to be sent in to the teacher using the digital drop box, access to which is on an individual basis.

The students work together in several parts of the course. For this particular topic, they submit CVs and application letters for peer review, using the group exchange function that the teacher has set up for each pair of students. The CVs and letters are written in *Microsoft Word*, the word-processing package that they use for all submitted work in the faculty. For peer reviewing they make use of the standard review functions in *Word*. Basic information on how to apply this function can be found in the teacher instructions accompanying the assignments. The reviewed letters are sent in to the teacher by means of the digital drop box. In addition, a special Frequently Asked Questions (FAQ) discussion list has been set up which allows them to ask questions and find answers about all kinds of procedural and technical aspects of the course.

The teacher occasionally comments on the work in progress as students exchange documents. She uses both group discussion and group e-mail for this, resorting to e-mail for personal communications and for contacting students who, for one reason or another, do not log onto the system regularly. Since e-mails in *Blackboard* are sent to students' regular e-mail accounts, this is one way of reaching potential dropouts from the course.

The teacher has set up columns in the student grade book for each mark to be obtained, making use of the latest innovation in *Blackboard 5.5*, which her institution is using, to assign weights to each of the marks. Students get credits for the submitted CV and application letter, and for their work as a reviewer. Because she considers mastery of relevant vocabulary an important aspect of this topic, she makes use of the quiz function to compose a 30-item vocabulary test. As input for the quiz she makes use of the vocabulary lists sent in by the students.

Finally, as a preparation for the job interviews to be conducted in the faculty's digital language lab, she asks students to use the group-based virtual classroom to conduct an online interview using the chat function to simulate the dialogue between applicant and personnel manager. The chat also involves the whiteboard, which is used to display the CV and application letter. The session is stored for review by the students and teacher. In this way, students can prepare for the spoken job interview to be conducted in the language lab in a couple of days.

As should be evident from this detailed description of how *Blackboard* may actually be used for task-based language learning, learning management systems go a long way to meeting the demands of modern Web-based teaching today. But there are several additional observations to be made about this scenario.

5. Analysis of scenario

This is an imaginary scenario at the University of Groningen, at least for English. To date using the potential of *Blackboard* to the full to develop realistic student-centred activities has been especially in evidence in the teaching materials at the Department of Communication Studies, possibly because computer-mediated communication (CMC) belongs to the 'core business' of the department involved. More importantly, however, developing task-based scenarios like that described above, writing them out in full and integrating them with live material on the Web is very time-consuming, even with easy-to-use programs such as *Blackboard*. In addition, using the facilities for interaction and communication as the course is running, even if it means cutting down on class time, does not necessarily mean less work for the teacher.

All of the activities described above could have been supported by a number of tools available at no cost, rather than by one single system costing tens of thousands of euros each year. In fact, Chizmar and Williams (2001) provide some evidence that faculty, if they had a choice, would prefer to use specific tools rather than make use of one tool that does everything. Their evidence, however, turns out to be rather inconclusive because the questionnaire they used to elicit responses from faculty is rather biased. For example, Statement 2 reads, 'I prefer to pick the one application I need to solve a specific pedagogical problem rather than having to adopt a Swiss-Army-knife Web tool that does everything' (Chizmar and Williams, 2001: 20), yet support for 'one Web tool that does everything' (Statement 3, Chizmar and Williams, 2001: 20) seems quite high. More important, they do not consider that providing adequate support for a wide range of tools may not be realistic for many educational institutions.

Quite often, individual teachers have little or no control over which system is adopted by the university or teaching institution. One could look at this negatively and suggest that the introduction of these systems is at the expense of individual freedom of choice and may not fit in with teachers' notions about putting pedagogy first. But at the same time, it promotes the issue of using technology for learning to the level of the institution. For online learning to be successful, educational institutions should develop implementation strategies and provide adequate support structures in terms of infrastructure, staff training, and technological assistance. Adopting and integrating a conceptual and organisational framework of learning constitutes an essential element of any such strategy. In the end individual teachers may be better served with one working technology that is properly supported than with a wide of range of incompatible tools for which no adequate training or support can be provided, and the same holds true for students.

Although the scenario shows that learning management systems may certainly be used for pedagogically driven language learning, an important aspect to consider is that they are largely teacher-controlled, i.e., the instructor is literally in control, since only he or she has access to the control panel allowing the authoring of material for language learning using the system. While this may not by itself be limiting to the range of tasks that may be defined for students, it does mean that many types of student work, most notably for student presentations, will actually have to be conducted outside the learning management system, using different authoring tools, and possibly requiring knowledge of HTML. If new 'multiliteracies' are defined in which technology skills and language skills are viewed as equally relevant (Warschauer, 2000), teachers will have to acquire ICT skills that go well beyond the basics of learning management systems.

It is interesting to note that learning management systems provide a suitable context for enhancing such skills. All too often, limited computer skills or frustrations about actually using technology prove to be obstacles that keep staff from trying out new educational concepts with ICT in the classroom. This aspect of the use of ICT in learning is often neglected. Computer-assisted learning will not truly catch on unless a significant number of staff are using it, and this holds for computer-assisted language learning too. Introducing an easy-to-learn system for delivering course content is an excellent way to increase computer literacy among staff and may serve as a focal point for training in educational institutions. The effectiveness of such approaches to language learning is reported by Gillespie (2000). Discussing the use of *FirstClass* for language teaching and learning at the University of Ulster, he suggests that the program provides 'the computer-based social context for staff and students', thereby fostering 'human connectivity', and contributes to the 'reinforcement of computer-skills' (2000: 24). This corroborates our findings at the University of Groningen, where providing a suitable context for promoting ICT skills was one of the primary reasons for introducing *Blackboard*.

This does not necessarily mean that learning management systems are mainly useful for teachers with little or no experience in ICT. As is obvious from several examples at the University of Groningen (including the use of *Blackboard* in the Department of Communication Studies), staff with considerable experience in using ICT, for instance those capable of writing their own Web pages or programming for the Web, have also started using *Blackboard*. From interviews and personal reactions, it is obvious that it is the combination of features that is appealing. Although most of the individual functions are less powerful than their counterparts available as separate tools (e-mail programs, Web boards, collaboration tools, Web-authoring packages), it is the combination of features, in addition to the support offered for this particular package, that carries the day. And of course, they can continue producing their own Web sites and integrate them into the Web-based course environment in the same way that they can ask their students to.

Learning management systems do not enforce a particular pedagogy. Although there may be a degree of variation between the individual packages, the most frequently used learning management systems have not been developed to support any particular learning philosophy. This does not mean that they are pedagogically neutral once they have been introduced into the classroom. Their use will in fact reflect the pedagogy explicitly or implicitly assumed by the course developer, teacher or institution. Since learning management systems are easy to use but hard to fill, perhaps the most common use is to regard the system as a convenient add-on to an existing course, thus using new technology for substitution rather than transformation of the learning process. At the University of Groningen, we have seen over a thousand courses brought online in just over half a year – an incredible success in terms of numbers (900 teaching staff, almost 20,000 students, more than 1,000 courses). But unless didactic support can be provided to instil a sense of the pedagogic potential of the new technology, old habits will persist and teaching will only be altered marginally. Fortunately, as we are entering the second phase of deployment, additional training programs are being set up focusing on didactic and pedagogic uses of *Blackboard*.

It should, however, be realised that in spite of the huge potential, it may sometimes be hard to implement certain methodological concepts. In language learning, as in several areas requiring a command of discipline-specific skills, there is a growing interest in the use of language portfolios (see, for instance, the Council of Europe's Web site on language portfolios: http://culture2.coe.int/portfolio). This is one area where programs like *Blackboard* fall short of actual user requirements, partly because of the teacher-centredness pointed out earlier. If electronic support of portfolios is required, users should, for the time being at least, turn to external programs or, if they have a choice, look for a particular system that does offer the functionality concerned.

6. Moving beyond English

Essential for language learning is the ability of a program to support languages other than English. In a comparison of *WebCT* and *Blackboard*, Siekmann concludes:

> In a foreign language learning context, it is important to create a target language environment that motivates students to use the second language. Ideally, it should be possible to present a language course site entirely in the target language. Both systems fall short of this goal at the time, but WebCT offers more opportunities to create a target language environment (for many western European languages) than Blackboard.
> (2001: 593)

There are in fact two major problems with regard to target language support. The first is that not all screen elements may be translated, which means that teacher and students will be confronted with a mixture of the target language and English. The use of diacritics and common characters for languages such as French, Spanish and German will be rendered correctly, but the target language text will be interspersed with English, which may be the only language for navigation. This may be a feature that teachers are willing to tolerate.

The second, more serious problem is that in certain contexts foreign language character sets cannot be rendered at all. This is the case for languages such as Russian, Hebrew, or Arabic, where results may vary depending on the operating system used and the fonts installed. Of course for these, language teachers can include texts in external formats such as *Word* or HTML to provide linguistic material in the target language, but even this is not a foolproof guarantee for correct representation of the text. They may have to resort to making specific fonts available, using the LMS for distribution. And even then, students will not be able to use the target language in quizzes and other interactive parts of the program.

The problems are mainly caused by the lack of localisation features and the absence of support for Unicode, an international standard for describing the characters of most of the world's languages (http://www.unicode.org). This lack of Unicode support may be in different parts of the program architecture, for example in the presentation layer (what you see on the screen), the scripting language (which handles user input) and database (where input is stored). Teachers may overcome some of these limitations, but, for the time being at least, the situation is less than perfect.

For anyone who has experience of using professionally created multimedia courseware with individual pathways, extensive feedback and reference capabilities, the interactive features of learning management systems may come as a bit of a disappointment. This points to an essential difference with multimedia CALL, traditionally distributed on CD-ROM. Most learning management systems have facilities for assessment (with standard exercise formats) but not for practice. Teachers should not expect to be able to set up a particular learning path with possibilities for branching depending on user input. Learning management systems have not been designed with that kind of use in mind. They have been designed with strong emphasis on information and communication features. They are best regarded as complementary to dedicated CALL programs.

Even when the overall perspective is integrative, there continues to be a place for interactive exercises allowing students to practice more structural or mechanical aspects of language use. We should not simply do away with dedicated CALL software just because it does not work on the Web. To make the best possible use of both types of programs, we should try to integrate them further. This calls for interconnectivity both in terms of pedagogy (to what extent is there a place for structure-driven exercises in an integrative language-learning program?) and in terms of technology (how can these different forms of CALL be made inter-operable in terms of access, presentation, storage, and so on?). This is one direction in which Web-based CALL may be developed further to serve the needs of language teachers and learners even better. As international standards for the integration and exchange of educational content on the Web are emerging (cf. the IMS Global Learning Consortium, http://www.imsproject.org, and SCORM, http://xml.coverpages.org/scorm.html), the feasibility of extending the functionality of CALL along these lines will increase significantly.

For the time being, progress towards more advanced, multimedia-supported exercise formats is also impeded by a number of well-known limitations of the Web. Most interaction on the Web today is form-based, which imposes severe restrictions on design. Most interactivity types are not nearly as advanced as some exercise types available for CALL five or even ten years ago. Together with bandwidth restrictions, preventing the use of high-quality multimedia on the Web, this means that Web-based interactivity types have not yet attained the same level of sophistication and attractiveness as some packages available on CD-Rom.

7. Conclusion

Exploiting the Web to its full potential for language learning is less a matter of technology than of methodology. The technology for setting up student-centred, task-based language learning on the Web is already available. Instead of being empowered by new technology, users may easily become overpowered, because of the vast range of options open to them. This is where learning management systems may make a difference: easy to learn and offering a lot of functionality in a single package, they may be useful for CALL practitioners with different ICT competencies and they may serve as a focal point for ICT-awareness in educational settings.

Technological limitations associated with the Web will most likely disappear. As bandwidth is increasing and permanent connections to the Internet are becoming available at home, the Internet will become the delivery medium of choice for almost any type of application. Limited interactivity types will disappear in a matter of years and full multimedia interaction, involving high-quality audio and video (absolute prerequisites for spoken language interaction) already available on several educational networks today, will soon be possible. This will open up even more opportunities for language learning, particularly in the areas of spoken language and interaction between tutors and peers. The true challenge, however, remains to determine how the technology can be put to maximum effect for language learning. This requires rethinking the way students learn, particularly how they learn second or foreign languages. Since learning management systems are usually introduced at the institutional level, this calls for institution-wide implementation strategies, including teacher-training programmes which focus on the didactic and pedagogic aspects of introducing new technology. These implementation plans should also take into account the preparation time for setting up properly designed courses and the actual time needed to keep the courses up and running. Compensation schemes based on the number of contact hours for each course are obviously inadequate for teaching online.

The organisational perspective on the potential of learning management systems (especially in institutions where language teaching is part of a broader educational setting) is most likely driven by more general considerations about online learning. This takes us back to the theme of e-learning introduced above. If learning is to be attractive, task-based, individualised, time and place independent, there will be increasing pressure on organisations to deliver learning online. Educational institutions may feel compelled to use learning management systems in an increasingly competitive, international market. Or as Warschauer puts it:

> Universities and schools will be under constant pressure to cut corners in favor of cheaper alternatives based on individual access to prepackaged materials with limited opportunities for student-teacher communication. Thus quality educational programs involving extensive personal interaction – whether in the classroom or on the Internet – will face mounting economic competition from inexpensive but pedagogically unsound programs.

> (2000: 526)

Even if limitations of technology may be overcome, the cost of putting teachers online may be prohibitive, or, even worse, good practices in language learning, such as face-to-face communication 'on the ground', may be put to one side for reasons of economy.

Web-based CALL has yet to establish its position in the larger context of e-learning. It is too early to offer full language learning on the Web, and it may very well never happen at all. The slow growth of Web-based e-commerce in the past two years demonstrates that the availability of alternative modes of delivery does not necessarily mean that people start using them. Web-based language learning, like Web-based commerce, must be rooted in well established practice and principles, if it is to become a successful method for language learning in the future.

Bibliography

Chizmar J.F. and D.B. Williams (2001) 'What do faculty want?' *Educause Quarterly*, 1, 18–24.

Debski, R. (2000) 'Exploring the re-creation of a CALL innovation'. *Computer Assisted Language Learning*, 13. 4–5, 307–32.

Felix, U. (1998) *Virtual Language Learning: Finding the Gems among the Pebbles.* Melbourne: Language Australia.

Felix, U. (1999) 'Web-based language learning: a window to the authentic world'. In R. Debski and M. Levy (eds.) *World CALL: Global Perspectives on Computer-Assisted Language Learning.* Lisse: Swets and Zeitlinger, 85–98.

Gillespie, J. (2000) 'Towards a computer-based learning environment: a pilot study in the use of FirstClass'. *ReCALL*, 12.1, 19–26.

Hogan-Brun, G. and H. Laux (2001) 'Specialist gateways through chaos: a changing learning environment'. *System*, 29, 253–65.

Ko, S. and S. Rossen (2001) *Teaching Online: A Practical Guide.* Boston: Houghton Mifflin Company.

Rosenberg, M.J. (2001) *E-learning: Strategies for Delivering Knowledge in the Digital Age.* New York: McGraw-Hill.

Siekmann, S. (2001) 'Calico Software Report: Which Web course management system is right for me? A comparison of WebCT 3.1 and Blackboard 5.0'. *CALICO Journal*, 18.3, 590–617.

Urdan, T. and C. Weggen (2000) *Corporate E-learning: exploring a new frontier.* WR Hambrecht and Co. Publication no longer available at original site. A copy may be retrieved from:
http://www.spectrainteractive.com/pdfs/CorporateELearingHamrecht.pdf

Warschauer, M. (2000) 'The changing global economy and the future of English teaching'. *TESOL Quarterly*, 34.3, 511–35.

Warschauer, M. (2001) 'The death of cyberspace and the rebirth of CALL'. *CALL in 21st Century*. IATEFL CD-ROM. Available:
http://www.gse.uci.edu/markw/cyberspace.html

Web sites

Learning management systems
Blackboard: http://www.blackboard.com
WebCT: http://www.webct.com
Intralearn: http://www.intralearn.com
Learning Space:
 http://www.lotus.com/products/learnspace.nsf/wdocs/homepage
 [Downloaded: 19 September 2003]
Edutools: http://www.edutools.info/course/index.jsp [Downloaded: 19
 September 2003]

Standardisation
The Unicode Home Page: http://www.unicode.org
IMS Global Learning Consortium: http://www.imsproject.org
SCORM: http://xml.coverpages.org/scorm.html

Other
Council of Europe Language Portfolio: http://culture2.coe.int/portfolio
Monster Careers Network: http://www.monster.co.uk/

3 Laying good foundations: The language resource centre as meeting-place of policy, pedagogical theory and practice

Jean E. Conacher and Siobhán Murphy

1. Introduction

Since the late 1970s, educational establishments throughout Europe have undergone enormous change in an effort to respond to the challenges posed by developments in global and national economic, social and political systems. In addition to this, rapid technological developments, pressing market demands and the desire for greater political integration have resulted in a growing requirement for lifelong skills development and increased mobility amongst the workforce (European Commission, 2001). At tertiary level, this has led to increased access to further and higher education courses, greater diversification of the learning population in age, knowledge and prior experience, and demands for flexibility in the design of learning programmes to meet these changing needs. These developments are seldom coupled with massive injections of capital and so, simultaneously, third-level institutions have been called upon to adopt a more business-like approach to their activities and to find more cost-effective ways of tackling the challenges posed by this changing learning environment (see, for example, Reichert and Wächter, 2000). Within the arts and humanities, language study, an area requiring more intensive class contact than other more library-based disciplines, has been particularly affected by these changes. While some solutions have been found in increased class sizes and reduced class contact time, the most significant development is undoubtedly the parallel emergence of a wide range of centres designed to support language learning beyond the classroom or lecture theatre (Benson and Voller, 1997: 15).

This phenomenon is not only a European one; language centres have existed, perhaps most notably in Australia and South East Asia, for many years. Indeed, such centres now exist in many different forms, types, sizes and dimensions in educational institutions across the world, and it is impossible to find one description to fit all. Within this chapter, we will use the generic term 'language resource centre' (LRC) to encompass everything from the corner of a library in a school or college to the virtual centres now emerging on the Internet. This is not in itself a problem, as it can be argued that no single type of resource centre suits every learning and teaching environment; rather each language resource centre aims to meet the needs of its users (learners, teachers, researchers, institution) while simultaneously reflecting in its practice the political and pedagogical thinking underlying its existence.

The aim of this chapter is, therefore, to examine both the theoretical and practical issues surrounding the establishment and evolution of language resource centres and to explore the extent to which any language resource centre does in fact reflect the interplay of policy, pedagogical theory and practice predominant in its local context. We begin with an account of the main types of language resource centres currently in existence, examining both their political and pedagogical rationale, before asking the question whether, despite their diversity, there are any factors common to successful LRCs which those wishing to establish such a centre might take into account. Finally, we look at how the role of language resource centres may evolve in future and argue that they are central to current debates on new learning environments. In so doing, we draw upon our combined expertise of working in and with such language resource centres as administrator, language teacher and researcher.

2. Language resource centres: Forms and functions

As indicated in our introduction, a language resource centre can take many forms and perform many different functions. In this section, we outline five main types of language resource centre currently in existence, providing illustrations which aim to highlight the importance of viewing such centres within their own individual context and to raise a range of issues which we will return to in later sections of the chapter. The five types of language resource centre examined, in order of their increasing sphere of influence, are:

- Classroom/school resource centre
- Departmental resource centre (inside college/university department)
- Institutional resource centre (inside college/university)
- Regional/national/international resource centre
- Virtual resource centre

2.1. Classroom/school resource centre

This is likely to be the smallest type of centre, often set up by an individual or small group and run out of an enthusiastic teacher's classroom or a corner of the school library. Materials may be limited to commercial audio, video and book materials, with a limited number of purpose-developed worksheets which are intended to consolidate and supplement classroom work. Teachers may, in particular, encourage student-directed selection of materials and themes for project work, but in most cases these are likely to be limited to fit into an overall syllabus or scheme of work developed by the teacher. None the less, this type of resource centre provides learners at a young age with important learning skills in relation to decision making in material evaluation and selection. In some countries, a number of schools, such as those awarded specialist Language College status in England, can access additional government funding to create a more stimulating environment:

> an authentic street/market place area was built which allows pupils to practise their languages in a very realistic setting. After all, you can't go to France or Spain every day, but here you can practise buying French Spanish [sic] goods in a shop with a native speaker of the language! There's also a newsagent's, a travel agent's, a market stall, a hotel reception area, a tourist information bureau and a clothes' shop. In the Centre, there are displays of visits abroad by staff and pupils, descriptions of career opportunities using languages and accounts of the work experience placements available at Palma Airport. (Greenbank High School Web site:
> http://www.greenbank.sefton.sch.uk/)

The Language Centre at Greenbank provides not only resources for its own pupils but also for other schools in the area, including primary and secondary schools. It is also used by evening classes in French, Spanish, Italian, Mandarin Chinese, Hungarian, and Arabic, thus going well beyond the possibilities open to many other schools. It shows, however, what can be done with policy-backed institutional and national commitment matched by adequate funding and resources. Arguably, this should be the norm rather than the exception, if any country is to establish itself as truly multilingual and multicultural, and such initiatives should be followed up with a broader programme of funding provision to a wider range of schools.

2.2. Departmental centre

This type of centre is generally located inside a university or college language department (or school of languages) and evolves in conjunction with that department. It is likely to have more extensive facilities available and to be used primarily by students registered for departmental language courses. Links between centre staff and language specialists are often good, as the latter have normally been party to the establishment of the centre and recognise it as fulfilling both their own needs and those of their students. Equally, as part of a university department, such a centre is likely to be very supportive of research activity. An example of this type of centre is the Language Resource Area (LRA) at the University of Limerick which was set up in the 1980s but expanded rapidly through the 1990s to provide both tailored learning and teaching resources and advice for students and teachers (http://www.ul.ie/~lcs/languageresourcearea/). Facilities include a materials resource base, two ICT laboratories and one audio-visual language laboratory, a self-access centre, and a teaching and recording room. These combine to support and enhance the work of teachers, learners, and researchers in the Department of Languages and Cultural Studies, the University of Limerick Language Centre, and the wider campus community. A resources budget is made available from the main departmental budget and a small committee with LRA, departmental, and Language Centre representatives meets regularly to make decisions on the development and implementation of new initiatives.

2.3. Institutional centre

Within an institutional centre, language-learning resources are located inside a distinct central or departmental unit established within a college or university, often in parallel to existing languages departments and with departmental status. Such a centre supports not only students studying languages as their main degree, but also, and often primarily, so-called 'language students of other disciplines'. As a distinct unit/department, it has more control of its own finances and policy-making than a departmental resource centre and is, therefore, more easily responsive to, and more rapidly affected by, institutional attitudes and national education policy. In many cases, teachers in such centres do not have an explicit research remit and funding for professional development must be found from the resource centre rather than the wider university budget. Two main types of institutional resource centre exist:

• centres with a learning/teaching remit only
These are common in many countries. For example in Germany, the teaching staff at the University of Rostock's Language Centre run courses for students of other disciplines and summer courses in German as a Foreign Language. Language centre staff in German universities seldom have a research remit and, therefore, receive little university support for such activity; language research of a more theoretical nature is carried out by the language departments situated in the Faculty of Arts. Rostock's Language Centre, supported by one technical/learning support member of staff, does, however, provide self-access multimedia facilities for students from all faculties (http://www.sprachenzentrum.uni-rostock.de/).

• centres with an additional significant commercial remit
These are becoming increasingly popular. An established example of such a centre is the University of Bristol Language Centre which has academic status within the Faculty of Arts and is well positioned to take advantage of commercial opportunities. As part of its many activities, the centre supports and teaches university students on accredited modules and offers custom-designed courses on a commercial basis to the wider community. Such an approach, of course, has its tensions and lays the centre more open to the vagaries of popular demand, but if successfully managed it may allow a resource centre to build up its stock (for example, within the Language Centre's multi-media facility) and activities rapidly on the basis of its own income generation, ensuring greater freedom of decision-making and introduction of innovation (http://www.bris.ac.uk/Depts/LangCent/).

2.4. Regional/national/international centre

Resource centres at this level have by their very nature a much broader remit and sphere of influence than the resource centres already mentioned, combining as they do the provision of a service for learners, teachers and researchers with a desire to inform language-education policy and practice. Ingram (2001) provides an extensive description and analysis of a number such centres, including the UK-based Centre for Information on Language Teaching and Research (CILT) (http://www.cilt.org.uk/) and the European Centre for Modern Languages (ECML), an institution of the Council of Europe based in Graz, Austria (http://www.ecml.at/).

The United Kingdom seldom considers itself a nation of language learners, so it is perhaps surprising that CILT should emerge in Ingram's eyes as such a significant influence in language education. Traditionally, CILT has operated largely as an information and resource centre for teachers in secondary schools, further education colleges, and to a lesser extent, universities, with most of its activities being generated from London. With the political devolution of Scotland, and to a lesser extent, Northern Ireland and Wales, the roles of the regional CILT offices have expanded and the London-based CILT office has had to redefine its own role to some extent, emerging more strongly as the support service for England and developing the concept of CILT UK which aims to encourage coordination between the four offices where possible. Such developments have raised a number of interesting issues, not least the increased vulnerability of the smaller regional/national centres and the tension between simultaneously providing services more appropriate to local educational needs and identifying common issues more effectively tackled at a broader level. Contrasting the development of Scottish CILT and the recently formed CILT Cymru in Wales highlights also the issue of the link between considered national language policy, political funding, and successful expansion. The former received increased funding following devolution, yet there has as yet been no developed language policy in Scotland. Indeed, Lo Bianco (2001) suggests that language policy in Scotland is largely characterised by fragmentation (60–62) and that the 'absence of decisive action [...] is a kind of choice or decision that implies a policy of "getting by" and "making do"' (Lo Bianco, 2001: 16). Wales, on the other hand, has been extremely active in developing a successful language policy to support and strengthen the role of the Welsh language in the school curriculum and public life, and appears to have recognised that the same must be done for modern foreign languages. In 2002, the Welsh Assembly provided substantial funding to launch CILT Cymru (http://www.ciltcymru.org.uk/).

The European Centre for Modern Languages (ECML) was established in Graz, Austria in 1994 (gaining status as a permanent institution in 1998), under the auspices of the Council of Europe. It offers an important meeting-place both for language advisors, researchers and multipliers (in the European Union sense of those responsible for the dissemination of information and good practice), and those interested in the development of innovative learning/teaching practices. Since September 2002, the ECML has had 33 member states who send representatives (advisors, teachers, textbook writers, or researchers) to regular seminars and conferences on agreed areas of national and European interest: in the period 2000–2003, such areas included language education (organisation, set-up, quality control), language awareness, intercultural competence, and ICT and language learning. The ECML is currently involved in a project entitled 'Improving support to language learning through language resource centres' which seeks to develop guidelines on good practice within resource centres (for more details, see http://www.ecml.at/activities/projectdetails.asp?p=7). The ECML disseminates the results achieved and promotes interaction between the different partners mainly through its Web site and 33 national contact points. Finally, the ECML is in the process of developing online thematic collections on specific areas such as ICT and multimedia, and learner autonomy which may prove useful for those wishing to explore these areas.

2.5. Virtual resource centre

Potentially the main challenges facing all of the above types of resource centres are the development of the Internet and the issue of what increased virtual mobility means for their centres. Learners have ever more pressures on their time and casual visitors are now much less likely to turn up at the door of a resource centre; centres are, therefore, faced with the challenge of ensuring that their resources are made available to existing users more easily and are on offer for a wider range of potential users. Already the Internet provides a range of virtual resource centres, such as Lingu@NET (http://www.linguanet.org.uk), and the Virtual Language Centre (http://vlc.polyu.edu.hk), while multilingual databases such as Lingu@NET-Europa (http://www.linguanet-europa.org/y2/) encourage teachers and researchers to share information and online resources with their international colleagues. In addition, existing centres are investing time and energy to converting many of their resources to the Web, so that the physical location of such resources becomes less of a barrier to their use (see, for example, the Humanities Computing and Media Centre at the University of Victoria (http://web.uvic.ca/hcmc/). The virtual environment opens up many opportunities for language resource centres to develop far beyond their current remits and has already fundamentally altered our understandings of the learning community and potential spheres of influence.

2.6. Balancing existing and future needs

Each of the above types of language resource centre has developed out of a perceived institutional need for such facilities. Whether emphasis lies currently on providing self-access learning resources, commercial taught courses, research-informed pedagogical support for teachers, or a combination of these, this emphasis is likely to change as the educational context changes. Centres which combine flexibility with a clear idea of their own objectives and how to achieve them are arguably best placed to cope with such short- and medium-term change. In the long term, from a pedagogical point of view, the issue of research-informed teaching and learning environments is crucial. If resource centre staff (be they teachers, administrators, or technical support) cannot keep themselves up to date on current thinking in language-learning technology and pedagogy as part of their own professional development, then dissatisfaction and disillusionment both on the part of teachers, and their learners, can occur. If teachers and resource centre staff are to help their students make the most of the facilities available to them, they must encourage students to explore what is available to them as learners and how they might best exploit materials and learning opportunities. Most of all, resource centre staff should help students understand the different learning environment within which they are operating and the challenges this poses. This can best be done, we would argue, through a concerted policy of combining pedagogical theory and practice through not only the structures but also the pedagogical ethos of any resource centre.

3. Language resource centres: Integrating pedagogical theory and practice

Although it is extremely important to be clear about the form and function of any language resource centre, the development of their unique identity cannot simply be ascribed to political and institutional factors. This identity is a result also of their position regarding language pedagogical theory and practice, not least in the area of learner-centred and/or learning-centred language learning. Significant examples of how such centres have emerged from the synthesis of research and practice are the Centre for Language and Communication Studies (CLCS) at Trinity College Dublin, around the work of David Little, the Centre de Recherches et d'Applications Pédagogiques en Langues (CRAPEL) at the University of Nancy II, around the work of Henri Holec, and the CTI for Modern Languages at Hull (now part of the Subject Centre for Languages, Linguistics and Areas Studies established in 2001). Each of these three centres has developed interesting theoretical positions which have influenced the shape and focus of many resource centres around the globe.

Little's work, as we have seen in Chapter 1, was central in developing the concept of autonomy as 'a capacity for detachment, critical reflection, decision-making, and independent action' (Little, 1990: 7). If adopted, this conceptual stance has many consequences for the language resource centre whatever its size, for to be successful, a centre must recognise that: a) such a capacity for autonomy is inherent in each student who walks through its doors or logs onto its Web site, regardless of which language they are studying and which level they are at; b) each student will be at a different level of development; and c) both external factors (e.g. time constraints, exam pressure) and internal factors (e.g.

confidence, motivation) will influence the individual's ability or willingness to exercise that capacity.

This raises not only important issues as to how we might measure or quantify 'levels of autonomy', but also poses the questions as to the way in which a language resource centre is set up and what it can, and should, offer students. Perhaps part of the answer lies in the work of Henri Holec at CRAPEL which, although primarily a research centre with largely self-selecting students, has likewise had a major impact on the work of others. Holec makes the useful distinction between self-directed learning and other-directed learning to focus our attention on the agency of any activity (Holec, 1981; 1988). It is important to note the use of the term 'other-directed' rather than 'teacher-directed'. The 'other' for Holec can be multi-faceted, for example, the strictures of institutional regulations, the curriculum and syllabus, the authorial voice within the very learning materials used and, not least, the form and system of assessment.

But developing self-directed learning is not just a case of creating the right conditions (although this is surely a pre-requisite); it is also a matter of enabling the learner to exercise their capacity for autonomy by directing their own learning. Holec is a strong advocate of the belief that such learning cannot be taught, but rather the learner must be given the freedom to discover for him/herself the extent of his/her own capacity for autonomy and how best to exploit it (Holec, 1987). This is an admirable stance in purely intellectual and philosophical terms, but it is not a luxury that many educational institutions, teachers, or even students (under increasing pressures to give evidence of cost-effectiveness and throughput) can afford.

Perhaps, in similar fashion to the argument posited in Chapter 1 that there exists a natural order of language learning which cannot be altered, only accelerated, there might well be a natural order of developing an individual's capacity for autonomy which can be accelerated by judicious intervention. This intervention might be interpreted on a broad scale in relation to the introduction of access to a different style of learning approach or more narrowly in terms of the types of support that might be provided by language teachers or language resource centre colleagues, be they technical, administrative, or learning support staff.

One of the most interesting developments from the University of Hull work has been the emergence of the concept of 'language advising' which is being explored through initiatives such as Project SMILE, (Strategies for Managing an Independent Learning Environment). This project, which ran from 1997 to 2000, sought to develop and disseminate good practice in the area of support for independent and open learning in modern languages (for more details, see http://www.ncteam.ac.uk/projects/fdtl/fdtl2/projectdescriptions/3-97.htm). Designed to bridge the gap between the provision of open learning facilities for languages and student use of these facilities, it aimed to disseminate best practice in the effective integration of learning resources, learner needs and student support. Its findings are based on the experience gained and the tools developed through extensive collaboration between language departments and the open learning advisory service for languages at the University of Hull, two main partner institutions (Nottingham Trent University and the University of Ulster) and several other universities with a wide spectrum of resources, learners, and courses. An extensive analysis of this project, including a discussion of the replicability of these findings in other institutions, can be found in Mozzon-McPherson and Vismans (2001).

Clearly one of the issues surrounding the potential or desirability of replicating the institutionalised function of the language advisor as advocated by Mozzon-McPherson and Vismans is the extent to which the overall educational context supports such an approach. Much work has been carried out by Phil Benson and colleagues at the University of Hong Kong English Language Centre on a wide range of aspects relating to the implications of putting theories of learner autonomy and self-directed learning into practice (Benson and Voller, 1997). Equally interesting is the work carried out by Mark Warschauer at the University of Hawai'i, not least in relation to the difficulties of introducing new learning philosophies into strongly traditional teaching environments (see Warschauer, 1999). Warschauer's more recent publications explore the emergence of virtual learning environments and their potential impact on com-munication and learning practices in the future (Warschauer and Kern, 2000; Warschauer, 2003).

Reports on the development of language resource centres frequently stress their role in supporting more learner-directed learning, and consequently their work is increasingly becoming a focus of research (see, for example, Little and Voss, 1997). This is highlighted by the development of European organisations such as CercleS (European Confederation of Language Centres in Higher Education) with its associated national bodies and regular conferences. International collaboration between centres in the areas of both teaching and research is increasingly encouraged through associations such as CercleS, International Association for Language Learning Technology (IALLT), and EuroCALL (see, for example, the joint policy statement of CALICO, EuroCALL and IALLT issued in 1999 on scholarly activities in computer-assisted language learning, http://www.iall.net/iallt_documents/ScholActCALL.pdf). For the institution seeking to establish a language resource centre or wishing to use existing facilities to their fullest potential, a range of useful research evidence now exists, but the question remains as to whether there is a clear set of charac-teristics related to any successful language resource centre which go beyond the individual institutional, learning and teaching context. In the section which follows, we outline a number of factors which, given the discussion above, would appear to contribute to the success of any language resource centre, and might serve as a useful starting point for any developing centre.

4. Contributing factors to establishing a successful language resource centre

In this section we suggest that although resource centres will have their own particular style and speciality, there are a number of common factors which, if present, might potentially increase the chances of creating a successful centre where the majority of learners improve their language and learning skills. These factors are distilled not only from the research literature outlined above, but also from our joint experience of being involved in the setting up, development and running of the Language Resource Area (LRA) within the Department of Languages and Cultural Studies at the University of Limerick, Ireland (Murphy as LRA Coordinator, Conacher as Senior Lecturer in German and member of the LRA Committee), and from our subsequent individual experience as Administrator within the expanding University of Limerick Language Centre (Murphy) and as Research Fellow within Scottish CILT, based at the University of Stirling (Conacher).

In order to establish common factors underpinning the development of a successful language resource centre, it is, of course, essential to tackle the constant dilemma of how to measure success. Each centre will have its own internal criteria, be they quantitative measures of the numbers of learners using their facilities on a daily, monthly, or annual basis, the frequency of visits to the centre by individual learners, the range of languages on offer, the sophistication and range of learning technology available and so on, or qualitative measures of the response by users of the facilities to the learning environment, the learning experience, and their improvement in the language they are studying. Whatever criteria are decided upon, the success of any language resource centre is likely to depend upon its ability to meet the institutional and pedagogical needs which are determined by its individual context. For this reason, it seems particularly important that the following factors are addressed on an ongoing basis as any language resource centre is set up and develops:

- the existence of a clear pedagogical mission, agreed and supported by all stakeholders;
- the establishment of a clear map of broad infrastructure and responsibilities of all stakeholders, taking into account the local context;
- clear planning and execution of implementation;

- an evaluation process in place which feeds back into cycle of planning and implementation.

4.1. Pedagogical mission

The primary aims of setting up and running a language resource centre forwarded by Sheerin in the late 1980s remain valid today; as she suggests, they are:

> to enable learning to take place independently of teaching. Students are able to choose and use self-access materials on their own and the material gives them the ability to correct or assess their own performance. By using such a self-access facility, students are able to direct their own learning.
>
> (Sheerin, 1989: 3).

Acceptance of this simple statement has major implications for any institution. It presupposes a commitment to the value of not just independent learning but also self-directed learning and self-assessment. Furthermore, it assumes the existence of a space where such learning can take place and materials which will support learners in identifying, and working at, their individual level and help them to monitor and improve their performance. Most fundamentally, it assumes support of Little's belief in the concept of autonomy as a capacity that each language learner possesses and can potentially tap into.

If the aim of the language resource centre in promoting such ideas is not to be constantly at odds with the department or institution within which it is based, then we must assume that the resource centre's success will be greatly dependent on the extent to which the pedagogical principles encapsulated by Sheerin's statement also form the basis of pedagogical thinking in the wider institutional context. Thus the ethos of the language resource centre is linked fundamentally to the relationship it has with the language department/school/study centre in which it is embedded. If there is support for innovative, new, and varied ways of learning within the department and institution, and if learners are made aware of this support and constantly receive reaffirmation of the potential advantages of independent and guided study, both generally and specifically in relation to their language learning, it is surely likely that users will be able to exploit more fully the opportunities offered them by the language resource centre.

In such an ideal situation, the mission of the language resource centre would support the fulfilment of the department's mission which in turn would contribute to the overall mission of the institution, and broader national educational priorities. This involves a significant level of exploration, discussion, and nego-tiation of where commonalities can be found between these different levels of educational management which can be espoused by all stakeholders (policy makers, educational managers, academic, administrative and technical staff, students) both in principle and in practice, through provision of adequate resources (staff, space, funding) and support for a complementary pedagogical infrastructure (via acceptance of flexibility in teaching/learning modes, timetabling, assessment and accreditation).

A recent survey reveals that there is indeed likely to be a greater level of suc-cessful use of such language resources in an institutional framework where staff are well-informed about current theories of learner autonomy, self-directed learning and new technologies (Littlemore, 2001: 50). It is hardly surprising that these two activities, the development of research and scholarship in the area of language learning on the one hand, and the application of this in the learning environment of the institution on the other, arguably go best hand in hand.

4.2. Infrastructure and responsibilities of stakeholders

If the principle of self-directed language learning is to be promoted within the language resource centre, then the fundamental will to make this happen still needs to be transformed into reality. For, as many writers in the field of learner training have emphasised, the assumption that the provision of a well-equipped and well-resourced language resource centre creates autonomous learners is misplaced (Dickinson, 1992; Ellis and Sinclair, 1989). Rather, an integrated rela-tionship between learner, teacher, resources, and language-learning support systems is necessary to ensure the successful development of learner autonomy within language resource centres.

As Sturtridge points out, 'the initial step towards the success of a self-access centre lies in the successful management of its introduction into the institution or educational system' (Sturtridge, 1997: 70). Adequate numbers of skilled staff with training in languages, a commitment to language learning, teaching, and research and an active interest in promoting the learning of languages through the use of various media (particularly newer technologies) are vital to the development and integration of the language resource centre.

A clear infrastructure needs to be established, so that, from a procedural point of view, it is clear where responsibilities for policy, pedagogical and budgetary decision-making lie and that, if certain elements of such decision-making are delegated to committee or individual level, these remits are clear, realistic and realisable. Regular, but time-efficient, reporting procedures are necessary to keep information and ideas flowing between the different areas of responsibility.

Above all, broader policy decisions within the institution and the department need to be communicated to those with responsibilities within the language resource centre, and opportunities must exist for resource centre staff to input ideas and comments to wider policy and pedagogical discussions.

The various functions performed by a language resource centre are similar, regardless of size or sphere of influence. They typically require the expertise of a librarian or resource manager, an administrator, a language teacher/advisor, a technician/IT specialist and reception staff. (In 2002, IALLT produced an extremely useful statement outlining the professional responsibilities of language technology specialists which highlights the varied nature of the work undertaken – available at http://www.iall.net/iallt_documents/IALLTProfessional.pdf). The reality in most centres is that many of these roles will be carried out by one or two individuals. Training and time should be factored into the resource centre's budget and work calendar in order to allow staff to support these various functions.

An important aspect of the work of the manager/administrator of any resource centre is liaising regularly with teaching staff both inside and outside the centre (depending on the LRC's structures) to determine their needs and those of their students, and to discuss what the language resource centre can, and cannot do, to fulfil those needs. This involves discussion of the overall aims of activities within the resource centre in the context of the programmes being followed. Teachers and learners also need to be kept up to date with new developments within the resource centre and to be encouraged to explore new ways of using the resources available. It is particularly useful to provide new teaching staff and learners with detailed individual or small group orientation in the language resource centre with specific reference to their subject area(s), but more established users should not be forgotten. Advice on new learning materials, activities, and technologies should be given on an ongoing basis to learners, tutors, and staff. This can easily be done via an up-to-date Web site, bulletin board, or regular sessions where users can try out new opportunities with the support of LRC staff. Clearly this requires a high level of organisation and effective communication; administrative systems within the language resource centre need, therefore, to include participatory mechanisms for information and feedback. A consultative committee may fulfil this role, supported by a discussion group including LRC staff, language teachers, and student representatives. Time must also be allocated within workplans to the maintaining of Web sites, bulletin boards, and so on so that these become an important information point for all stakeholders within the language-learning process.

The teacher plays an important role in what happens within the LRC, whether it is based within a department or operates in parallel to the language departments of a given institution. In particular, the teacher who takes an active, participative approach to the resource centre (Benson and Voller, 1997: 94), liaising with librarians and technicians and recognising the LRC as an important element of the learning space within which students operate, is likely to have a positive impact both on the development of the LRC and the integration of its activities within the overall learning experience of students. The teacher can provide students with important support, encouraging and advising students in their self-study, providing pointers for further areas to explore, and assisting learners in their discovery of different learning strategies and their development of new skills.

Many schools/language departments also expand upon the staffing possibilities available to them by using the services of students in the school/department to do part-time hours in the resource centre. They act as reception staff and advisors to students (especially if they are final year/postgraduate language students themselves). This appears to have many positive advantages in the sense that the students are usually interested in languages and language study; they may be perceived as more approachable than other staff; they have recent and current experience of language learning and so are in a position to advise; and they can give students a sense of involvement in, ownership of, and responsibility for, the resource centre.

One area of expertise which is not easily accommodated within this multifunctional approach is that of the technician/IT specialist who is generally required on at least a part-time basis for most language resource centres that utilise any level of technological equipment. Major ICT advances, from e-mail and chat-rooms to video conferencing and electronic learning environments, can be successfully harnessed for the promotion of language learning and language use, as subsequent chapters in this volume will show. However, the other pressures on language teachers may mean that they are reluctant to integrate such opportunities into their regular teaching and may not recommend these to their students if there is no support from qualified IT/technical professionals available at all times.

Arguably the most important stakeholders in the learning that takes place in any language resource centre are the learners themselves, for the success of the LRC will largely depend on the extent to which learners, whether they are paying directly for its facilities or not, believe that this facility helps their language learning. It is important that learners see the work that they do in the LRC as being part of a broader learning experience. A resource centre which is efficiently and professionally run encourages students to treat staff and fellow learners with respect and to take their own learning seriously. Clear information should be provided to students of what facilities and materials are available; advice on learning and instruction in the use of different technologies should be on offer; students should also be aware of the layout, staff structures and standard opening hours of the LRC, so that they know whom to contact about individual issues and when. Much of this information can, as indicated above, be provided via bulletin boards and the Web site, and again provision should be made for students both to provide feedback and suggestions for improvement of facilities/services and to have representation on decision-making committees of relevance to the LRC. In this way, students are encouraged to see themselves as important stakeholders in the language resource centre with reasonable expectations of the support they will receive and clear responsibilities towards the centre, fellow learners, and themselves.

It is vital that the role and responsibilities of all stakeholders in the development of any language resource centre are clearly defined and agreed by all concerned. It may well prove beneficial for these to be clearly mapped out and made available to anyone using the facilities. Equally, wherever possible such a mapping exercise should be integrated into the creation of a development plan which will gain institutional support and financial commitment; such a document can then provide a clear point of reference both for ongoing review and future planning.

4.3. Implementing plans in the language resource centre

Forward planning is vital to any language resource centre looking to develop smoothly and successfully. While different institutional frameworks will, of course, impose different constraints on the establishment and running of the language resource centre (Little, 1998: 34–7), there are a number of key aspects which need to be addressed when first planning the centre and subsequently reviewed on a regular basis.

The main challenges to establishing a good language resource centre are finding suitable space and regular funding. While many institutions seek to free up space from existing buildings (a common strategy adopted to create school and departmental resource centres), others which have adopted the model of an institutional resource centre existing as a central or departmental unit parallel to the language departments have been able to attract university and government funding to build purpose-built facilities. Both models have their advantages and disadvantages in a number of areas. Siting the resource centre in an existing building close to, or inside, the departments which most frequently use it, easily establishes the LRC as an extension of the work that is already done within the department. It is likely to be handy for students and staff to access and use, and work carried out there can easily be integrated into work done in the classroom (it may even be possible to let students use the facilities for part of the classroom period and then incorporate their findings into the next section of the lesson). If the LRC is a separate unit, perhaps some distance from the departments from which it draws students, this will have an impact on the type of work that can be carried out there and more energy will have to be put into attracting staff and students to avail fully of the facilities on an integrated basis. Liaison, too, with different stakeholders may prove more complex. However, a separate LRC has the advantage that the building is custom built and can therefore be configured in such a way that the potential of the space available is fully realised. Where the LRC is set up in an existing building, there may well be restrictions on what can practicably be done with the space available, or it may prove very expensive to reconfigure the space to the optimum design. Finally, the existence of a separate LRC may make it simpler to introduce a new ethos of learning within the unit and establish a clearer identity for this learning space than might be the case if the LRC is simply integrated into an existing building. Whatever the space available, however, key decisions need to be made on how to divide this up to best effect, and many examples are now available for language resource centres, whether newly established or undergoing redevelopment, to draw upon (see for example, the case studies provided in ICT4LT, Module 3.1. at http://www.ict4lt.org/en/index.htm).

Developing a strong funding base is of utmost importance to the development of a successful language resource centre, and again here the infrastructural basis of the LRC is likely to be a fundamental issue. Where the LRC is located within a school, department, or school of languages, it is likely that it will be funded out of that budget, with some element of transfer payment from other departments whose students use the facilities. This may mean that the funding available is limited and only becomes known once the departmental budget has been allocated and subdivided; it does mean, however, that in any one year the department may decide to allocate additional funding to the LRC for upgrading of equipment and resources with little bureaucratic red tape to be negotiated. Where the LRC is located in a separate unit, funding is likely to be higher and to be allocated earlier in the budget planning cycle, making it easier to plan for the next academic year. The LRC itself then has greater control over how it spends its budget, and will have direct access to transfer payments from other departments. It will, however, have to argue its case on an annual basis for funding against larger units, and this will require major time investment on the part of the manager/administrator, which must be taken from other activities. Whichever model the LRC is working within, it is likely that there will be increasing pressure for language resource centres to attract funding from outside sources by offering their facilities on a commercial basis. This has implications for both models in terms of staffing and security issues – implications which need to be balanced out in planning and budgeting (it may, for example, be much simpler, yet much more expensive, to provide evening support and security staff in a purpose-built resource centre which can be open when other parts of the institution are closed).

With the level of space and overall funding available established, plans need to be implemented to maximise these resources through the establishment of a suitable physical layout (taking into account issues of access and security) and agreed budgetary priorities. As was stated at the outset of this chapter, great variety exists in the size and layout of resource centres. The ideas presented here are examples of the kinds of physical features that might be included, particularly within a purpose-built space. It is not a definitive list but may provide pointers to any resource centre, beyond the simple classroom-based model, in adapting any space available to the needs of users.

4.3.1. PHYSICAL LAYOUT

The importance of large, comfortable, well-lit, well appointed, custom-designed space, containing moveable furniture and fixtures to facilitate variation of activity, should never be underestimated. The ideal is to use custom-designed space in a building where there should be raised floors, which would conceal an intensive level of data and power servicing, and a structural grid with lightweight walls to allow for computing arrangements and teaching room configuration to be changed within a week. The room configuration should be set out in such a way as to provide the lightest and most attractive environment for students working in open-access areas. There should be a reception area for handling queries, leading to turnstiles, with a card entry system, computer teaching rooms, and an e-mail room. The guiding principle is to allow access to wide-ranging multi-media resources so that at any one time a multitude of media is being used, ranging from newspapers, music scores, records, CDs, and books through to CD-ROMs and the Internet. The nature of the equipment in use in the open-access area would mean that headphones would need to be worn at most user places, enabling those involved in language practice to speak aloud without disturbing others.

In order to enable all audiovisual and ICT resources to be smoothly integrated, they need to be security-tagged and catalogued. Where possible, there should be a PC-based catalogue with resources being issued from a single service point or available on an open-access basis. Resource centres benefit from maintaining close links with the IT department and the library, as the centre draws on all aspects of the integrated services in its daily operations, not only in the preparation of audio-visual resources and language reference books, but also in the provision of CALL, networked computing, and Internet services.

The resource centre would include viewing positions, bookable viewing rooms for groups, CD/audio positions, catalogue networked points, language audio positions, networked computers, networked printers, and study spaces for users of reference material. Live satellite broadcasts, pre-recorded films and documentaries, bookable rooms for group viewing and discussion, software, multimedia language courses, language reference books, and foreign newspapers should all be available to learners, teachers and researchers. In addition, there will be a need for language teaching rooms, equipped with 20–25-position language laboratories, overhead projectors, televisions, VCRs, and multimedia PCs. Again, the physical layout of the centre will have implications for access to, and security of, the facilities, so these matters should be considered carefully before embarking on the setting up of the centre. At the same time, users are likely to appreciate a welcoming, non-threatening atmosphere, and so a balance must be found.

4.3.2. ACCESS AND SECURITY

Access is not simply an issue of removing barriers to the successful use of the LRC – barriers like inadequate or inappropriate opening hours. More importantly, access should focus on making the facilities as easy to use and as relevant as possible to the target users. As discussed already, the physical layout should be arranged in such a way as to provide the lightest and most attractive environment for students working in open access areas. Lack of familiarity with new technologies may immediately prove a barrier to access for some potential learners, and LRC staff need to overcome this difficulty in an open and supportive way. Equally, open access for everyone has to be ensured, with premises, materials, and technology being easily navigable by learners with particular special needs, be they related to mobility, sight, hearing, dyslexia, or whatever (see, as one example, the University of Hull Dyslexia Project at http://www.hull.ac.uk/langinst/olc/dyslexia.htm).

To open up access to the centre and create a sense of the potential of the centre within the target users, motivational activities may be considered. These may include open days in which learners are involved, cultural events, food fairs, dancing, singing, competitions with a language theme, crosswords, games and treasure hunts. 'Language Exchange Meetings', based on the tandem principle, may also be considered as a means of promoting authentic communication in the target language between native speakers. Such a system can be equally successful in helping integrate incoming exchange students from a variety of language backgrounds. (see, as one example of such language exchange meetings, http://www.ul.ie/~lcs/languageresourcearea/facilities_and_services.htm).

As we have seen, opening up access to the centre raises the issue of security. Staff of language resource centres are constantly trying to walk the fine line between 'full cupboards that are locked and open cupboards that are empty'; in other words, striking a balance between self-access and self-service (Esch, 1994: 63–7). The ideal solution is to tag all items of material and create a central database where items are recorded when borrowed, akin to the operation of a library. Most large resource centres now install these systems as a matter of course. Some centres still struggle on with a paper-based method of controlling the borrowing of material; various efforts at increasing security are made: installing video cameras; keeping bags outside the centre; signing in and out all material. These systems work to a large extent but are cumbersome to administer and are not as successful as the automated tagging and security bar system.

Modern language resource centres also face security-related issues surrounding ICT resources and there is a need to prevent the possibility of tampering with programs or pirating of programs by users. Electronic trespassing (hacking) is increasingly becoming an issue for resource centre managers, and steps need to be put in place in conjunction with IT support personnel to prevent this type of activity. Anti-virus software and virus checkers are usually installed as standard on PC networks and are adequate to prevent most rogue ICT activities.

4.3.3. BUDGETARY PRIORITIES

As with the physical size and shape of the resource centre, funding will vary considerably from institution to institution. Regardless of size, however, the major areas for which ongoing funding will be required include staffing, equipment, resources and training (for LRC staff, teachers and students).

The multiple functions required by LRC staff are, as we have already discussed, frequently encompassed by one or two staff. While this may well be adequate for a small resource centre offering students limited support, a centre which lacks well-trained staff to ensure desired levels of access and skilled support and which offers little or no technical support cannot hope to realise its full potential. Ideally, core staff should be employed on a permanent basis to encourage their commitment to the language resource centre and to permit the building of a strong team who can bring forward the agreed mission of the LRC and act as powerful advocates of its work.

In many institutions, the overall budget is divided from the outset into pay and non-pay budgets, so that staffing costs are kept separate from those for other expenditures. In dividing up the non-pay budget, Davies offers a useful model of the balance between different demands: 30 per cent hardware, 30 per cent software (including learning resources), 30 per cent staff training and materials development, and 10 per cent contingency (for unforeseeable costs). Davies argues that many problems in relation to the development of successful learning environments are caused by the weighting of this balance falling away from staff training towards hardware and software which then lie underutilised (Davies, 2002: 2–3).

Hardware (including computers, televisions, video recorders, and cassette recorders) constitutes a substantial cost for a new language resource area. Beyond that, it is important that any resource centre keeps reasonably up-to-date with technological advances, so that learners, teachers, and researchers with an active interest in ICT can fully explore the potential of these in language learning. PCs, for example, can have a good shelf life of three years, even with heavy usage by students, but will generally need to be replaced at that stage. Older technologies may develop less slowly and thus be more durable. They should certainly not be rejected just because newer equipment appears on the market, as they can frequently be incorporated into new ways of learning and teaching. Fortunately, most resource centres do not have the luxury of indulging in the kind of wastefulness which sees any old technology being quickly abandoned in favour of the new, and so they can frequently experience a more thoughtful building upon what has gone before.

Policy on funding software and learning resources will dictate what is possible for learners, teachers and researchers in the resource centre, and the resources budget will mark the limitations and potential of the centre. Those responsible for the centre will have to decide whether there is a necessity for a certain amount of material in many media in many languages or whether there is a need for the centre to have a basic level of material in many languages and a deeper, stronger collection in the languages on which the centre focuses. All centres will implement cost-saving measures which suit the local environment. One example is buying single copies of many different varieties of course books, multimedia courses, and software packages to be used by learners working individually in guided study groups and only buying multiple copies/site licences when the item has a more universal appeal across languages/skills levels. Copyright is an important issue which no language resource centre can afford to ignore. Guidelines for educational establishments on how to interpret copyright legislation are readily available (see, for example, ICT4LT Module 3.1 at http://www.ict4lt.org/en/index.htm) and should be made available to all staff, teachers, and students working in the language resource centre.

There will be major differences from one language resource centre to another in the amount of money available for material resources. That said, each resource centre needs a core set of resources as a baseline upon which to build. This includes paper dictionaries, dictionaries on CD-ROM, text books at various levels, reference materials in paper, CD-ROM, or increasingly on the Internet. Adding new resources and adapting existing resources to new requirements will be a continual process. Language resource centre staff will need to develop policy both on materials acquisition and on adapting, organising, storing, and cataloguing resources. A detailed multilingual catalogue is one of the central components of any language resource centre. The cataloguing system will evolve and develop according to the specific needs of the centre, and ideally it should be available directly to users so that they themselves can choose appropriate resources to use for their language study (McCall, 1992: 31).

Davies also draws attention to the need to allocate funding for staff training and materials development. In many cases, time pressures mitigate against the large scale development of in-house learning materials specifically catering for students' needs. This is, however, a desirable aim and at the very least such funding could contribute significantly to the development of a regularly updated informative Web site which both keeps regular users informed of new developments and functions as an important marketing tool for the language resource centre inside and outside the home institution. Beyond that, the most overlooked aspect of funding in resource centres is arguably that of staff training. In a developing and evolving resource centre which seeks to offer excellent language-study opportunities to its users, there should be recognition of the fact that, without regular, funded staff training in relevant areas, there will be no ongoing development. Depending on the current skills of the resource centre staff, in-service training might include courses in ICT, second language acquisition theory, learner autonomy, language advising (helping learners develop learning skills and promoting self-directed learning), educational management, promotion, and marketing. There are already various examples of staff training possibilities in existence. For example, within the UK context, the University of Hull offers both a Postgraduate Certificate in Advising for Language Learning (University of Hull: PG Cert), which is a new programme, developed specifically as a professional qualification for Language Advisers, and a taught postgraduate degree programme, MA/Diploma in Language Learning and Technology, focusing on the application of computer technology to language learning, teaching, and research (University of Hull: MA).

Training is not only required, however, for the language resource staff; funding also needs to be available so that they can offer training opportunities for teachers and learners in the use of the language resource centre and promote a more learner-centred approach to language learning. Training sessions for teachers are often best arranged in non-teaching periods of the year, when teachers are already devoting some of their time to revising past courses and developing new ones. Sessions might be language or technology specific depending on the needs of teachers, or might cover more generic areas such as integrating self-access learning into the curriculum or promoting self-directed learning in the classroom. Collaborative sessions between resource centre staff and teachers experienced in using the facilities with different groups and levels of students can be particularly successful in encouraging established colleagues to integrate new ideas into their teaching. For new teaching staff, sessions should be available before the beginning of the academic year to introduce them to the facilities, resources and staff of the resource centre.

Unlike training opportunities for teachers, training sessions for students are likely to take place on a regular basis throughout the academic year. Training in the use of particular facilities and the range of materials available in specific language areas is usefully done at the beginning of each semester or term, but it is likely that ongoing support and advice will be required by individual students throughout the year. Programmes such as the European Computer Driving Licence (ECDL), The Online Netskills Interactive Course (http://www.netskills.ac.uk/TonicNG/cgi/sesame?tng) or the modules contained in ICT4LT (http://www.ict4lt.org/) can be recommended to learners (and teachers) so that they acquire the skills required to gain access to the potential of ICT and language learning. Once the technicalities of using the facilities have been understood, it is important that students also learn to appreciate that they are operating in a rather different environment from any they may previously have encountered. Group training sessions can be arranged to introduce students to the fundamentals of language learning within an independent learning environment and then followed up as appropriate on an individual basis. Possible topics include: learner needs analysis, learner profiling, the development of study plans and learner diaries/portfolios, the organisation of learning circles (peer learning) or tandem learning networks, and the provision of learner training workshops (listening strategies, reading, mnemonic skills, time management, goal setting, understanding grammar, and independent learning skills).

Some institutions have begun introducing optional or compulsory modules directed towards developing independent study skills and self-directed learning. For example, in Ireland, where the Leaving Certificate syllabus remains largely teacher-directed, and students arriving at university level have little experience of taking control of their learning, universities have tried to address the difficulties encountered by first-year language students in various ways. The Centre for Language and Communication Studies at Trinity College Dublin, for example, has established a specific course entitled 'Introduction to Language Studies', which is compulsory for all first-year language students. The module emphasises that learning a language is a lifelong project, and includes areas such as grammar and linguistic competence, language acquisition, language variation, language planning, language change, and basic techniques of linguistic description and analysis. In addition to this, students are encouraged to think about how language learning occurs, how it might be better managed (including planning, monitoring, and evaluation), and how identifying individual strengths and weaknesses can help informed choice-making about their language learning (for more information, see http://www.tcd.ie/CLCS/courses/intro_lang_study.html). Such interventions in the learning process continue to be valuable well after the learner has completed formal language education or ceased to use the resource centre on a regular basis, as learners develop patterns of learning which can be continued after the course has been completed. Research has shown that learners react positively to attempts to increase their ability to learn independently (Sheerin, 1997: 56), and thus language resource centres have an important contribution to make to any institution's policy on lifelong learning. Indeed, supporting the development of such a module and its integration into the overall learning programme of students is a clear signal from any institution of its commitment to lifelong learning and to the type of learning environment fostered within many LRCs.

4.4. The evaluation–planning–implementation cycle

It is important that, once initial decisions have been made regarding the location, staffing and day-to-day running of the language resource centre, mechanisms are put in place to ensure that these decisions can be reviewed regularly, thus ensuring that the LRC can proactively address changing circumstances, whether of a financial, pedagogical, or technological nature, or simply arise from the fact that the resource centre is swamped by visitors. The danger always exists that resource centre staff are so busy there seems no time to take a step back reflect on their own activities and achievements, and on the facilities on offer and how these are being exploited. However, a centre which has been established to support directly the needs of specific stakeholders (policy makers, educational managers, academic, administrative and technical staff, and students) depends for its continued success on sustaining a cycle of evaluation, planning, and implementation.

Feedback from all stakeholders is, therefore, essential. This can be gathered in different ways, directed towards the particular target group, and the focus of the feedback sought. Tracking Web site hits allows the LRC to see who is using what facilities and the extent to which interest is confined to students, users within the institution, or beyond; a feedback feature on the Web site allows comments to be posted by visitors; ideally policy-makers, decision-makers, education managers, and teachers could be surveyed at intervals to measure their awareness of the LRC and its work. Such indicators provide invaluable information on per-ceptions of the LRC's activities while also providing an opportunity to raise its profile. LRC staff might well benefit from the opportunity to take time away from the centre to meet and discuss short and long-term plans. Such 'away days' can also be used to review practices, discuss new initiatives, and explore alternative training possibilities with teaching staff.

Additional systems of monitoring and evaluation should be kept simple and easy to implement, lest they are abandoned because of more immediate demands on LRC staff members' time. User evaluation may include informal queries about activities, questionnaires, interviews, and surveys (see Esch, 1994: 78–80 for examples of needs analyses and evaluation questionnaires). Learners, too, as the primary users of the facilities, can provide invaluable feedback on their use of the centre in terms of frequency of use, average length of stay, whether visits are compulsory (i.e. dictated by a tutor/assignment) or voluntary, types of materials used and found to be useful or not, opening hours, and comfort levels within the centre (temperature, noise, access, access to support). They will undoubtedly also have suggestions for improvements. All systems need to be updated regularly and if procedures exist for monitoring, evaluating, and implementing change, the LRC will be better placed to make informed planning decisions. Of course, there is little point in gathering such information if changes are not, or cannot be, implemented, but even within a situation where the LRC has limited control over its own development, such feedback data can provide valuable ammunition in funding and policy discussions at every level.

5. Future perspectives in language learning and the role of the LRC

The proliferation of language resource centres over the last twenty years has, as we have seen, arisen from particular political, economic, and pedagogical circumstances. In responding to the challenges posed by this context, such centres have contributed significantly to an expansion of research on self-instruction and autonomy in language learning (Benson and Voller, 1997: 12), as well as a gradual change in the role of the teaching profession and a move towards a more learner-centred approach. 'Teachers are seen as "facilitators of learning", [...] curriculum designers and producers of multimedia module study materials' (Littlemore, 2001: 50), and take increasing advantage of the flexibility and choice offered by both older and newer technologies in developing more varied approaches to the learning and teaching process.

Much more research needs to be done, however, on how learning takes place within the language resource centre, on the extent to which the emphasis on the value of self-directed learning is actually carried through in the materials and support systems provided, and on the extent to which such self-directed learning not only contributes to the development of greater learner autonomy (in itself a laudable educational aim), but also to improved language performance. At present, much of the research work is undertaken by academic staff situated in languages or language education departments who are at least one step removed from the work of the language resource centre. As frequent visitors to the centre and avid observers of the work which goes on there, they provide an invaluable insider/outsider research perspective. However, the frequently institutionalised decision to establish posts within many language resource centres which do not include a research remit (or even prohibit it) means that much research potential, which could feed back into pedagogical discussion and professional development, is wasted. Language resource centre staff who interact closely with learners are ideally placed to become involved in major research projects whose findings are invaluable to the development of our understanding of learner autonomy, lifelong learning, and second language acquisition.

Much interest has been shown in recent years in the development of learning management systems (for an analysis of their potential in language learning, see Chapter 2). As such systems become more sophisticated and flexible, they may well provide an important model for institutions to draw upon in integrating policy and pedagogical thinking in practical ways. The processes by which integration does or does not take place will impact significantly on the future existence of language resource centres in their present form. Many teachers and language resource staff are rightly sceptical of the prospect of language learning based exclusively on ICT, arguing that as language performance is fundamentally social and communicative in nature, the role of ICT is merely to support the learning process, and that this role will vary considerably depending on institutional settings, cultural traditions, and individual learner and teacher preferences. The art of designing technological support for language learning in a resource centre, therefore, lies in identifying the needs of a given set of language learners in specific social and cultural settings, and using the rapidly evolving technologies to support this particular learning environment in the most effective way possible (Esch and Chanier, 2000: 5). It is vital, therefore, that the language resource centre has a strong voice and makes itself heard in institutional discussions on the development and introduction of such learning management systems, if it is not to find itself sidelined and its facilities slowly run-down as being superfluous and outdated.

6. Conclusion

In the current economic and educational climate, the language resource centre has a vital role to play in supporting many students in their language learning. It provides an important framework within which such students can develop skills and strategies through their learning of languages which they can exploit in their other studies and future careers. It also provides a wealth of potential data (all too often untapped) on how students learn, how they interact with one another, and the media and technologies they exploit in their language learning. Without turning the language resource centre into a laboratory within which researchers conduct experiments on unsuspecting subjects, there is much scope for involving teachers, researchers, LRC staff, and students in better understanding what goes on within the language-learning process.

This becomes all the more vital, as technological advances increasingly make the delivery of teaching possible either in the learner's home or in his/her place of work. As a result, it is likely that language resource centres will become more facilitators of distance learning than library-like places where students go to study. Informed decisions on how this transformation might take place can only be made on the basis of a sound, research-driven understanding of the practical and pedagogical implications of such a move. Furthermore, while the multimedia materials currently produced frequently fail to exploit the full potential of the available technology, such potential may well in future produce materials of design and intention which differ significantly from the paper, taped and electronic materials we know today. As the creation of Web-based language-learning resources grows more complex, the danger increases that, as happened in the initial stages of CALL development, many teachers and learners will be effectively excluded from participating creatively in Web-authoring and Web-enhanced language learning. This, once again, moves those with pedagogical experience and relevant research expertise one step further away from the activities of the language resource centre. In contrast we would argue that language resource staff, teachers and researchers need to work more closely together in helping identify and evaluate new approaches which promise to enhance student learning.

Any language resource centre with the right institutional support has the potential to play a pivotal role in the development of language-learning policy and practice at all levels within its host institution and beyond, and, in so doing, to feed into broader educational discussions on lifelong learning, flexible educational modes, and new learning environments. The language resource centre can, therefore, be seen as an important touchstone by which one can determine, through an analysis of its structures and institutional role, the degree to which it, and the institution within which it is based, are indeed working positively towards developing as a meeting-place of integrated policy, pedagogical theory, and practice.

Acknowledgements:

The authors would like to thank the following people for providing information on which sections of this chapter are based: Graham Davies, Sabine Heinzius, Catherine Jeanneau, Pat McQuade, Breffni O'Rourke, Ray Satchell, Catherine Seewald.

Bibliography

Benson, P and P. Voller (eds.) (1997) *Autonomy and Independence in Language Learning*. London and New York: Longman.

CALICO, EuroCALL, and IALLT (1999) 'Scholarly activities in computer-assisted language learning: Development, pedagogical innovations and research'. Joint Policy Statements of CALICO, EuroCALL, and IALLT, arising from a Research Seminar at the University of Essen, Germany, 30 April–1 May 1999 (http://www.iall.net/iallt_documents/ScholActCALL.pdf).

Chapelle, C.A. (2001) 'Innovative language learning: Achieving the vision'. *ReCALL*, 13, 3–14.

Davies G.D. (2002) 'ICT and modern foreign languages: Learning opportunities and training needs', *International Journal of English Studies*, Monograph Issue 2, 1: *New Trends in Computer Assisted Language Learning and Teaching*, edited by Pascual Pérez Paredes and Pascual Cantos Gómez, Servicio de Publicaciones, Universidad de Murcia, Spain, 1–18.

Dickinson, L. (1992) *Learner Training for Language Learning*. Dublin: Authentik.

Ellis, G. and B. Sinclair (1989) *Learning to Learn English – A Course in Learner Training*. Cambridge: Cambridge University Press.

Esch, E. (1994) *Self-Access and the Adult Language Learner*. London: CILT.

Esch, E. and T. Chanier (2000) 'The contribution of Information Communication Technology (ICT) to language learning environments, or the mystery of the secret agent'. *ReCALL*, 12.1, 5–18.

European Commission (2001) Making a European area of lifelong learning a reality. Brussels: European Commission (http://europa.eu.int/comm/education/policies/lll/life/communication/com_en.pdf). [Downloaded 19 September 2003]

Holec, H. (1981) *Autonomy in Foreign Language Learning*. Oxford: Pergamon (First published 1979, Strasbourg: Council of Europe).

Holec, H. (1987) 'The learner as manager: Managing learning or managing to learn?'. In A. Wenden and J. Rubin (eds.) *Learner Strategies in Language Learning*. London: Prentice Hall, 145–57.

Holec, H. (ed.) (1988) *Autonomy and Self-directed Learning: Present Fields of Application*. Strasbourg: Council of Europe.

IALLT Statement of Professional Responsibilities: (http://www.iall.net/iallt_documents/IALLTProfessional.pdf)

ICT4LT (Information and Communications Technology for Language Teachers), Module 3.1 (http://www.ict4lt.org).

Ingram, D. (2001) *Language Centres*. Amsterdam: John Benjamins.

Little, D. (1990) 'Autonomy in language learning'. In I. Gathercole (ed.) *Autonomy in Language Learning*. London: CILT, 7–15.

Little, D. (1991) *Learner Autonomy 1: Definitions, Issues, Problems*. Dublin: Authentik.

Little, D. (1998) *Technologies, Media and Foreign Language Learning*. Dublin: Authentik.

Little, D. and B. Voss (eds.) (1997) *Language Centres: Planning for the New Millennium*. Plymouth: CercleS.

Littlemore, J. (2001) 'Learner autonomy, self-instruction and new technologies in language learning: Current theory and practice in higher education in Europe'. In A. Chambers and G. Davies (eds.) *ICT and Language Learning: A European Perspective*. Lisse: Swets and Zeitlinger, 39–52.

Lo Bianco, J. (2001) *Language and Literacy Policy in Scotland*. Stirling: Scottish CILT.

McCall, J. (1992) *Self-access – Setting up a Centre*. Manchester: The British Council.

Mozzon-McPherson, M. and R. Vismans (2001) *Beyond Language Teaching Towards Language Advising*. London: Centre for Information on Language Teaching and Research.

Reichert, S. and B. Wächter (2000) The Globalisation of Education and Training: Recommendations for a Coherent Response of the European Union. Brussels: European Commission (http://europa.eu.int/comm/education/programmes/eu-usa/global.pdf). [Downloaded 19 September 2003]

Sheerin, S. (1989) *Self-Access*. Oxford: Oxford University Press.

Sheerin, S. (1997) 'An exploration of the relationship between self-access and independent learning'. In P. Benson and P. Voller (eds.) *Autonomy and Independence in Language Learning*, 54–65.

Sturtridge, G. (1997) 'Teaching and language learning in self-access centres: Changing roles?' In P. Benson and P. Voller (eds.) *Autonomy and Independence in Language Learning*, 66–78.

Warschauer, M. (1999) *Electronic Literacies. Language, Culture, and Power in Online Education*. Mahwah, NJ: Lawrence Erlbaum Associates.

Warschauer, M. (2003) *Technology and Social Inclusion: Rethinking the Digital Divide*. Cambridge, MA: MIT Press.

Warschauer, M. and R. Kern (2000) *Network-Based Language Teaching: Concepts and Practice*. Cambridge: Cambridge University Press.

Web sites

Centre for Information on Language Teaching and Research: http://www.cilt.org.uk/

encompassing also:

CILT Cymru: http://www.ciltcymru.org.uk/
NICILT: http://www.qub.ac.uk/edu/nicilt/
Scottish CILT: http://www.scilt.stir.ac.uk
Centre for Language and Communication Studies, Trinity College Dublin: http://www.tcd.ie/CLCS/courses/intro_lang_study.html
European Centre for Modern Languages: http://www.ecml.at/
European Computer Driving Licence: http://www.ecdl.ie/
European Confederation of Language Centres in Higher Education: http://www.cercles.org/
Greenbank High School: http://www.greenbank.sefton.sch.uk/
Information and Communications Technology for Language Teachers (ICT4LT): http://www.ict4lt.org
International Association for Language Learning Technology (IALLT): http://www.iall.net/
Lingu@NET Virtual Language Centre: http://www.linguanet.org.uk/
Lingu@NET-Europa Multilingual Resources Centre: http://www.linguanet-europa.org/y2/
SMILE Project, Language Institute, University of Hull: http://www.ncteam.ac.uk/projects/fdtl/fdtl2/projectdescriptions/3-97.htm
The Online Netskills Interactive Course (TONIC): http://www.netskills.ac.uk/TonicNG/cgi/sesame?tng
University of Victoria, Humanities Computing and Media Centre: http://web.uvic.ca/hcmc/
University of Bristol, Language Centre: http://www.bris.ac.uk/Depts/LangCent/
University of Hull: Dyslexia and Learning a Modern Foreign Language: http://www.hull.ac.uk/langinst/olc/dyslexia.htm
University of Hull: Open Learning Advisory Servicehttp://www.hull.ac.uk/langinst/olc/adv.htm
University of Hull: MA/Diploma in Language Learning and Technology: http://www.cti.hull.ac.uk/malang/
University of Hull: Postgraduate Certificate in Advising for Language http://www.hull.ac.uk/languages/prospective/courses/pg/langlearn/
University of Limerick, Language Resource Area: http://www.ul.ie/~lcs/lan-guageresourcearea/intro.htm
University of Rostock, *Sprachenzentrum* (Language Centre): http://www.sprachenzentrum.uni-rostock.de/
The Virtual Language Centre: http://vlc.polyu.edu.hk

INTEGRATING ICT IN LANGUAGE TEACHING AND LEARNING

4 Essential evaluation criteria in multimedia CALL and WELL environments

Liam Murray

1. Introduction and background

There are many evaluation checklists of variable length already in existence whether on-line (see Thompson; Chekhouni *et al.*; Stevens) or printed (Rowley, 1993) as well as several criticisms of their use (McDougall and Squires, 1995). Some are offered as strict taxonomies, others are of a generic nature providing basic but very useful help to teachers sometimes in the form of an evaluation framework that has been widely piloted in schools beforehand (see National Centre for Technology in Education guide, 2001), whilst still others have designed evaluation grids and methodologies aimed specifically at language teachers with little experience of CALL evaluation (Bertin, 1999). Susser cogently defends the continued use of checklists against attacks from researchers, while at the same time accepting that 'studies confirm that there is little agreement on the essential criteria for evaluating courseware' (2001: 263). One may suspect that the main reason for this is because there are so many different types of courseware aimed at different types of learners and learning situations for the acquisition of different bodies of knowledge. Apart from these 'dedicated' programs, there are still more generic programs and of course Web sites that may be used for language learning. Even within our particular area of CALL, there is evidence of much diversification in opinion and in emphases when evaluating language software, as may be gleaned from even a short examination of Susser's 'Checklists for CALL or L1 Language Arts Courseware' and his accompanying bibliography (2001: 272–6). One possible response to this cognitive overhead is to follow Hubbard's lead in creating an evaluation framework and 'not to propose a specific evaluation process but rather to identify the elements involved in evaluation so that teachers and reviewers can set up their own evaluation forms and procedures' (Hubbard, 1996: 27).

Another possible answer is that guides and checklists must continue to be produced because many evaluative criteria must change and others be updated on a regular basis as additional research into their use either improves upon or rejects their inclusion in such lists (Bertin, 1999: 11). Checklists for CALL courseware and for the growing number of Web-Enhanced Language Learning (WELL) sites will change because learners' expectations, uses, and experiences change, and also because pedagogical software capabilities and functionalities will become more powerful if not better, for example with the creation of newer types of exercises such as those in the *Hot Potatoes* products on the Web site: http://www.halfbakedsoftware.com. Students and teachers with even a small exposure to CALL are demanding better design and more functionality from their products, for example with more flexible and 'fuzzy' acceptable answers to set questions and of course the expectation that each product contain multimedia features. The demands are even greater from more experienced CALL practitioners who wish to move on to authoring suites. However, this paper need not be concerned with evaluating authoring tools as this subject has quite recently been extensively covered elsewhere (Bickerton *et al.*, 2001). With these demands come new and different challenges both for prospective developers and for evaluators. In addition, different teaching styles are becoming more prevalent – witness the growth of constructivist and autonomous learning techniques, with students gaining greater responsibility for their own learning and understanding their own language-learning styles earlier – visual-textual, visual-graphic, auditory, or kinaesthetic.

It is our goal here to offer fundamental and important criteria to teachers to help them make the necessary decisions in assessing, purchasing, and integrating putative CALL software through whichever platform, CD-ROM-based or Internet-based. In addition, it is hoped to augment a sense of self-confidence in teachers' own value judgements and convey a sense of open-mindedness in approaching new software – as they should have in assessing different teaching methodologies – as this would assist greatly in 'futureproofing' teachers in their preparation for encountering newer generations of programs and sites. Such futureproofing would mean achieving a critical yet appreciative mindset, because as Susser points out, 'the checklist serves as an educational instrument that can help teachers rethink their assumptions and practice' (2001: 271). In addition, some discussion of the theoretical issues in CALL is necessary, giving an historical context in which to judge current and future CALL offerings. This discussion will include pertinent and critical comments taken from second-year students at the University of Limerick who completed hands-on CALL and

WELL tasks, evaluation sessions, and essays as part of a language technology module. Their practices and opinions prove to be forthright and revealing.

2. A brief history of CALL evaluation

The use of computers in education has a long and chequered past that is rarely acknowledged. Despite the flashy visuals and sounds that accompanied the latest generation of educational software, almost all CALL exercises up to the last decade of the last century were based on a 'programmed-instruction' workbook method that included exercises that one might term as being the 'classical triumvirate of CALL' i.e., gap filling, text reconstruction, and multiple choice questions. For over two decades, computer variations on this basic theme have been hailed time and again as the greatest breakthrough in educational technology and the culture has yet to see any evidence for that claim. It is not necessary to look far to discover the reasons for what many educationalists regard as the disappointing rate of progress in educational technology (Sloan, 1984). An affirmation that has been compounded by the claims and fears of some educationalists that 'economic interests' are attempting to railroad or simply ignore criticisms of the educational value of certain digital tools and promote their own educational technology-driven agenda. These educationalists have pointed out that:

> New 'partnerships' of designers and developers committed to technology for its own sake now create products for the 'education marketplace', with little or no experience of, or interest in, underlying *educational* goals, while explicitly educational theories are supplanted by a re-purposed economistic discourse.
>
> (De Castell *et al.*, 2000)

Education is the development of people and people are not machines, nor even machine-like. The need to make sense of an increasingly confusing world of 'men and machines' often induces us to blur the distinction, first in the way we speak, then in the way we act. Indeed, we have anthropomorphised machines (Baddeley, 1976) by calling them 'electronic brains', 'mechanomorphised' people in phrases such as 'what makes them tick' and we appear to be allowing ergonomics, the science of adapting machines to people, to merge into a darker science of adapting people to machines.

We learn, speak, and impart knowledge in many different ways, and our modes of intelligent thought are created from many different sources. However, it is also true that we constantly seek to apply logical structures to help us to learn better and to teach more efficiently. Baddeley (1983) discusses, *inter alia*, these issues from the aim of attempting to discover how to optimise our memory recall. Effective memory recall appears to be achieved by following logical 'memory link paths'. It must now be said that if we can create software to help us strengthen these logical paths then this will induce better memory recall and, thus, better learning. The question must always be that of imitating, improving, and assisting the human model as certain eminent artificial intelligence experts have claimed (see, for example, Haugeland, 1985).

There exist several other important differences between people and machines which make person–machine interactions quite unlike person–person ones. A machine can only respond, it does not initiate; its responses are either totally rigid or random in an unmistakably machine-like way. Machines are lacking in subtlety, they cannot satisfy social needs; people need people and learners need teachers in ways in which they do not need machines. Obviously we do not wish to support any kind of neo-Luddite, anti-technologist stance, but it needs to be reiterated and understood that it is only possible to use machines to support teachers in a proper pedagogical environment.

There are other reasons why CALL and WELL have taken so long to be successfully adapted into our educational establishments. The major reason is that they have been frequently misunderstood. Computers are not brains, nor do they possess brains. They do not think; they process. They are extremely fast and totally infallible in what they do, but they are still mindless. Last maintains that they cannot be 'sensibly used as a substitute for either teachers or books' (1984: 118)..Although this statement was made before the arrival of the World Wide Web (WWW), Last is still guilty of making a sweeping generalisation in his use of the generic term 'books' and of them being used 'sensibly'. Is he referring to works of a pedagogical nature or to fiction or to other types of writing? Whilst many people would claim that books, of any nature, should not be substituted or replaced by electronic texts, one can say that works can be produced and are currently being used within the electronic medium to support and develop intelligent reading and learning. This is of course true to a greater degree with many CALL packages and WELL sites where reading and writing skills are practised and tested as standard.

3. Asking the basic questions

Generally speaking, the essential limitations of software packages are revealed not by what they do, but by what they fail to do. As Richard Ennals writes in his chapter entitled 'Humanities and computing':

There are two questions that one must ask,
1. What can be done with computers? And
2. What cannot be done with computers?

(1987: 46)

While these appear to be two obvious questions, they are questions which have been overlooked in the past. Ennals also gives us a caveat, in that the computer must not, as he puts it, 'be used simply for its own sake' (1987: 74). The computer – or more particularly the software package – should help to clarify the decision procedures involved in solving a problem and enhance the learning experience of the user. As well as that, it should not be too complex, yet at the same time it should not be too simple. A good CALL/WELL package should seek a happy medium here. A very good package should have different levels of sophistication and complexity so that it may provide a constant challenge to the user/learner. Falling into the trap of using software packages as substitute tutors must be avoided, because they will simply end up like the old teaching software of the past – hidden away and forgotten. It would be wrong to destroy the educational reputation of computers/software packages simply by casting them in the wrong role. Computers are, after all, very versatile educational aids. They have progressed from being used for recording students' progress, for administering and scoring objective tests, and for presenting and manipulating extremely large databases of knowledge and information. They are now being used more extensively with multimedia learning applications, sometimes erroneously and inappropriately and other times where imaginative teachers have gone beyond the original teaching applications of the designers (see, for example, Murray and Barnes, 1998).

4. Re-evaluating theories and practices

It is therefore necessary to re-evaluate the theories and practices that currently exist and those which originally lay behind CALL packages and WELL sites in order to see if they are still valid and if they can be improved upon if we are to help the language teacher to acquire up to date evaluation skills. Let us take Barker and Yeates as our starting point, as they provide a list of questions for evaluating putative CALL/WELL courseware. These are:

1. Is the courseware easy to use?
2. Does it teach?
3. Does it cater for individualised instruction?
4. Does it utilise ancillary media?

5. Does it use these to optimum effect?
6. Is there good technical support?
7. Is it easy to modify if the need arises?
8. Is it free from technical/procedural errors?
9. Does it motivate the student?
10. Is it cost effective for what it does? (1985: 19–35)

Questions 1 to 10 are based on several assumptions, with regard both to inherent value judgements and implicit priorities which really require empirical or theoretical support. For example, is it necessarily an advantage to employ 'ancillary media'? How much more effective – especially in terms of time, effort, and expense – is individualised instruction than a less flexible approach? 'Does it teach?' This is the most fundamental question of all and is one that must be answered and measured convincingly by the evaluator. 'Easy to use?': is this necessarily beneficial in educational software or could it be that the requirement to master a degree of skill in order to use the package might confer its own advantages? For example, on a more general level the learning of Web skills in searching for, navigating and reading Web pages more effectively as a prerequisite to using a WELL site would bring more widely applicable skills to the user in utilising the Web for other educational purposes.

Much evaluation of software – both educational and otherwise – has tended to be based on the intuition of the evaluator/s. Whilst this is acceptable (and inevitable), there are certain limitations to restricting oneself to this basis alone. For example, teachers with greater experience of teaching may possibly have a different intuition than those with lesser experience. Of course, the intuition may be no better or worse than that of others, only different.

As part of the background to the overall evaluation of CALL/WELL courseware packages, the interactive aspects of these packages must be examined. The semantic concepts used in the design of the user interface may, to paraphrase Shneiderman (1986), be organised notions of the computer system. This is because when one comes to deal with syntactic information, the learning of such information depends on practice and/or repetition. However, such information is easily forgotten and often peculiar to a limited number of systems. Where syntactic knowledge has to be used, it enhances 'ease of use' if, for example, (a) the keypresses can be made to seem less arbitrary, X for eXit, Q for Quit, or LO for Log Out, (b) items are consistent throughout the system, and (c) where the actions are quite arbitrary there are ever-present prompts for the user, for example menus or reminders on the monitor screen.

All of the above help the user by reducing the quantity of information to be remembered, allowing greater opportunity for learning to take place, for example, through practising and repeating exercises with sufficient error feedback using possibly different types of media. Thomson (1985) argues cogently that systems designers must allow for the characteristics of human memory, and Long (1987) puts forward a more general argument in favour of the cognitive ergonomics approach. But perhaps the most relevant characteristic of human memory is that only meaningful material can be effectively encoded into the long-term memory.

Thus (a) and (b) try to render essentially arbitrary information meaningful, while (c) tries to get around using memory at all. But again as regards (c), menus can make operations very slow and tiresome, especially if the list is long and the user is experienced. Ideally, the user who has learned the syntax should be able to circumvent such prompts. With the possible exception of a few generic key-presses, such as the Alt key for jumping between text boxes, the Ctrl+C, Ctrl+X ,and Ctrl+V for copying, cutting, and pasting respectively, many CALL and WELL site designers appear to have forgotten, ignored, or perhaps never to have learnt these rules. One may speculate on the reasons for this, but this author suspects that it may be due to the ephemeral nature of many sites and programs. Therefore we may add to Barker and Yeates's list regarding cost effectiveness and ease of use: is there enough content for long-term use and a possibility for quickly acquiring any required syntactic knowledge to facilitate better engagement with the learning aspects of the program or site?

The representation of information which a system presents to the user (in whatever form) must be congruent with the user's representations, or the assumptions s/he is likely to make. Thus Hammond and Barnard mention the difficulties caused by a system where pressing a key marked 'end' calls up the previously displayed screen (1985: 65). Last (1989) also gives several examples of programming where there has been little evidence of foresight or forward planning. The well-established phenomenon of pro-active interference in memory and particularly the effect of item-similarity on such interference (see, for example, Baddeley, 1976), suggests that entirely arbitrary representations (for example 'Ctrl+X') will be acquired more easily than those which are closer to items (for example, words), which the user already knows. Therefore, such items must be readily interpretable in already-known terms (for example, the Apple and later Microsoft convention of a 'trash can' icon for deletion of unwanted files or the simple direction arrows on Web sites) or in entirely new terms, so as not to be interfered with by prior knowledge.

From Hammond and Barnard one crucial lesson can be learned on how to evaluate an interactive program. They found that the effects of aspects of dialogue (such as consistency or 'meaningfulness') on ease of use alter over time with the user's experience, and, above all, depend upon the cognitive contents where this 'includes mental representations and cognitive processes relating not only to the explicit structure and content of the dialogue, but also to the general cognitive demands imposed by the system' (Hammond and Barnard, 1985: 56–7).

The implication here is that there are no general rules yet devised which can necessarily predict the ease of use of a system, and so the empirical testing of users on any particular system is an absolute necessity for its evaluation in terms of ease of use. Comments from two of our students serve to illustrate this point. In separate essays, both students were evaluating the *travlang* site (http://www3.travlang.com) which is aimed at tourists. One student found that there was an excessive amount of advertising, causing disorientation and demotivation, whilst the other reported only minor irritation with the ubiquitous advertising banners and pop-up pages. As Student 1 said, 'the word that immediately comes to mind when describing this Web site is "clutter" [... later referring directly to the banners] "Propaganda" was another word that came to mind'.

5. Screen layout and design

Much has already been written about the concepts behind successful screen layout and design, and it is still worth mentioning some of these here for various reasons. The most important reason is that a relatively good level of knowledge in this area is to be welcomed, when one comes to evaluate screen designs for hopefully extensive and long-term use with language learners at whatever level of proficiency. Smith and Mosier (1984: 180–89) present us with 162 guidelines for data display and also five 'high-level principles', three of which are particularly relevant to a CALL/WELL program:

1. Consistency of display;
2. An uncluttered screen;
3. The grouping of items according to their functions

These are three principles which have perennially been found to aid usability. Smith and Mosier (1984: 194) also proved that whereas functional grouping of material was closely associated with efficiency of the display, subjective user preference was determined more by the density of material displayed on the screen (i.e. there was a high preference for low density). In his highly-researched and exemplary book, *Designing the User Interface*, Shneiderman offers guidelines, which would be equally useful to the software evaluator and to the Web page authoring teacher, on how to highlight material, underlining the use of pointers, putting material in 'boxes' and 'blinking', and the sparing use of colours. One particular dictum from Shneiderman's thirteen rules for colour is worth noting:

'Use colour sparingly, systematically and with regard for user's expectations and conventions'(1986: 79).

Teachers and learners must also beware of eyestrain. If colours from opposite ends of the spectrum are used with various other colours, then this will cause visual fatigue in the user after a very short time period (Tannenbaum, 1998: 426). One solution is to use yellow and green because they are middle-frequency colours. This solution can be found in the writings of Lester (1995: 43), where he describes the use of the colour-wheel method, yet it continues to be ignored in many CALL packages and WELL sites. As further evidence to support Shneiderman's findings, Dillon *et al.* have carried out a study comparing reading from paper to reading from a screen. They concluded that '[r]eading from a screen is up to 30% slower than reading from paper; reading from a screen is more fatiguing; and reading from a screen gives rise to more errors' (1988: 459). In attempting to find the causes underlying these findings the authors reported the following factors as being significant:

1. The orientation of the screen
2. Eye movement across the screen
3. The visual angle subtended by the screen (i.e. the distance from the eye to the screen)
4. Aspect ratio (height/width ratio)
5. The dynamic aspects of screen filling and refresh rates
6. Flickering due to the refresh rate
7. Image polarity-colour of foreground versus colour of background
8. The users (i.e. were they habitual users of the program?) (Dillon *et al.*, 1988: 462–3)

The major conclusion was that it was the display quality and colour polarity which had the most significant effect on the performance. In support of this, some of our students wrote about feedback answers from several sites and packages, reporting that the mixed use of colours (in their examples: red, green, and blue) was quite 'off-putting after a bit of time' and even more so when combined with audio files playing 'applause' for a correct answer and 'shattering glass' for an incorrect response. However, it is interesting to note that learner customs and expectations may be changing, with a discernible minority of students requesting more visually engaging screen designs. Here are two of their reported comments which would appear to suggest that more up-to-date research is required in this important area where immediate reactions to a screen design often prove to be the most lasting:

> If I were to suggest some improvements to the Web [of the Spanish sections of http://www3.travlang.com ...] with regards to Web design, the dull and identical pages became very monotonous to look at after a while.

> There are no striking visuals to keep you interested and there is a strain on the eyes especially if a site has a dark or too bright a background.

6. Interaction

It must always be remembered that, with the exception of chatroom-type activities and community forums, we are dealing with a strictly circumscribed and limited form of interaction between a computer and a human user. One may also question the efficacy and popularity of using target-language chatrooms in language learning especially amongst post-beginner learners. Many of our students at this level reported that they felt excluded, particularly the male students and even some female students if they assumed a 'male name'. Typical of their comments was that it was 'difficult to get beyond the first stage of getting-to-know-each-other phrases, many of the conversations were stilted, most of the time lacking expression'. Returning to the issue of human–computer interaction, there are invariably two questions that will arise when one studies this form of interaction:

1. Is the limited form of interaction in a particular CALL package or WELL site the best that is currently available for achieving the software's stated and implied aims?
2. How should one set about evaluating the quality and effectiveness of the interaction?

When attempting to answer these questions it is worth considering Skinner's principles, which are crucial from the point of view of programmed learning. These principles deal with:

1. The power of positive reinforcement as a means of increasing the probability of a desired behaviour.
2. The requirement for an organism to emit a response before it can be reinforced.
3. The supposed need for reinforcement to be temporally contingent upon the response.
4. The supposed ineffectiveness of punishment (not negative reinforcement) as other than a temporary suppressor of responding.

(Skinner, 1983)

The knowledge that was gleaned from Skinner's work indicates that there are substantial differences in individual learning, that people learn better when they are interested, and that they learn just as much from finding out why they are wrong as from being told that they are correct. The conclusion, that 'people learn better when they are interested', may seem slightly obvious, yet evaluators must keep in mind the question of whether the teaching software is exploiting and helping to prolong the users' initial learning interest and enabling them to go beyond the 'wow' factor (see Murray and Barnes, 1998).

7. Establishing and established features in evaluation

Three established features are absolutely essential when evaluating any CALL package or WELL site:

1. The need to establish the objectives of the software, because without this knowledge it is impossible to evaluate the package's success.
2. The necessity for testing the relevant knowledge of subjects – who are as typical as possible of the intended users of the package – both before and after using the program.
3. Eliciting these subjects' opinions of the software.

In asking what the objectives of the software are, this complex and thorny question must be approached by (a) reading any relevant information from the author(s) of the package, and (b) roughly estimating the priorities that informed the program by noting the emphasis given to the various topics that are treated within it. In response to a request for his own set of criteria in evaluating a CALL package, Davies offers a 'Golden Rule for evaluating an interactive CALL program', namely, to define the objectives of the package (Davies, 1990). However, this describes a task which is barely possible, even for someone who would be fortunate enough to be able to ask the creators of the item to be evaluated. There are simply too many levels of objectives. One could work downwards (or upwards given one's objectives) from 'education' through 'maintain the student's interest' or 'be comprehensive and accurate', to 'limit the contents to one subject area' or 'use all the colours available'. This rule could be qualified so as to be user-orientated: 'Define the objectives of the package in terms of who the users will be and what new accomplishments they will have gained as a result of experiencing the CALL program or WELL site'. This redefinition would better allow objective assessment, the more so if the 'new accomplishments' could be quantified. It is the difficulty of quantification of educational objectives that makes it so hard to assess a WELL site and CALL program in isolation. On the other hand, whose standards are appropriate for evaluating a program? Is it the group of intended users or someone relatively (very relatively) knowledgeable in the area? The answer will ultimately depend upon the aim of the evaluation. If the question is asked, 'does this item fulfil its stated objectives?' (in terms of user performance), then measurement of user performance and opinion may be appropriate. If, however, an eye is being kept on long-term development and on establishing a good reputation for the site or product, then the above question should be supplemented with a second one: 'does this item fulfil its objectives as well as it possibly could, given the current state of knowledge?'

One further fundamental question has to be approached: is there a need for such a package? By 'need', we mean a package for which there is a widely perceived educational requirement, and/or a demand from would-be users and/or a requirement for specified individuals to apply the knowledge that the program aims to impart. We may state at this point that the role of computers in education is a recognised one and, with the constantly increasing number of WELL sites and CALL programs, there is a definite growing tendency for reinventing a less than perfect wheel. Given that there exists a definite need, each package should be designed with at least these five factors in mind:

1. Ease of use;
2. Presentation of information;
3. Degree and nature of interaction;
4. Efficacy as a CALL/WELL package;
5. Contents: accuracy, appositeness and priorities.

Also, with respect to the important notion of 'usability' there are four aspects to be taken into account:

1. Effectiveness;
2. Learnability;
3. Flexibility;
4. Attitude.

All of which we may include and expand upon to create our current essential checklist specifically for MFL teachers.

8. A current essential evaluation checklist

The pedagogical tools may have changed, but only in so far as they have been compressed into one workspace and into 'one piece of hardware' – a computer.

The media will continue to develop and so must teachers when employing their professional judgement and experience in evaluating CALL and WELL tools. The 'software' in the final checklist below refers to both CALL software and WELL site materials, and they must provide suitable answers to the following questions which are offered in no intended order of importance:

- Does the software provoke and maintain student interest to a satisfactory degree? (Which is related to how likely it is that the information will be retained.)
- Does the software incorporate manageable and meaningful input?
- How is new language introduced? Is sufficient (optional) practice possible before learners produce language?
- Does the software make optimal use of the writing medium?
- How credible/authoritative is the information which the program imparts? (This is related to our earlier reference to the notion of 'attitude'.)
- Does the software attempt to create a target language context?
- Is there sufficient aesthetic appeal (colour, layout, legibility, style of presentation)? Or as one student said, 'What is the eye candy quotient to decent information?'
- Does the software perpetuate cultural stereotypes, i.e., how objective is the content?
- How authentic and accurate is the target language used?
- How authoritative is the content and who exactly produced it?
- How current is the content?
- Does the software incorporate suitable language-learning activities and offer scope for additional activities away from the computer?
- How practical is integration of the software into the classroom context?
- How serious is your intention to integrate the software into the classroom context?
- How well does the software match pupils' expectations and the needs of the course?
- Does the software cater for all types of learners?
- What form of (self-)assessment, learner feedback or profiling is provided?
- Is the multimedia dimension exploited with regard to grammar and language patterns?
- How are language items presented on screen to the learner and can the learner control the order of their presentation (this is also known as 'ease of comprehension of contents' which is also related to how likely it is that the information will be retained)?
- How clear are the instructions for users?
- Is the software aimed at autonomous learners, i.e. is there a self-directed learning potential?

- What support for teachers is provided?
- What is the cost of the software, i.e. can it be free or are there hidden charges or impositions such as advertising banners?

This checklist is by no means comprehensive, nor is it meant to be, but from our readings we hope to have included only currently essential items for language teachers and evaluators. We should finish on the question of checklists in stating that, if we have no lists, then what else do we offer teachers? The creation of lists are intended to order our thoughts, to offer us a framework for evaluation and enable us to go beyond that to deeper considerations. Should the criteria listed above be given enough practice, then they will become instinctive to teachers and futureproof them in expectation of newer generations of sites and programs for which they must be critically prepared.

Acknowledgements

Sincere thanks must be offered by this author to the following people for their essential help in compiling and completing this chapter: Phil Hubbard, Jean-Claude Bertin, Bernard Susser, Deborah Masterson, Carmit Romano Hvid, and finally http://www.nachtclub.org

Bibliography

Baddeley, A.D. (1976) *The Psychology of Memory*. New York: Harper and Row.

Baddeley, A.D. (1983) *Your Memory, a User's Guide*. Harmondsworth: Penguin.

Barker, P. and H. Yeates (1985) *Introducing Computer Assisted Learning*. Englewood Cliffs: Prentice Hall.

Bertin, J.-C. (1999) , 'L'évaluation des matériaux multimédias de formation en langue'. *Contrat de plan État-Région*. Le Havre: Université du Havre, 35–48.

Bickerton D., T. Stenton and M. Temmerman (2001) 'Criteria for the evaluation of Authoring Tools in language education'. In A. Chambers and G. Davies (eds.) *ICT and Language Learning: A European Perspective*. Lisse: Swets and Zeitlinger, 53–66.

Crawford, C. (2000) *Understanding Interactivity*. C. Crawford Web Publishing, http://www.erasmatazz.com/library/JCGD_Volume_7/Fundamentals.html

Davies, G.D. (1990) *CALL Pamphlet and Questionnaire*. London: NCCALL, Ealing College of Higher Education.

De Castell, S., M. Bryson and J. Jenson (2000) 'Object lessons: Towards an educational theory of technology'. *First Monday*, Peer-Reviewed Journal on the Internet, http://www.firstmonday.org/issues/issue7_1/castell/index.html

Dillon, A., C. McKnight and J. Richardson (1988) 'Reading from paper versus reading from screen'. *Computer Journal*, 31, 457–64.

Ennals, R. (1987) 'Humanities and computing'. In S. Rahtz (ed.) *Information Technology in the Humanities*. Chichester: Ellis Horwood Ltd., 45–78.

Hammond, N.V. and P.J. Barnard (1985) 'Dialogue design: Characteristics of user knowledge'. In A. Monk (ed.) *Fundamentals of Human–Computer Interaction*. London: Academic Press, 54–73.

Haugeland, J. (1985) *Artificial Intelligence: The Very Idea*. Cambridge, MA: MIT Press.

Hubbard, P.L. (1996) 'Elements of CALL methodology: Development, evaluation, and implementation'. In M. Pennington (ed.) *The Power of CALL*. Texas: Athelstan, 15–32.

Last, R. (1984) *Language Teaching and The Microcomputer*. London: Basil Blackwell Ltd.

Last, R. (1989) *Artificial Intelligence Techniques in Language Learning*. Chichester: Ellis Horwood Ltd.

Lester, P.M. (1995) *Visual Communication: Images with Messages*. Belmont, CA: Wadsworth.

Long, J.B. (1987) 'Cognitive ergonomics and Human-Computer Interaction'. In P.B. Warr (ed.) *Psychology at Work*. Harmondsworth: Penguin, 23–47.

McDougall, A. and D. Squires (1995) 'A critical examination of the checklist approach in software selection'. *Journal of Educational Computing Research*, 12.3, 263–74.

Murray, L. and A. Barnes (1998) 'Beyond the "wow factor": Evaluating multimedia language learning software from a pedagogical viewpoint'. *System*, 26.2, 249–59.

National Centre for Technology in Education (2001) *Evaluating Educational Software: A Teacher's Guide*. Dublin: Dublin City University.

Rowley, J.E. (1993) 'Selection and evaluation of software'. *ASLIB Proceedings*, 45.3, 77–81.

Shneiderman, B. (1986) *Designing the User Interface*. Reading, MA: Addison-Wesley.

Skinner, G.G. (1983) *Practical Information Processing*. London: Hodder and Stoughton.

Sloan, D. (1984) *The Computer in Education: A Critical Perspective*. New York: Columbia University.

Smith, S.L. and J.N. Mosier (1984) *Design Guidelines for the User Interface for Computer-Based Information Systems*. Bedford: Mitre.

Susser, B. (2001) 'A defense of checklists for courseware evaluation'. *ReCALL*, 13.2, 261–76.

Tannenbaum, R.S. (1998) *Theoretical Foundations of Multimedia*. New York: Freeman Co.

Thomson, N. (1985) 'Human memory: Different stores with different characteristics'. In A. Monk (ed.) *Fundamentals of Human-Computer Interaction*. London: Academic Press, 97–110.

Examples of evaluation sites

Thompson, University of Hawaii, National Foreign Language Resource Center: 'Taxonomy of features for evaluating foreign language multimedia software' at: http://www.nflrc.hawaii.edu/aboutus/ithompson/flmedia/evaluation/general/gencriteria.htm

H. Chekhouni *et al.*, 'Medial gestütztes, selbstorganisiertes Lernen', at: http://www.nachtclub.org

V. Stevens, 'Software Selection, Evaluation and Use' at: http://www.orst.edu/Dept/eli/vstevens/day1.htm

5 Communication with a purpose: Exploiting the Internet to promote language learning

Jeannette Littlemore and David Oakey

1. Introduction

Throughout the development of CALL, theories of language and language learning have influenced the way in which the current technology has been used, while the technology has also had an impact on the theory underlying the pedagogical techniques employed. Unusually the Internet has managed to do both these things simultaneously.[1] The huge amount of resources available on the WWW has permitted authentic purposeful communication within the communicative language-teaching paradigm, whereas the many-to-many interaction afforded via the Internet has contributed to new forms of language and language-learning theory.

In order to clarify this statement, let us first situate the Internet within the wider CALL context. During the 1970s and 1980s the computer was seen predominantly as a vehicle for providing exercises and drills designed to promote accuracy. With the growth of the communicative movement in the 1980s, efforts were made to create exercises of a more communicative nature. This involved a shift towards language-learning tasks aimed at engaging learners in real communication about topics in which they are genuinely interested (Gitsaki and Taylor, 1999: 48). Recent technological developments have meant that the Internet now provides opportunities for purposeful communication with a worldwide community of speakers and learners of the target language. Educators have spent the last decade attempting to exploit these opportunities for language learning.

These developments have been described by Warschauer (2001: 6) as a shift from 'structural', to 'communicative', and finally to 'integrative' CALL. He claims that each phase has had as its focus a principal teaching objective, i.e. accuracy, fluency, and agency respectively. The concept of 'agency' chimes in with a current focus of critical applied linguistics, in which language is used as a means of constructing, maintaining, and altering power relationships in the language user's world. Thus the main purpose of the current 'integrative' phase of CALL is to help learners enter genuine discourse communities, and communicate with the members of those communities about authentic issues and in so doing 'make their stamp on the world' (Warschauer, 2001: 7).

However, with much writing on CALL by those at the forefront of theoretical research such as Warschauer, there is sometimes the danger of the researchers disappearing over the technological horizon in pursuit of esoteric notions such as agency, while teachers are often left behind in a cloud of publications trying to obtain funds from their administrators and support from technical staff in order to implement what was fashionable a few years previously (see Lam, 2000: 390–91; Littlemore, 2001: 45). We argue that a lot of useful work has been done using the Internet in current and earlier CALL paradigms but this has not been fully disseminated to language teachers who are new to the field. We feel that an overview of the ways in which the Internet can be used to develop accuracy and fluency, agency notwithstanding, is necessary.

This chapter thus discusses some of the main ways in which the Internet can be used to promote all of the above. First it considers the most effective ways of searching the World Wide Web (WWW). It then looks at the WWW itself, focusing on Web sites that are designed specifically for language learning. The pedagogical rationale that lies behind these Web sites is often 'structural', rather than 'integrative', and the exercises themselves do not always promote 'agency'. As we argue above, there is none the less still much of value for language teachers to be found in such sites. We also look at how the Internet can be used as a stand-in for reference tools such as dictionaries, concordancers, and grammar-checkers. The chapter then outlines more communicative activities, using sites that are not explicitly intended for language learning. In the final section, we move on to discuss the more 'integrative' aspects of Internet-based language learning. In this section, the relative merits of discussion lists, e-mail, multi-user object-oriented dimensions (MOOs), and so on are discussed.

At regular intervals throughout the chapter we evaluate different CALL activities in order to show how different types of activities meet different types of criteria. We use Chapelle's (2001: 59) 'criteria for CALL task appropriateness', as they are wide-ranging and respond to structural and communicative, as well as integrative concerns. These criteria include the language-learning potential of the activity (does it provide sufficient opportunity for beneficial focus on form?), learner fit (can it be adapted to fit the needs of different groups of learners?), meaning focus (is learners' attention directed primarily toward the meaning of the language?), authenticity (will learners be able to see a connection between the activity and second language activities that they may engage in outside the classroom?), impact (will learners learn more about the target language and language-learning strategies?), and practicality (are sufficient hardware and software resources likely to be available?). It is, of course, for teachers themselves to decide the relative importance of each of the above, depending on their intended learning outcomes.

2. Using the Internet as a resource: The World Wide Web

There are many ways in which the WWW can be used for language learning. In this section, we look at a number of sites that are dedicated specifically to language learning and practice. We then look at ways in which the WWW itself can be used as a language reference tool, duplicating functions such as dictionary, concordancer, and grammar checker. Finally, we consider ways in which sites that are not specifically designed for language-learning purposes can be used for language learning. Before beginning this discussion, brief consideration is given to the various ways in which it is possible to search the WWW.

2.1. Searching the World Wide Web

The first point of call when accessing the WWW is the Internet browser. This simply refers to the toolbar of an Internet Service Provider. In order to find a Web site, it is usually necessary to type its full address beginning with http://www, but a short cut is just to type 'go' or 'find' followed by your keywords. When the exact address of a Web site is not known, a variety of tools is available to help one search the WWW. These fall into three categories, directories, search engines, and metasearch tools (see Dudeney, 2000: 17–27, for more information on this subject).

Directories use people to search the Web and to review and categorise the sites by topic. *Yahoo* is the most popular, and has versions in different languages. Search engines are compiled automatically by Web 'spiders', automatic search tools which regularly visit sites and update their files (Teeler and Gray, 2000). *Google* is thought by many to be the best, while *Altavista* is probably the biggest, and *Lycos* is often described as one of the most effective. *Infoseek* has some human editing, and *Excite* is the most frequently updated. Metasearch tools are search tools that provide simultaneous access to a number of other search engines. *Ask Jeeves* is probably the most user-friendly as it allows the user to write questions, using the same forms of syntax that would normally be employed in conversation (see Appendix 1 for the addresses of the above).

2.2. *Web-based resources explicitly intended for language learning*

There are many resources for language learning available on the World Wide Web, including stand-alone courses, integrated courses, and integrative task-based exercises. Felix, who provides excellent practical information on the use of ready-made sites for language learning, argues that teachers can outsource significant parts of their teaching to the Web (1998; 1999). A few resources for learning languages online are listed in Appendix 2. As it is impossible, in this short section, to do justice to the large number of resources available on the WWW for learning virtually every language, we consider here a few examples of the type of resources that are available, including sites of two types. Some contain a variety of language-learning activities, whereas others pull together links to a selection of useful language-learning sites. Given the extent of language-learning resources available on the Internet, these 'compendium' sites can be a useful resource for teachers.

For learners of French, *Bonjour de France* offers exercises in grammar, vocabulary, idiomatic expressions, and provides virtual contexts in which the language can be practiced. *Hometown French* contains various grammar exercises and annotated texts. Unfortunately the site is rather slow as it has a large number of graphics. *French Resources* contains a wide variety of links to media resources, online dictionaries and cultural Web sites for learners and teachers of French.

As for English, Susan Clarke's EFL page contains grammar exercises that focus on parts of speech, clauses, and phrasal verbs. She also provides exercises on writing skills, particularly business writing. The *Grammar Safari* Web site contains activities in which learners look for words and grammar in context. It also suggests assignments that can be completed in order to practise using the grammar. Dave's ESL café offers a range of English language-learning activities, including information and exercises on phrasal verbs, idioms and slang, as well as useful lesson plans for teachers of English.

For learners of Spanish, *Si Espana* provides a wealth of information on Spanish current affairs, historical development and culture. Juan Ramon de Arana's homepage provides a number of grammar exercises, some on a self-check basis and others that would need to be checked by a teacher. The exercises come in a variety of formats and are intended to provoke discussion between students and teachers on the subject of different approaches to learning. *Sussex University Spanish Resources* provides links to language-building exercises, online dictionaries, Spanish media, and discussion groups. *News Stories* provides a number of topical articles that can be used for discussion purposes. Finally, *Academic Info* provides links to a number of online Spanish schools, although a number of these charge fees.

As for multilingual sites, the *Halls of Academia* site offers resources and exercises in a range of European and Asian languages. Another useful site is *1stop languages,* which contains links to different types of exercises in thirty different languages. Jim Becker's homepage contains a large number of well selected Web sites for learning French, Spanish, German, Russian, Italian, Japanese, Latin and Chinese. The trouble with these sites is that they are aimed primarily at students whose first language is English. One of the few sites to take account of the native language of the learner is *travlang,* which contains short language-learning exercises in over fifty languages. Another site which takes account of the student's native language is the Goethe Institute site, which contains vocabulary and grammar tests in around fifty languages.

Web-based resources that are intended explicitly for language learning meet some of Chapelle's 'criteria for CALL task appropriateness' (2001: 59). In general, they provide adequate opportunities to focus on form, and there are relatively few practicality issues. However, the main problem with these activities lies with learner fit. As the majority of the activities have been designed with a particular group of students in mind, it is difficult for teachers to find a set of ready-made exercises that meets the requirements of their own group of students. This could be turned into an advantage if teachers were to ask their students to assess the appropriateness of the exercises for their own particular learning needs. They could then identify the parts of the exercise that correspond most closely to their needs. They could also rate various aspects of the exercises in terms of difficulty. This might help the students to identify their own learning profiles and zones of proximal development, which Vygotsky defines as 'the distance between the actual developmental level as determined by independent problem solving and the level of potential development as determined through problem solving under adult guidance or in collaboration with more capable peers' (1978: 86). Another approach would be for teachers to make more use of Web sites that contain free, downloadable authoring software. For example, *Hot Potatoes* software (see Appendix 3) allows teachers to create their own gap fills, quizzes, re-ordering exercises, and multiple-choice questions. Empty exercise shells are provided by the Web site, and the teachers simply need to provide appropriate texts. They can thus tailor the exercises to the needs of their students. Other Web-based authoring tools are described and evaluated in ICT4LT (see below).

A second problem with ready-made activities is that it is very difficult to measure their impact. The activities are likely to contain a mixture of familiar and unfamiliar material, making it difficult for both teacher and student to gauge what exactly the student has learned from the activity. Paradoxically, one might say that in this respect the ready-made activities resemble authentic encounters with the target language, where a mixture of familiar and unfamiliar material is inevitable. A further criticism of ready-made activities is that they tend not to promote strategic awareness. On the other hand, if students are encouraged to engage in some kind of 'metadiscussion' about the activities (What are the activities testing? Do they match my own language-learning aims? Of what personal relevance is the vocabulary used?), then the ready-made activities become a powerful tool for the development of both strategic awareness and learner autonomy. Another possible solution may lie in increased use of authoring programs. If students were given the opportunity to create exercises for each other, using these programs, then this might give them further insight into their own language-learning needs, as well as those of their peers. It might also give them better insight into the rationale behind the exercises created for them by their teachers. Finally, these types of activities tend to vary in terms of meaning focus and authenticity. Although activities such as 'News stories' and the student publications are both meaning-focused and relatively authentic, grammar exercises, quizzes, and gap fills are less so. On the other hand, as we have argued above, there is a place for structure-focused activities, at some point, in most language classrooms.

2.3. Using the WWW as a language reference tool

The WWW can be used to focus on language structure via its numerous reference tools. Various dictionaries, thesauri, and spell checks are available free online. The yourdictionary Web site calls itself 'the most comprehensive and authoritative portal for language and language-related products and services on the Web with more than 1800 dictionaries with more than 250 languages' (http://www.yourdictionary.com/about.html). These reference tools can also be accessed via the Onelook Web site, which is linked to a database of 746 dictionaries in a wide variety of languages. Another useful source of links to dictionaries is the Linguist list (see Appendix 4). Of course, it is possible to use the WWW itself as a language reference tool, without referring to electronic dictionaries at all. A good way of finding out the meaning of a new word is to type it into a search engine and to follow up the links to see it used in context. In many cases the meaning can be inferred from the context. In the case of specific terminology, particularly business terms, it is not uncommon to find recent definitions, usually in lecture notes that academics have put up for their students. The definitions provided are often more thorough and up to date than those provided in dictionaries.

The role of concordancing in language learning is discussed elsewhere in this volume (Chapter 9, by Chambers and Kelly). The WWW itself can, of course, be used as a corpus, as any successful search for a word will result in a list of uses in context. This means that learners are able to search for collocations of a given word, helping them to become familiar with the common collocations words in the target language. Furthermore, these collocations help learners to infer whether a word has positive or negative connotations, or to identify the types of discourse in which it is usually found. Finally, search engines can be used to learn and check grammatical and lexical 'rules'. For example, a student of French might use a search engine to verify the difference between 'visiter' and 'rendre visite', by simply typing those combinations, in inverted commas, into a search engine. A search for 'visiter' leads to expressions such as 'musées à visiter', 'visiter Versailles', whereas a 'rendre visite' search leads to expressions such as 'venez nous rendre visite' and 'comment nous rendre visite'. A student might infer from this that 'rendre visite' is more appropriate when inviting someone to their house. A similar approach could be taken to investigate grammatical points, such as the difference between 'ce qui' and 'ce que' in French, or 'sondern' and 'aber' in German.

2.4. Creating activities using sites not explicitly intended for language learning

It is, of course, possible to think up language teaching ideas using Web sites that were not specifically intended for language learning. One activity which we have found to be particularly successful for use with university-level students of English is 'That's got to be the Loch Ness Monster!' (see Appendix 5). This exercise, which was created by David Oakey at the University of Birmingham, uses one subject to frame the use of the WWW as a source of information to complete a task, and as a source of listening materials to focus on the forms used in the expression of certainty. The subject of cryptozoology is a lively area which occupies more than its fair share of sites on the WWW. Many examples can be found of complete nonsense, which although an authentic real-world use of language, is not perhaps the best model for students. However, some serious analytical sites also exist which treat the subject with some degree of rigour. One particular site accompanies a TV documentary on the Loch Ness Monster and contains streaming audio eyewitness accounts, together with transcripts. Once downloaded, these transcripts make a very small but useful corpus of unscripted spoken discourse which yields several illustrative uses of adverbs and modals of certainty. These can be used to raise awareness of how speakers highlight the difference between observation and evaluation. They give a plain factual description of what they saw, and then follow it up with a more personal evaluation of what it was that they saw. Thus a speaker says, factually, 'It was an object, it was huge', before evaluating this object, 'I must say that it was the monster, really'. The subject of the Loch Ness Monster also produces useful cross-cultural opportunities for classroom discussion, since many countries round the world have their own 'lake creatures'. Furthermore, teachers of languages other than English will be able to find equivalent cryptozoological phenomena for their own language.

Teachers may not always have the time to create original Internet-based language-learning activities like the one described above. When pressed for time, they may prefer to use, or to adapt ideas presented in the increasingly popular 'practical ideas' books that are being made available to language teachers. The year 2000 saw the publication of three books containing practical ideas on how to use the Internet in English Language Teaching: Dudeney (2000), Teeler and Gray (2000) and Windeatt *et al.* (2000). Two of these (Dudeney and Windeatt *et al.*) have accompanying Web sites. As each of the three books has a slightly different focus, they will be briefly discussed below and consideration will be given to some of the specific activities that they include.

Teeler and Gray's book, which contains a chapter on using the Internet as course book, is the most original, and is likely to be most relevant to those teachers who have a high degree of autonomy in their teaching; few teachers will have the freedom to replace their entire course with activities which use the WWW. The activities in their book do, however, tend to be rather complex. For example, in one activity, entitled 'A quick tour of the Internet', students are first asked to use a search engine to find the meanings of a number of computer-specific words. They are then asked to group the words into categories, and compare their categories with those of another student. Following this, the teacher gives a number of tips on how to use the Internet and the students are asked to take notes. The teacher then gives the students a list of questions to be answered using the Internet. In the final, most complex part of the activity, students are sent to a site containing language-learning tasks and asked to complete one of the tasks. At the end, they are asked to list the new words they have learned during the activity. The amount of autonomy given to the students gradually increases within this activity as their confidence in using the Internet for language learning grows. However, this activity does not need to be carried out exactly as specified in the book, and could be adapted in several ways. For example, different search engines could be used. The words that the students are asked to find could be made less computer-specific. This might be necessary for young learners, who are likely to know quite a lot about the Internet already. The questions that they are asked to answer could be turned into a competitive quiz. They might also be expanded or adapted to suit particular groups of learners, or the students may be asked to write questions for each other. The tasks at the end of the activity can be altered for students of languages other than English.

The book by Windeatt *et al.* contains the largest number of practical ideas for using the WWW in the classroom. The book's Web site contains downloadable worksheets for use alongside the activities described in the book, an invaluable asset for teachers who have a limited amount of preparation time. Again the activities in this book are easily adapted. For example, one of the activities involves sending students to a jokes page on the Internet, and asking them to find their favourite joke, translate it into their own language, then discuss the problems inherent in the translatability of jokes. Different sites could be found for different languages, students could create their own Web sites with their own jokes on them, or the teacher could get the students to focus on jokes that have a particular grammatical structure or lexical theme. It could also be extended to include sayings and proverbs rather than just jokes.

Dudeney's book presents a range of activities for teaching, all clearly indexed by level and theme. He suggests ways in which the activities can be adapted to different learning situations, and explains the Internet add-ons that are frequently necessary to make some of the activities work. The book also has a Web site which contains, amongst other things, an online discussion forum, and updated Web site addresses relating to the ideas presented in the book. This goes some way towards overcoming the problem of obsolescence intrinsic to any of book about the Internet.

These three books are not intrinsically different in design from other methodological books. As Hardisty (2001: 3) points out, good pedagogical exploitation of the Internet involves principles similar to good pedagogical exploitation of other resources, and, in general, a good practical ideas book should have a basis in theory and contain usable ideas. Each of the three books mentioned above meets Hardisty's criteria, although their strengths lie in different areas. In all three cases, the pedagogical aims of the activities are transparent, and clear indications are given as to the required preparation, likely duration of the activities, and the technical requirements. Furthermore, most of the activities in these books lend themselves to a high degree of variation. The best part of Dudeney's book, the section on how to search the WWW, gives advice on how to narrow down a search, therefore making it both more rapid and more accurate. It also has a useful section on advanced Internet applications for the more experienced teacher. The book's one weakness is that the activities are not grouped particularly well, and one has to rely heavily on the mini-index at the beginning of the activities section. Teeler and Gray's book is good in that it goes beyond the usual scope of the average practical ideas book by suggesting ways in which the Internet can be used in teacher development. However, the book contains relatively few classroom activities, and the presentation of these ideas is quite wordy. Finally, the book by Windeatt *et al.* contains by far the largest number of activities, carefully categorised according to their skills focus. Any language teacher looking for ideas for things to do in class would find this book by far the easiest to use.

A number of ways have been suggested in which Internet activities can be adapted to suit different groups of learners in different learning situations. According to Hardisty (2001: 3), further variations could include changes in level, time, aims (linguistic and other), technical requirements, software used, place (is the activity done in CALL lab or self-access or home mode), procedure, and so on. He also points out that when adapting activities, it is important to be aware of methodological principles – for example, realising an idea is based on an information gap may allow the teacher to retain the underlying aim whilst introducing considerable surface change.

Ideas such as those mentioned above are designed to provide teachers with broad outlines showing what kind of things are possible. The teacher's responsibility lies in developing the skills to adapt and extend the ideas from the book to suit particular learning situations. Web sites linked to books can be used as a forum to share such work. The strengths of the activities mentioned above clearly lie in the realms of meaning focus, learner fit, and authenticity. However, the practicality of such activities is sometimes questionable, as fast, reliable Internet access is a real necessity as well as add-ons such as sound and video capability. Another problem is that it may be difficult for the teacher and the student to gauge the amount and the type of language that has been learned in a given activity. It is important to include both self-evaluation and consciousness-raising tasks if the activities are to meet this criterion.

3. Using the Internet for communication beyond the WWW: CMC

Unlike Warschauer's first two phases of CALL, the current 'integrative' phase of CALL has been stimulated by changes in what is technologically possible. The structural and communicative CALL phases were driven by behavioural and cognitive views of language and language learning, whereas the integrative phase was enabled once many computers could be connected, via the Internet. This has allowed language learners to communicate directly with other learners and speakers of the target language. This 'Computer Mediated Communication' (CMC) is a new use of language permitted for the first time by computer applications such as online learning environments, e-mail, discussion lists, chat rooms, MOOs, and videoconferencing. Before examining these applications in this section, we first discuss the nature of CMC.

3.1. CMC

Warschauer (1997: 471) argues that communication by computer is different from 'normal' communication primarily because it is text-based and computer-mediated, allows many-to-many interaction, is time- and place-independent, and can occur over long distances. While it is time-independent, a distinction is normally made between synchronous and asynchronous CMC, since important differences in the language used arise.

CMC brings a number of benefits to language learners, particularly in terms of the interaction between many group members, as has been discussed by Warschauer in relation to the work of Krashen and Vygotsky (Warschauer 1996: 4). CMC provides a more egalitarian interaction environment, although it can reduce conformity and convergence as compared with face-to-face group discussion, partly because of information overload: students receive so many messages that they ignore the bulk of contributions from group members, and the conversation becomes 'a set of asocial monologues' (Moran, 1991: 52). CMC has also been found to improve students' levels of intercultural understanding, make them better able to consider their audience in their writing, and display advanced levels of critical thinking (Boggs and Jones, 1994; Chun, 1994; Cooke, 1996; Hogget, 1996; McWhirter, 1996). Furthermore, it has been found to have positive effects on motivation (Warschauer *et al.*, 1996: 12) although, as Dunbar *et al.* (2000: 304) point out, choice and achievability of task are crucial factors in determining levels of student motivation. Finally, Kern (1995: 463) found that the use of CMC helped his students to produce more complex linguistic output than face-to-face communication. One reason for this may be that the time pressure was removed whilst authenticity remained.

Applications which allow CMC via the Internet vary in accessibility. Some, such as online learning environments, require professionally produced software for restricted access, whereas others such as e-mail, discussion lists, chat rooms, and MOOs, are open to all.

3.2. CMC within restricted environments

This section deals with applications which create restricted Internet environments dedicated to a particular group of learners. Many such software applications have been developed for use in non-language-specific contexts, but offer many of the benefits claimed for communicative, collaborative, task-based language learning familiar from contemporary language-learning theory. Several of these platforms were developed at universities and then spun off as commercial ventures. Such platforms include *Blackboard*, *WebCT*, *FirstClass*, and *Merlin* (see Appendix 6). These all can be used for teaching groups of students within an institution or for courses where students are geographically dispersed. The common core features are that they enable the teacher to manage a group of students, to assess group performance, to structure and sequence course content, to provide online learning resources, and allow communication with and between members of the group. The strength of these environments is the ease with which members of these environments can communicate via CMC. Teachers are able to create discussion fora for asynchronous communication, and several of them also allow for synchronous 'chat' (see Section 3.3.3, below and also the chapter by Jager in the present volume).

Where students are geographically dispersed, such channels of communication are essential to create a sense of community in which learning can take place. Palloff and Pratt, for example, point out that while 'the power of community is great [...] the power of a learning community is even greater, as it supports the intellectual as well as personal growth and development of its members' (1999: 163). They outline six elements critical to the success of distance learning: honesty, responsiveness, relevance, respect, openness, and empowerment.

3.3. *CMC outside restricted environments*

3.3.1. E-MAIL

E-mail is one of the easiest and most practical ways of enabling language students to get in contact with native speakers of the target language. The most popular sites for obtaining free e-mail addresses are listed in Appendix 6 (though some of them tend to be rather slow). The most straightforward way to use e-mail as a language-learning tool is to see it as a provider of electronic pen pals (sometimes updated to 'key pals'). Such pals can be found at the addresses listed in Appendix 6. More in-depth information on the subject of pen pals can be found in Dudeney (2000: 128). The main advantage that electronic pen pals have over traditional pen pals is that response times are shorter, which can have an important effect on motivation. A second possible advantage is that a more relaxed style of writing is generally deemed appropriate for e-mails. This means that students may be more likely to focus on communicating their ideas, rather than worrying too much about the more rigid structure of traditional letters. In some cases, the fact that they have managed to communicate their ideas using less-than-perfect language may provide an important boost for a student's confidence. Students may also feel that they are using real language that is used in the target country, rather than the sometimes more artificial-sounding 'textbook' language.

However, simply pairing students with e-mail partners does not necessarily promote a language-learning focus. This is why it is often necessary for language teachers to provide some kind of organisational structure within which an e-mail exchange can take place (Ushioda, 2000: 126). For example, a group of English students learning French might be paired up with a group of French students learning English. The teachers of the two groups might then agree on a suitable research project, for example, local customs. Responsibility would then lie with the students to provide each other with sufficient information to help them put together a report on local customs in their partner's country. Box 1 – 'A Sample E-mail Exchange Project' – shows one way in which such a project might work.

Box 1: A Sample E-mail Exchange Project

1. A French teacher in England finds a class of French students learning English who are interested in exchanging e-mails.
2. Students are each allocated two partners in the other country, bearing in mind any preferences that they might have.
3. Students in both countries send brief descriptions of themselves to both partners.
4. The teacher gives the students a broad topic area (for example, local customs), within which students choose an area of interest.
5. They spend some time in class writing to their e-mail partners. The first half of the e-mail should exchange information on the topic. The second can include any personal content they want.

It is important that both groups have the same level of commitment to the project and that the structures of the academic years allow for periods of time when they are both able to work on the project at the same time. According to Ushioda (2000: 126), the advantages of 'tandem learning' are that students are required to 'take control of the learning process, select its content, set themselves objectives, and plan, monitor and evaluate their own learning'. This means that e-mail learning can serve as an excellent vehicle for self directed learning. More in-depth information on the use of e-mail as a language-learning tool can be found in O'Dowd's Chapter 7 in this volume.

3.3.2. DISCUSSION LISTS

Learners may also engage in authentic communication with native speakers via discussion lists, which can be found in most languages and cover a wide variety of topics. Their only danger is that they can be too popular, and learners may be overwhelmed by the number of messages. However, if used in a structured way, they can serve as a useful learning aid. For example, Warschauer (1996: 16) describes a project involving discussion lists for students of English for Science and Technology (see Box 2).

Box 2: A language-learning activity involving discussion list

1. The students search the WWW for articles in their area of interest and study them.
2. The students write their own drafts online.
3. The teacher evaluates these drafts online and creates electronic links to his/her own comments and to pages of appropriate linguistic and technical explanation.
4. Using this assistance, the students prepare and publish their own articles on a Web site set up by the teacher, together with reply forms to solicit opinions from readers.
5. They advertise their articles on appropriate discussion lists.
6. When they receive comments they can take these into account in editing their articles.

Useful sites containing discussion lists can be found in Appendix 6. Teeler and Gray (2000) provide lists of sites and discussion lists that can be used by teachers who are interested in keeping up to date with new ideas on how to use the Internet in language teaching.

3.3.3. CHAT ROOMS

Chat rooms are unrestricted places on the Internet where people can communicate in real time. A number of people can type synchronous messages, reading, and replying to what others in the room are saying. Some chat rooms contain graphics and images that enable participants to be represented by animated characters. High school teachers may experience problems using chat rooms as many schools have strict policies preventing their students from using them. However, schools may be more lenient towards the use of chat rooms that have a specific language-learning focus (see Appendix 6).

3.3.4. MOOs

As we have seen, MOO stands for 'multi-user object-oriented dimension'. These permanent sites exploit various metaphors in the way they construct the virtual communication interface. There are no illustrations so participants and metaphors are described only in words. It is possible for participants in a MOO environment to converse in different 'rooms', to 'whisper' to each other, or to 'shout' to the whole room. They may also create notice boards, or record conversations on a virtual tape recorder, and play them back later. MOO environments therefore enable groups of language students to create their own individualised learning environments. A number of researchers are enthusiastic about the capability of MOOs to improve language learning. Von der Emde *et al.* (2001), for example, who position themselves somewhere between the communicative and integrative paradigms, refer to the ability of MOOs to provide opportunities for authentic communication, autonomous learning, peer teaching, individualised learning and for experimentation. The autonomous learning angle is also emphasised by Shield *et al.* (2000: 40). Of all these claims, opportunities for experimentation are the most distinctive advantage of MOOs, whereas the other claims could be made equally strongly for all the Internet-based means of CMC presented in this chapter.

A major disadvantage of MOOs is that the new user is faced with a daunting list of abbreviations and symbols that need to be mastered before beginning to communicate in the MOO environment. Many language learners may not be prepared to invest the amount of time required for this activity, as it is not directly related to language learning per se. Another problem is that the metaphors used in the description of the environment ('shout', 'whisper', 'message board' and so on) may be open to different interpretations, especially if the medium is being used by students from different cultures. Whether or not students benefit from using MOOs is likely to depend heavily on their personality and learning preferences. It seems to be an environment that some love, but which others hate. Nevertheless, they can be worthwhile, and some useful MOO sites for language learning are listed in Appendix 6.

3.3.5. VIDEOCONFERENCING

Videoconferencing allows participants to communicate directly with each other and to see each other at the same time. Although it is still fairly expensive to run a video conferencing session, the cost is likely to fall significantly over the next few years, enabling language teachers to organise discussions between their students and speakers of the target language in co-operating institutions. The language-learning potential of this tool is enormous. However, unlike the other applications included in this chapter, the equipment necessary for its use is not yet widely available, so a more detailed account of it is not included here.

3.3.6. DISTINGUISHING BETWEEN 'PUSH' AND 'PULL' MEDIA

Of all the Internet-based activities discussed in this chapter, CMC comes closest to meeting the needs of Warschauer's 'integrative CALL'. Furthermore, it meets most of Chapelle's criteria for appropriateness, as the communication is likely to be meaning-focused, authentic, and well suited to the learners who are using the technology. The aforementioned activities, outlined by Ushioda (2000: 126) and

Warschauer (1996: 16), show that, when used in a controlled manner, it can also provide opportunities for focus on form as well as giving learners insight into their own language-learning processes.

It is useful at this point to draw a distinction between 'push and pull media'. 'Push media' tend to 'push' their contents at the user, whereas 'pull' media allow the user to select when and how they use the contents. Within the context of CMC, discussion lists would probably fall within the category of 'push media', as unsolicited messages tend to arrive, on a daily basis, in a user's in-tray. In order to use discussion lists to meet their individual learning needs, learners must therefore be selective about which messages they choose to read and, whenever possible, contribute to the list themselves, asking questions that are likely to provoke a response from other list users. With other types of CMC, such as e-mail, students have more control over the content, making autonomous learning more attainable.

4. Conclusion

The information presented in this chapter has necessarily been limited to that which can be presented in a single book chapter. For a much more detailed account of the various ways in which the Internet can be used for language-learning purposes, readers are referred to Uschi Felix's (2002) book, which offers a wide-ranging presentation of current developments in Web-based language learning, including extensive examples of Web-based language-learning resources, as well as in-depth discussions of current research issues. Another comprehensive source of information on the use of the Internet for language teaching is via ICT4LT (Information and Communications Technologies for Language Teachers), a training course for language teachers in the use of ICT for language teaching. Developed by a team of European experts in the area and funded by the European Commission under LINGUA, it contains sixteen modules in total, one of which is entirely devoted to uses of the WWW. At present, ICT4LT is free and open to all.

As we have seen, the Internet provides activities for teachers working within any one of Warschauer's structural, communicative, or integrative paradigms. For example, stand-alone grammar exercises available on the WWW are able to provide learners with knowledge of linguistic form and structure. Web-based activities, such as those outlined in Section 2, allow students to identify and fill information gaps, thus providing opportunities for authentic communication within the communicative paradigm. Finally, the types of CMC described in Section 3 correspond most closely to the integrative paradigm, as they allow students to communicate with the target language community about issues in which they are genuinely interested. As we saw in Section 3, with CMC the onus is on language teachers to create activities for their learners that encourage them to pay attention to form.

The potential of the Internet as a language-learning resource is considerable, yet teachers need to know what uses they want to make of it. The problem of information-overload is likely to remain significant, and language teachers will have to deal with the difficult task of limiting the amount of information with which their students have to work. This is why practical ideas books are likely to become an increasingly useful resource for teachers. As facilities such as chat rooms, discussion lists, MOOs, and videoconferencing become more accessible to language teachers, a new generation of practical ideas books is likely to appear. In the meantime, teachers and materials writers are likely to use the WWW itself as a forum for the discussion and dissemination of ideas.

Note

1. A distinction is made in this chapter between the terms 'Internet' and 'World Wide Web'. The Internet comprises all computers in the world that are linked, whereas the WWW consists of individual Web sites hosting content. Thus there are uses of the Internet, such as e-mail, videoconferencing, and data transfer, which are not via the WWW.

Bibliography

Information and Communications Technology for Language Teachers. An Online Training Course in Information and Communications Technology for Language Teachers. Available at http://www.ict4lt.org/en/index.htm

Gateways – Information Technology in the Learning Process: A collection of Teacher-Practice from Australian schools. (1996) Canberra: ACT Department of Education and Training, and Children's Youth and Family Services Bureau. Available at: http://www.edna.edu.au/sibling/learnit/

Boggs, R. and D. Jones (1994) 'Lessons learnt from connecting schools to the Internet'. *Australian Educational Computing, September,* 29–32.

Chapelle, C.A. (2001) *Computer Applications in Second Language Acquisition.* Cambridge: Cambridge University Press.

Chun, D. (1994) 'Using computer networking to facilitate the acquisition of interactive competence'. *System,* 22.1, 17–31.

Cooke, M. (1996) 'Networking across the globe'. In *Gateways – Information Technology in the Learning Process.*

Dudeney G. (2000) *The Internet and the Language Classroom*. Cambridge: Cambridge University Press.

Dunbar, E.J., S. Linklater, and D. Oakey (2000) 'The mystery project: Bridging the gap online'. *Educational Technology and Society*, 3.3, 293–307.

Felix, U. (1998) *Virtual Language Learning: Finding the Gems Amongst the Pebbles*. Melbourne: Language Australia.

Felix, U. (1999) 'Exploiting the Web for language teaching: Selected approaches'. *ReCALL*, 11.1, 30–37.

Felix, U. (2002) *Beyond Babel: Language Learning Online*. Melbourne: Language Australia.

Gitsaki, C. and R.P. Taylor (1999) 'Internet-based activities for the ESL classroom'. *ReCALL*, 11.1, 47–57.

Hardisty, D. (2001) 'Themes and variations: Internet lesson ideas'. *CALL in the 21st Century*. IATFFL CD-ROM.

Hogget, B. (1996) 'Towards 2000'. In *Gateways – Information Technology in the Learning Process*.

Kern, R. (1995) 'Restructuring classroom interaction with networked computers: Effects on quantity and quality of language production'. *Modern Language Journal*, 79.4, 457–76.

Lam, Y. (2000) 'Technophilia vs. technophobia: A preliminary look at why second language teachers do or do not use technology in their classrooms'. *The Canadian Modern Language Review*, 56.3, 389–420.

Littlemore, J. (2001) 'The relationship between learner autonomy, self-instruction and new technologies in language learning: A comparison between current theory and practice in European institutions of higher education'. In A. Chambers and G. Davies (eds.) *ICT and Language Learning: A European Perspective*. Lisse: Swets and Zeitlinger, 39–52.

Moran, C. (1991) 'We write, but do we read?'. *Computers and Composition, 8.3*, 51–61.

McWhirter, D. (1996) 'Student collaboration across cultural boundaries'. In *Gateways – Information Technology in the Learning Process*.

Palloff, R.M. and K. Pratt (1999) *Building Learning Communities in Cyberspace*. San Francisco: Jossey-Bass.

Shield, L., L. Davies, and L. Weininger (2000) 'Fostering (pro)active language learning through MOO'. *ReCALL*, 12.1, 35–48.

Teeler D. and P. Gray (2000) *How To Use the Internet in ELT*. London and New York: Longman.

Ushioda, E. (2000) 'Tandem language learning via e-mail: From motivation to autonomy'. *ReCALL*, 12.2, 121–8.

Von der Emde, S., J. Schneider, and M. Kotter (2001) 'Technically speaking: Transforming language learning through virtual learning environments

(MOOs)'. *The Modern Language Journal*, 8.2, 210–24.

Vygotsky, L.S. (1978) *Mind in Society: The Development of Higher Psychological Processes.* Cambridge, MA: Harvard University Press.

Warschauer, M. (1996) 'Computer-assisted language learning: An introduction'. In S. Fotos (ed.) *Multimedia Language Teaching.* Tokyo: Logos International, 3–20.

Warschauer, M. (1997) 'Computer-mediated collaborative learning: Theory and practice'. *The Modern Language Journal*, 81.3, 470–81.

Warschauer, M. (2001) 'The death of cyberspace and the rebirth of CALL'. *CALL in the 21ˢᵗ Century.* IATEFL CD-ROM.

Warschauer, M., L. Turbee, and B. Roberts (1996) 'Computer learning networks and student empowerment'. *System*, 24.1, 1–14.

Windeatt S, D. Hardisty, and D. Eastment (2000) *The Internet.* Oxford: Oxford University Press. Oxford Resources Books for Teachers.

Appendix 1: Directories, search engines and metasearch tools

Directories
Yahoo: http://www.yahoo.com
Yahoo in French: http://fr.yahoo.com
Yahoo in Spanish: http://es.yahoo.com
Yahoo in German: http://de.yahoo.com

Search engines
Google: http://www.google.com
Altavista: http://altavista.digital.com
Lycos: http://www.lycos.com
Infoseek: http://www.infoseek.com
Excite: http://www.excite.com

Metasearch tools
Ask Jeeves: http://www.askjeeves.com

Appendix 2: WWW language-learning resources

Web-based language-learning resources for French
Bonjour de France: http://www.bonjourdefrance.com/
Hometown French: http://hometown.aol.com/glorybfree/index.html
French resources:
http://lang.syr.edu/Grad/MainMenu/French/gfresources.html

Web-based language-learning resources for English
Susan Clark's EFL page:
http://home.earthlink.net/~sclark98/ESLonLine/ghwelcome.htm
Grammar safari: http://deil.lang.uiuc.edu/web.pages/grammarsafari.html
Dave's ESL café: http://www.eslcafe.com/

Web-based language-learning resources for Spanish
Si Espana: http://www.sispain.org/
Juan Ramon de Arana: http://mld.ursinus.edu/~jarana/Ejercicios/
Sussex University Spanish resources:
http://www.susx.ac.uk/langc/spanish.html
Academic info: http://www.academicinfo.net/langspanish.html

Web-based language-learning resources for all languages
The Halls of Academia: http://www.tenet.edu/halls/forlanguage.html
1stop languages: http://www.1stop-language.com/resources.htm
travlang: http://www.travlang.com
Jim Becker's Web site: http://www.uni.edu/becker/
Yourdictionary: http://www.yourdictionary.com/grammars.html
The Goethe site: http://www.goethe-verlag.com/tests/

Appendix 3: Authoring software available on the Internet

Hot Potatoes: http://web.uvic.ca/hrd/halfbaked/

Appendix 4: Reference tools

Yourdictionary: http://www.yourdictionary.com
Onelook: http://www.onelook.com/
The Linguist List: http://www.linguistlist.org/

Appendix 5: 'That's got to be the Loch Ness Monster!'

Student Task 1
'Cryptids' is a term used to describe 'unverified animals; that is, animal species or forms which have been reported in some manner but which have not been scientifically proven to exist.' The study of such "hidden or unknown animals" (Bates 2004) is known as Cryptozoology http://www.cryptozoology.com/articles/wic.php. Click on a cryptid in the table below and look at the pictures and descriptions of the animal. Then complete the table:

Cryptid	Location	How much do you believe that this animal exists?				
		100%	50%	0	-50%	-100%
Bigfoot (Sasquatch)						
Chupacabra						
Inkanyamba						
Kraken						
Loch Ness Monster						
Mokele-Mbembe						
Tasmanian Tiger						
Woolly Mammoth						

When you have finished this task, talk to the person at the computer next to you and see if they have completed the table in the same way as you.

Student Task 2

There are many ways of saying how certain or sure you are that something is true or not. This lesson you will look information about one of the above cryptids, the Loch Ness Monster. Because this information has been produced by people with very different opinions about whether the Loch Ness monster exists or not, it is important to pay attention to the words they use to discuss it.

Loch Ness is a very large lake in the Scottish Highlands. For many years there have been reports of a large unknown animal or 'monster' living there. Hundreds of people say they have seen 'Nessie', and hundreds of photographs have been taken and presented as proof of the creature's existence. Some eye-witnesses have been accused of lying, and many photographs have been exposed as hoaxes. Until the 1970s there was little scientific study of the loch, and there is still no conclusive evidence to show that a large unknown creature lives in the loch.

A zoologist friend from your country has been given a scholarship to conduct research at Loch Ness during the first week in July this year. The scholarship covers transport expenses and up to £40 a night towards accommodation. The scholarship committee will pay transport fees directly, but your friend can keep any accommodation money left over. Look at the map of the area and then find suitable flights to the nearest international airport. Then decide whether rail or bus would be more convenient for getting to Loch Ness from the airport. Work out your friend's travel itinerary and accommodation arrangements and fill in the table:

Outward journey							
	Carrier	Date	From	To	Departure time	Arrival time	
Flight 1							
Flight 2 (if necessary)							
Train 1							
Train 2 (if necessary)							
Bus 1							
Bus 2 (if necessary)							
Return journey							
	Carrier	Date	From	To	Departure time	Arrival time	
Bus 1							
Bus 2 (if necessary)							
Train 1							
Train 2 (if necessary)							
Flight 1							
Flight 2 (if necessary)							

Accommodation								
Hotel name	Arrival date	Departure date	Number of nights	Type of room	Room rate	Smoking/ non-smoking	Meals included	Deposit

When you have finished this task, talk to the person at the computer next to you and see if they have got their friend a better deal than you. Find out who got their friend the cheapest accommodation.

Student Task 3

Modal verbs

That's the Loch Ness Monster.	That's got to be the Loch Ness Monster.
It isn't anything.	It can't be anything.
It was the monster.	It must have been the monster.
I've seen it!	I've actually seen it!
I saw it.	I actually saw it.
It wasn't a fish	It certainly wasn't a fish
It was the monster.	It was the monster, really.

An American TV company interviewed five people who say they saw something alive in the Loch. Click on their names to hear them describe what they saw. Match each group of words with the person who says them.

Val Moffat	1.	'I've actually seen it!'
	2.	All I can say is that I suppose looking at the Loch, that somewhere in there is the Loch Ness monster.
	3.	And as far as I'm concerned, I've seen it.
Richard White	4.	But I saw it, and nothing can take that away.
	5.	I mean, I actually saw it.
	6.	I myself obviously think I saw the monster, but I certainly saw that.
	7.	I saw what I saw.
Gary Campbell	8.	I thought, 'No, it can't be anything,'
	9.	I would say it was black, sort of a dark black color,
	10.	It certainly wasn't a fish,
	11.	It certainly wasn't a seal,
Ronald	12.	It must have been the monster.
Mackintosh	13.	It was a large, black object — a whale-like object
	14.	It was a mixture of browns, greens, sludgy sort of colors.
	15.	It was an object, it was huge.
	16.	It was gray-brown, massive.
	17.	Must have seen it three or four times, and the last time I looked, it was gone!

	18.	That's got to be the Loch Ness Monster that everybody has spent thousands of pounds searching for,
	19.	That's what I actually saw with my own eyes,
	20.	The nearest I can tell you is it looked like a boat that had turned upside down.
Ian Cameron	20.	Therefore I must say that it was the monster, really.

Help for Student Task 3
If you find the eyewitnesses' accents unfamiliar, click here to read what they say.

Appendix 6: Computer Mediated Communication

Online learning environments
Blackboard
http://www.blackboard.com
WebCT
http://www.webct.com/
FirstClass
http://www.firstclass.com/
Merlin
http://www.hull.ac.uk/elearning/merlin/

Popular sites for obtaining free e-mail addresses
http://mail.yahoo.com
http://netaddress.com
http://egroups.com

Sites for obtaining electronic pen pals ('key pals')
Penpals: http://www.penpals.com
The Tandem network: http://www.slf.ruhr-uni-bochum.de/

Discussion lists
Listserve (access point to various English discussion lists for language students): listserve@latrobe.edu.au
Francolistes (French discussion lists) http://www.francopholistes.com/
Spanishpass (Spanish discussion list):
http://www.tees.ac.uk/langc/lancent/spanishpass.html

Multilingual chat rooms
Chat4all: http://www.chat4all.org/
Links to multilingual chat rooms:
http://www.theorderoftime.com/cyber/to/chatting.html

MOO Connections
SchMOOze University (English MOO):
http://schmooze.hunter.cuny.edu: 8888
MooFrançais (French MOO):
http://www.umsl.edu/~moosproj/moofrancais.html
MundoHispano (Spanish MOO):
http://www.umsl.edu/~moosproj/mundo.html
Terravista (Portuguese discussion list):
http://www.terravista.pt/ancora/1833/moo-pt.html

6 A task-based approach to Web authoring for learning languages

Freda Mishan

1. Introduction

The Internet is fast becoming the primary medium of our age. As a marketing and publicity medium, the public face of everything from private businesses to state institutions, the Web site has far overtaken other media due to the sheer size of its global audience.[1] Electronic literacy – the ability to find, organise and make use of information as well as to read and write in the new medium (Shetzer and Warschauer, 2000: 173) – is, therefore, arguably the core enabling skill of our era. The reciprocity of language learning and electronic literacy adds a new dimension to the area of ICT and language learning: 'Whereas previously educators considered how to use information technology in order to teach language, it is now essential also to consider how to teach language so that learners can make effective use of information technology' (Shetzer and Warschauer, 2000: 172). This justifies a greater emphasis on tasks such as authoring a Web site that combine these fields. The rationale of this chapter is that in terms of the range of skills it deploys and its language-learning potential, Web authoring is among the most valuable of the many learning opportunities – asynchronous and synchronous communication, virtual access to the TL culture, self-access language practice activities and so on – that the Internet offers students. It will be demonstrated that learner Web authoring combines 'the three A's', authenticity, authorship and autonomy. The first two are the twin tenets of the communicative approach to language teaching (CLT) (Kramsch *et al.*, 2000: 78), the third, autonomy, is the contemporary educational ethos and might be seen as the natural heir to CLT facilitated by the freedom of access to communication and information that technology has given us. The approach to learner Web authoring detailed in this chapter is underpinned by theories of experiential learning and draws on the principles and frameworks of Task-Based Learning (TBL). The first section of the chapter situates learner Web authoring within the context of the emerging research in this area. Next, the principles, features and a detailed description of the task-based approach to Web authoring are given. Following this, the language-learning potential of the approach is assessed, with reference to core factors for language acquisition such as motivation, input and output. The conclusion looks to the potential for development of learner Web authoring in view of the ever-increasing usability of Web tools and the general shift in pedagogical orientation from teacher to student-directed learning.

2. Background

Language practitioners have been quick to recognise the potential of the Web as a medium as well as a resource (see the distinction refined in Conacher and Royall 1998: 38), in particular its interactive and communications capacity. However, although extremely common in other sectors of education,[2] the opportunity for learners of languages to author their own Web pages appears not to have been fully exploited or researched. While there are accounts of Web-authoring projects by language students to be found on the Web itself (such as Fox, 1998; Kimball, 1998; Mills, 1996; A'Ness's case study in Kramsch *et al.*, 2000) and in print (for example Warschauer, 1995; Atkinson, 1998; Kubota, 1999, Warschauer, 2000: 44–5), many published studies in this area are still effectively anecdotal reports: 'There is a growing body of anecdotal evidence […] suggesting positive effects of task-based learning using the Web in a variety of projects, approaches and languages' (Felix, 1999: 94). Studies tend to claim that skills have 'improved', for example, without indicating sufficiently strict criteria by which improvement is evaluated or clear methodologies by which such results were achieved (Schultz, 2000: 122). Indeed few such projects offer methodological frameworks that are grounded in SLA theory: 'Much more can be accomplished if CALL designers regularly consider CALL task design in view of […] conditions hypothesised for SLA' (Chapelle, 2001: 163). Shetzer and Warschauer's framework, which focuses on electronic literacy, is among the most comprehensive available, and identifies Web authoring as a core skill for electronic literacy (2000: 180–81). On the whole, however, the bulk of the research on Web authoring still tends to focus on the teacher as author. That the autonomous modes of learning involved in the proposed approach to Web authoring have been slow to be applied in this area may be attributed to the perceived complexity (both technical and/or organisational) of the authoring task or, indeed to practical reasons (access to networked computers, levels of computer literacy).

Notwithstanding this apparent gap in the research, the refrain of factors being associated with this and comparable creative, ICT-based activities, and which coincide with factors identified with the promotion of language acquisition, is too insistent to be ignored. Significantly, the most frequently recurring factor is motivation (see, for example, Warschauer, 1996) – arguably the critical factor in learning in general (Corder, 1974: 22). For learners of English if not for others, this motivation is effectively circular (Warschauer and Whittaker, 1997: 27) in that, at present, English remains the dominant language of the Web,[3] and is thus essential for electronic literacy (an acceptable end in itself). Aspects of this instrumental type of motivation include the empowerment that electronic literacy offers (Warschauer, 1996: 9) and 'the opportunity to gain an authorial voice outside the authority of the teacher and the educational institution' (Kramsch *et al.,* 2000: 79). As Kramsch *et al.* demonstrate in that paper, computer-mediated communication such as learner Web authoring implicate key factors essential to language learning which underlie the Communicative approach, namely *meaningful communication* and *agency* ('the power to take meaningful action and to see the results of decisions and choices', Murray, 1997: 126). Writing for the Internet on discussion lists, bulletin boards, or in the context of this chapter, Web pages, gives not only greater meaning but more focused purpose to communication and, by vastly broadening the audience for learner output, has been shown to impact positively on accuracy levels (Warschauer and Healey, 1998: 64, see also Willis, 1996: 14). Provision of that most essential element of language learning, authentic target language input, could be no better served than via that limitless database of authentic materials that is the Web (Kramsch *et al.,* 2000: 79). The requirement in the authoring project not only to search for, access and read authentic texts on the Web but to evaluate and process them implicates cognitive and language processing skills that are essential to language learning. These and other factors emerge in the exposition of the proposed approach to learner Web authoring that follows.

3. The task-based approach to learner Web authoring: Principles and features

For its pedagogy, the proposed learner Web-authoring framework draws on a number of approaches and methods. Learner autonomy, in terms of its pedagogical ethos; collaborative learning (an essential element of autonomy, see Konohen, 1992: 19) in terms of its model of interaction; experiential learning or 'learning by doing' (for example, Kolb, 1983) in its cyclical learning model based on concrete experience; problem-based learning (PBL) in its use of an evaluation stage (for example, Barrows 1985); and most directly, Task-Based Learning (TBL). In TBL, the concept of task is developed and concretised and placed at the centre of a methodological framework (see especially Willis, 1996). Defined as a 'goal-oriented communicative activity with a specific outcome' (Willis, 1996:

36), the task is customarily described as an activity involving genuine communication, focusing therefore on meaning rather than form, as having a relationship to the real world, and as being assessed in terms of its completion and its outcome (Skehan, 1996: 38), rather than the correctness of the language forms in which these are achieved. The inherent authenticity of the concept of task makes it an ideal pedagogical model to apply to such an authentic activity as creating a Web site: 'The Web is best suited for task-driven activities in which students […] have some degree of control over their learning' (Felix, 1999: 94). The task-based approach conceived here draws on the TBL framework constructed by Willis, notably in its language focus element (Willis, 1996: 101–15).

The task-based approach to learner Web authoring contains three basic elements which correspond to the three stages of authoring a Web site: conception, creation, and post-construction. Each of these involves technical and non-technical aspects (see Figure 1). Conception, or planning the site, involves such aspects as decisions on function and content of the site, evaluating other sites (non-technical), and designing the navigational structure (technical); the creation stage includes producing text (non-technical) and constructing the site using Web-authoring tools; the post-construction phase involves the mainly technical aspect of maintaining the site and the (non-technical) summative evaluation. Each element or phase consists of a number of stages and ends with a reflective, evaluation stage that includes a language awareness-raising session. The latter is intended to maintain the language-learning balance in a task where the technical aspect can tend to be all-absorbing. The overall tripartite framework is therefore iterative and cyclical in its reprise of evaluation.

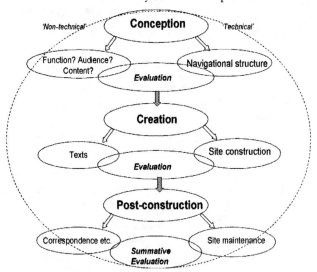

Figure 1: Framework for the task-based approach to learner Web authoring

The three elements of conception, creation, and post-construction correspond to the three stages of authoring a Web site; however, this does not mean that every task undertaken within the framework has to involve creating a Web site from start to finish. A teacher may opt for a literacy focus, for example, concentrating on the text creation element, doing other aspects of the Web site creation task him/herself or having this done by the institution's IT section. Learners might focus only on the conception and creation elements, handing over the technical aspect to the teacher/technologist. Alternatively, a collaborative approach could be adopted where learners with technical expertise construct the Web site, with the content contributed by others in the learner group. This flexibility broadens the applicability of the framework: possible selective routes within the framework may be visualised from Figure 1.

Two of the key features of the approach mentioned above are the evaluation stage and the language awareness-raising session which it includes. Others are the pre-task briefing and conception of the teacher's role. As in other autonomous learning contexts, the teacher's role in this task-based framework for learner Web authoring, is fundamentally that of *enabler* in that s/he 'opens the way' for autonomy. The teacher has to act as guide, facilitator, resource (Benson, 2001: 171; Willis, 1996: 40–41) and – to be realistic, especially in a technical task – trouble-shooter. As guide, the teacher is responsible for inducting the students into the approach being taken and explaining its rationale (Mills, 1996) and for giving clear instructions for the procedure of the specific task in hand and the students' roles in it. The teacher-guide's *pre-task briefing* (see below) is an essential element in the task. Mills emphasises that this leadership can affect the outcome of such a project, contrasting student performance in a poorly-led project and one led by an enthusiastic and involved teacher (Mills, 1996). The role of facilitator is to provide support for learning (Benson, 2001: 171). In a task with a language-learning purpose this includes maintaining the language focus of the task while informally monitoring the learners' work. As resource, the teacher retains the traditional role of serving as source of knowledge and expertise (Benson, 2001: 171–2). In this language-learning context, this includes advising on language use. The resource role also involves being active in the sessions specifically dedicated to language awareness-raising (which round off each stage, see *evaluation* below), although these should ideally be learner-led.

Each element or phase undertaken within the learner Web-authoring framework begins with a pre-task briefing. Because of its introductory function, this will usually be teacher-led, but could usefully include the learners themselves doing some background research into key concepts. Good basic introductions to Web authoring can be found in the *Yale Style Manual* on http://info.med.yale.edu/caim/manual/contents.html and on http://www.ict4lt.org/ (*Module 3.3 Creating a World Wide Web site*). The pre-task briefing is a vital stage in that it introduces the learners to the approaches being taken (autonomous and collaborative learning, learning by doing, Task-Based Learning) and their rationale. However, it should be borne in mind that such approaches are not necessarily appropriate to all learning styles (see below). This introduction should include an indication of the range of skills, both language and technical, that will be employed in the task, linking these to the various stages and aspects of the task. This is the stage at which instructions for the task can be given and various roles allocated, on the basis of learners' expertise, preference or, most importantly, their learning styles. Not all students are the type of 'holistic' learners amenable to the autonomous and collaborative modes of learning required in a task framework. A teacher aware of the diversity of learning styles of members of his/her class can anticipate this potential for frustration. One way to do this might be to encourage learners to reflect on their learning styles, and acquaint them with the range of learning style options open to them (Tudor, 1996: 123). There is some research evidence to show that this can induce learners to adopt different learning styles (see, for example, a study by Little and Singleton, 1990: 14–16; Tomlinson, 1998: 18). Alternatively, the teacher may prefer to accept individual differences and match activities to learning styles. In Web-authoring tasks, the analytic type learner might be involved in the technical side of site construction which requires such modes of work (especially if coding HTML or XML), or could be asked to design interactive language exercises if these are a feature of the site.

The concluding stage of any task undertaken within the learner Web-authoring framework is evaluation. The evaluation stage is essential in autonomous and task-based modes of learning as providing an opportunity to reflect on and thus make explicit what has been done during the task. This reinforces or even, according to the tenets of experiential learning, prompts learning, since the process of learning is 'the recycling of experience at deeper levels of understanding and interpretation' (Kohonen, 1992: 17). Reflection is a key psychological component of autonomy (Benson, 2001: 90), one that is not only intellectual but affective (Benson, 2001: 207 citing a study by Lor, 1998). Benson points out that reflection is bi-directional in this respect, potentially induced by positive or negative feelings or, conversely, boosting morale, confidence, and motivation. As reflection is probably best instigated by writing (Benson, 2001: 95), one way to prompt this is by asking learners to keep journals throughout the task (Benson, 2001: 204–8). In these, learners can record what they have done during each period of working on the task and then add 'reflections' on this (degree of satisfaction with their own performance, achievements, failures, frustrations, ideas for improvement, and so on). Reflection can be particularly important for analytical type learners who have a systematic approach to learning and who benefit from explicitness.

In the context of language pedagogy, the language awareness-raising session is a crucial part of the evaluation stage of the task (Willis's TBL framework in Willis, 1996: 102–10) also concludes with a 'language focus' session. In the prevailing climate of the fluency-focused communicative approach, recent SLA research (see Carter *et al.*, 1998) has indicated the benefits of a return to a focus on form albeit in a more organic way (see also Tomlinson, 1998: 13–14). Language awareness raising is an appropriate way to do this in task-based activities which involve authentic texts. Learners will have 'experienced' much language during the task (Willis, 1996: 41) and inferred meanings and uses of particular structures/lexes from their context. A language focus session allows learners, once removed from the pressure of performing the task, to test the hypotheses they have formed about the language structures/lexes they have encountered and explore them in more detail. This can be done by such means as concordances (see the chapter by Chambers and Kelly in this volume) or through research and practice on language-learning Web sites or conventional grammars. These sessions are ideally learner-led, since the language issues are raised by the learners themselves, with the teacher acting here as 'resource'. The teacher may also, of course, wish to draw attention to language points noted while monitoring the task.

4. The task-based approach to learner Web authoring: Description of procedures

4.1. Element one: Conception

The conception stage of building a Web site should take place well away from the computer. In collaborative work such as this, ideas might best emerge in a brainstorming session. The first aspect of conception is a definition of the function of the Web site. Is it to be a channel of (intercultural) communication for learners; for dissemination of students' work; to make other resources available (on site or via links); a language-learning resource containing interactive exercises or merely have entertainment value? The function of the site is related to its target audience and in a pedagogical and foreign language context, the language proficiency of the target audience (native speakers [NSs] or non-native speakers [NNSs] of the language of the Web site?) will need to be considered. The function or functions of the site will also determine its content. For example, if the site's function is dissemination, content will probably comprise learner- and possibly teacher-authored material; if the site is serving a resource function, content may include authentic material either uploaded, downloaded or via links to online newspapers, magazines, literature, and so on. Linguistic register should be considered in relation to content; is the site to have a uniform register (as do many commercial sites), or will the variety of content prevent this?

The technical aspect of the conception stage is *visualisation* of the *navigational structure* of the site itself, i.e., how the home page links to other pages on the site. This is often best done on paper or on a blackboard as a tree diagram. At this stage, outlines of the pages and content in block form can be drawn, and some ideas about the desired technical features of the site will probably emerge (e.g. navigational tools, frames, graphics, internal and external links, e-mail links, discussion forums, search function). Depending on the familiarity of the learners with the Web, this step might include a survey of Web sites with similar parameters to the one being planned. Many of the criteria in the chapter by Murray in this volume may be applicable here. From such a survey, learners will be able to draw some generalised conclusions about the features of Web sites; for example, that the quality of a Web site depends more on its appearance than on the quality of its text content, what Shetzer and Warschauer call 'the value of the visual' (2000: 174); and that there is a sort of symbiotic relationship between appearance and text. It is not as simple as 'starting with a text and then prettifying it' as Shetzer and Warschauer put it (2000: 174).

The main aspects of the conception element as described here are planning and design. In accordance with the structure of the framework, whether the learners are to go on to construct the site themselves or give the brief to the teacher or technical assistant, this element is rounded off with an evaluation session. This will include the features described above, general reflection on concepts, processes, language, and possibly cultural aspects of the TL that have been encountered, skills that have been used, and so on. If learners are keeping journals (see above) they may wish to review them at this stage and extract recurring observations, either positive or negative. These can be shared with the group or with the teacher if desired. The language awareness-raising session may be incorporated into the evaluation session or may take place separately, depending on the amount of language research work anticipated and the interest of the learners. In this first language session of the task, a useful way to focus on the technical vocabulary encountered is via translation techniques, asking learners to translate the Internet-related lexes into their own languages and then compare translations in mixed-language groups. This should have the (positive) effect of reassuring learners by revealing that the language of the Internet is truly international, as the tendency is for the English source word either to be adopted or directly translated (Italian, for example, uses *il Web* but translates the Net – *la Rete*). Some of the other means of raising language awareness in this session have already been mentioned above, notably, language-learning Web sites and concordances.

4.2. Element Two: Creation

The creation element consists of two main aspects, creating the text sections to be transferred to hypertext and the technical construction of the Web site. Writing for the Web involves a good deal of preparation, as Web text is both a medium and a unique discourse type. Preparation for this task can be done by original research, for instance, a corpus of Web texts may be complied (see Chapter 9 by Chambers and Kelly in this volume) and analysed for recurring/distinguishing features using concordancing software. Alternatively, learners may source material already written about this discourse type on the Web or in print (such as Pemberton and Shurville, 2000). In fact, the discourse type engendered by this new medium is not as yet extensively researched (Amitay, 2000: 25). Its main rationale is readability within the constraints of the Web page format, i.e., clarity; hence the preponderance of the present tense and avoidance of complex linguistic structures (Amitay, 2000: 31). Other aids to Web page readability are 'scannability' and presentation of information in clearly marked and easy-to-process chunks (Eayrs, 1999).

Creating hypertext documents is not only a matter of appropriate discourse type, however, but requires a radical shift in conceptualisation of text, from a linear, sequential model to one that has a non-linear branching structure. The technical capacity to link from one text to another is given not only to the author but to the user; this effectively wrests the text from the author's control: 'The original author(s) must consider that the reader will link to the other site in the middle of reading and thus engage in the two (or more) pieces in a back and forth fashion' (Shetzer and Warschauer, 2000: 175). Web authors are constrained, in other words, by loss of context; they have no assurance that their text is being read in sequence (Henriquez, 2000: 6). This is one of the reasons why hypertext documents need to present text in short, self-contained units of information. On the other hand, this also makes the text dynamic and interactive, 'readers also become co-constructors, as they play a more active role in piecing together texts to make meaning' (Shetzer and Warschauer, 2000: 175). All these aspects need to be borne in mind by learners, whether writing their own texts or compiling and editing material from other sources. 'Creating' material for the Web based on other sources is arguably even more demanding than writing one's own text because it calls on further electronic literacy skills of searching, evaluation, culling, and reformulating (see Section 5.5.).

Integrating other people's material into one's own also involves, of course, issues of plagiarism and copyright. The Internet's provision of instant access to vast quantities of information, has blurred these principles and provided opportunities for plagiarism on an enormous scale. Learners need to be aware of the complex legal and moral aspects of the technically simple act of 'cutting and pasting' from Web texts. A useful preliminary to writing or 'assembling' their own materials is to look at some of the information about copyright on the Web.[4] Learners wishing to reproduce large sections of text should be encouraged to write to the original authors requesting permission to do so. Where they wish to quote short passages or to paraphrase, learners should apply the conventions of referencing.[5]

If the technical construction is to be done by the learner group or sub-group, they will at this stage have to decide on an *authoring tool* (unless the teacher has already done so). The criteria for choosing an authoring tool are, as with the choice of any 'tool' from a car to a camcorder, variable and personal. The most important criteria are the size and the range of features (for example, e-mail, discussion board, search function) on the planned Web site. Other criteria include features of the tool (e.g. views, ease of publishing), compatibility with existing software, the user's level of computer literacy, and cost. Once these criteria have been established, learners can set about evaluating and comparing available tools. This can most conveniently be done on the Web, consulting online magazines such as *PC Magazine on-line* (http://www.pcmag.com/).

Authoring tools fall into two categories: code-based (i.e. for coding in HTML) and visual or WYSIWYG (What You See Is What You Get), although the latest generation of tools[6] give both views (i.e. of WYSIWYG or HTML code) in different windows, or allow the author to toggle between views. Code-based tools allow the author to directly edit the HTML code of Web pages. HTML was until recently the 'lingua franca' for publishing hypertext on the Web but is currently being surpassed by XML, eXtensible Markup Language, the next-generation Web-authoring language. XML is far more flexible than its predecessor because it separates style from content and because unlike HTML, it allows the user to define his/her own tags. Code-based authoring is possible using as basic tools as a simple text editor such as *Notepad* or *Wordpad*. Visual (WYSIWYG) tools are probably more suitable for novice Web authors who are not interested in knowing 'what is going on under the bonnet', as Riley and Davies (2000) put it. Probably the simplest of these tools is available on the simple word-processor; *Microsoft (MS) Word 97* onwards incorporates Web-authoring tools so Web pages can be prepared in *Word* and saved as HTML ready for uploading to the Web server. Of the current crop of authoring tools, *Macromedia Dreamweaver 4.0* is the most popular with professional Web builders,[7] although it is intended for building more complex sites. *FrontPage 2002* is recommended for its ease of use and navigation features (it has options for setting up e-mail response forms, discussion groups, and a search function).

If learners are to create their own interactive language exercises, the current authorware of choice appears to be *Hot Potatoes*. *Hot Potatoes*, from Half-Baked Software Inc., is user-friendly, has six exercise templates (multiple-choice, gapfill etc.) and is freely available to download from University of Victoria (http://web.uvic.ca/hrd/halfbaked/) for non-profit educational users using it on sites available on the Web. *Quia*, also free from http://www.quia.com/, has a range of 11 exercise templates, such as hangman, flashcards, and popups which can be fun for students to use. *Quia* allows authors to create exercises which are then accessible to the authors' site via a link. Half-Baked Software has also produced *Quandary*, an application for creating Web-based action mazes.[8] Although the concept and structure of the interactive maze is conceptually challenging enough, *Quandary* is simple to use from the technical and linguistic point of view so is suitable for interested learners to use. All three of these applications have online tutorials which are easy to follow.

Whatever the authoring tools selected for the construction of the Web site, learners will find it easier, and more beneficial to language learning, to follow printed instructions, printed off from the Web or using a manual. Once the site has been constructed and saved on disc, it will have to be uploaded to a server to make it available on the Web itself. Many educational institutions now have their own Web servers, usually managed by the IT section, so it may be as simple as giving the file to whoever manages the institution Web site. Alternatively, free Web space can be gained on most Internet Service Providers (ISPs), a comprehensive list of which can be found on http://thelist.internet.com/, or from Web account providers such as *Tripod* (http://www.tripod.lycos.com/), *Yahoo* (http://www.yahoo.com), and so on. It is worth bearing in mind when selecting an authoring tool, however, that with the latest authoring software, such as *FrontPage 2002*, uploading is as simple as clicking the appropriate button.

Another option, in cases where an institution does not have access to a remote site, or where confidentiality is required, is the Intranet – essentially a private Internet that operates on the institution's internal network. This gives it greater speed of access, privacy and reliability but limited access to the Internet. A useful starting point for those interested in using an Intranet is http://www.intrack.com/intranet/index.cfm. Most of the large computer corporations nowadays also deal in Intranet systems, for example, http://www.microsoft.com/solutions/msi/.

More than in the previous conception element, there is a marked divide in the creation element between the technical and non-technical aspects of Web site construction. Unless the former aspect has been delegated (to the teacher/IT staff), the evaluation session might best be structured in two parts. Whether the learner group all worked on both aspects or whether it split into technical and non-technical 'teams', this will allow learners to focus on language on the one hand or on technical aspects on the other. In both evaluation sessions (which can run in parallel if the learner group was divided) the main emphasis is on 'creative reflection', i.e. reflection on language experienced and/or technical skills employed with the aim of consolidating this into learning. Technical skills and techniques can be consolidated by applying some form of the experiential learning model, i.e., making observations and reflecting on concrete experience, generalising from these, and then testing the implications derived in new situations. If learners had worked on some aspects of site construction alone or in small groups, this could involve them comparing how they achieved particular technical tasks. The language awareness-raising session can involve previously mentioned Web-based activities and ones such as writing a humble vocabulary list, often the best way to revise new language, particularly for the kinaesthetic learner for whom the physical act of writing assists memorisation.

4.3. Element three: Post-construction

The post-construction element comprises a mainly technical aspect, site maintenance and a non-technical aspect, summative evaluation. If site maintenance is to be included in the Web-authoring project, the job of site editor will go to one or a group of students. Otherwise it will fall to the teacher or a member of the institution's IT staff. Site maintenance is, of course, a continual process and can be a useful way for learners to consolidate and develop the language and technical skills that they have learned. The basic task is to keep the site current: updating contact details, class lists, adding new material if the project is on-going and checking that links are still 'live'. If the site has a discussion board, this will need to be maintained and e-mail correspondence dealt with.

Whatever elements/stages of the learner Web-authoring task have been done, the summative evaluation is mandatory. As has been emphasised above, evaluation is integral to the approach, as it is considered an essential part of the learning process and habituates learners to autonomous ways of learning. The summative evaluation is basically a reflective stage in which the learners review and assess the entire project in terms of achievements in both language learning and electronic literacy. The fact that the psychological process of reflection is instigated by writing was the basis for the suggestion of learner diaries (see above). A practical 'non-threatening' starting point for reflection in the summative evaluation is the use of questionnaires with open-ended questions. These are useful for both the information that they garner and the reflective process that they prompt. Once they have completed the questionnaires, learners might gather in small groups to compare and discuss their responses. Groups can be asked to pull out some generalisations from this discussion (such as 'We found Web searching very complex' 'We liked the research aspect of the project'[9]) – this method preserves confidentiality if learners are shy about personal comments. A similar group analysis approach can be used to summarise and generalise the comments in learner journals, if these have been kept. A more quantitative approach is to issue questionnaires listing breakdowns of skills (language learning and technical) and asking learners to indicate their proficiency in them on a numerical scale, as a result of working on the project.

5. SLA rationale for the task-based approach to learner Web authoring

The basic rationale of the task-based approach to learner Web authoring is that all three elements, conception, creation, and post-construction, hold great potential for language learning, both in the range of SLA factors that they invoke and the skills that they deploy. This section gives the SLA rationale for the task-based learner Web-authoring approach described here, showing how it creates many of the conditions identified as conducive for language learning, most notably motivation, exposure to authentic TL in context ('input'), opportunities for meaningful language use ('output'), and for autonomous learning. The approach also supports language learning by giving learners opportunities for developing and honing language (and general) learning skills. These include interactional (communication) skills and ones associated with using the Internet; reading skills such as skimming, scanning, and related cognitive skills of searching for, evaluating, and processing information.

5.1. Motivation

Motivation, always a crucial pre-requisite to learning, is the core factor influencing the two basic outcomes of the Web-authoring task. The first outcome is the achievement of the task's short-term goal; a functioning Web page. The second is the long-term objective; enhanced language learning in its participants. Motivation as incentive (to finish the task, to make a good job of it) works at a relatively superficial level. This is underlain by the individual participants' personal motivations regarding language study in general, be these intrinsic, the motivation being the learner's own interest or curiosity, or extrinsic, the motivation coming from external forces (Arnold and Brown, 1999: 14). Part of the motivational aspect of writing for the Web comes from the sense of authorship (Kramsch *et al.*, 2000: 79) and this has been shown to positively affect language proficiency: 'When students perceived they were contributing something of value to the public arena, they put in a great deal of effort in the process and attention to the product, yielding positive results in their learning to write in a second language' (Warschauer and Healey 1998: 64). Although the relationship between motivation and achievement is, as Ellis notes, probably an interactive one (1994: 515), successful completion of so complex a task as Web authoring, with its combination of technical and language elements, is bound to give learners more confidence in using the Internet and this itself will have an indirect effect on language learning. Leloup and Pontiero note this in the context of accessing authentic materials and the Web: 'When students realise they can successfully deal with and understand authentic texts, confidence in their own TL abilities soars and they are more apt to attempt further investigation of TL materials' (1995).

Finally, the autonomous aspect of using the Internet is itself motivating to many students. Information is sought and acquired rather than directed at them as in traditional teacher-directed set-up. Information is, as Baker puts it, 'pulled' rather than 'pushed' (1997).

5.2. Input

In learner Web-authoring tasks, all the material the students are dealing with is authentic, from the Web sites they evaluate, to the authentic texts they may adapt for the site under construction, and to the instructions for the authoring tools. The language-learning benefits of exposure to authentic TL texts in preference to purpose-written or simplified materials is by now well-grounded in language learning/SLA research (see, for example, Little *et al.*, 1989; Swaffer, 1985; Yano *et al.*, 1994; Larsen-Freeman and Long 1991; Krashen, 1989). Of relevance to the Web-authoring task is the impact of the prodigious quantity of authentic materials to which learners are exposed and the implications for information and language processing of the way in which this material is presented. The potential for cognitive overload of the hypertext environment, in terms of navigation and of its structure is only now being assessed (see, for example, Chun and Plass, 2000). The hypertext environment is demonised by some for its density and non-linear structure which is said to interfere with thought processes (see, for example, Murray, 1997; Laurillard, 1993: 122). Others claim that 'information age' learners are quite accustomed to information overload and are practised in screening out/ignoring superfluous information. This coping strategy for ICT is advantageous for language learning in general as it gives a higher tolerance of non-comprehension. Indeed, it has been claimed that, far from interfering with thought processes, the hypertext structure of the Internet realises the full potential of human thought processing and is even analogous to natural language-learning processes: 'The multi-layered structure of hypertexts can mimic the didactic spiral of language instruction and thus provides an intuitive gateway to the understanding of grammar and to the construction of grammatical knowledge' (McBride and Seago, 1997: 21). What is less controversial is that the text-based nature of the technology is ultimately responsible for an improvement in learners' writing skills, the electronic discourse that learners participate in being 'lexically and syntactically more complex' than their oral discourse (Warschauer, 1997: 474). One of the many reasons for this is that the increase in interaction with written language material increases the potential for 'noticing' characteristics, lexes and patterns in the TL, as pointed out by Warschauer (1998b). This is also the rationale for the emphasis on language awareness-raising sessions in the approach proposed here.

5.3. Output

Another crucial condition for language learning after motivation and input is, of course, output. In a Web-authoring task, the learners' output is of two main types: the first is the spontaneous oral communication in connection with the task/s in hand and involves the famous 'negotiation of meaning' embedded in the rationale of CLT. This is discussed in Section 5.5. below. The second type of output is written text, which may include editing or reworking of existent downloaded texts. The latter is the sort of 'pushed output' (output which makes demands on the learner for correct and appropriate L2 use) which has been claimed by some SLA research,[10] as vital for development of certain grammatical features (Ellis, 1994: 27).

However, the actual process of producing written output in the ICT environment might have implications for language learning (and for thought processes), as there is a growing tendency to compose on-screen. In on-screen composition, thought processes are in a sense 'enacted' and developed on-screen, in the form of deletions, substitutions, revisions, and editing. The possible negative repercussions of composing online are that, far from developing thought processes, the actual physical and technical process of typing, correcting and editing and the technical expertise they call on, can interrupt and curtail the train of thought. And because word-processing 'obliterates' previously written words, unlike revising on paper, which involves crossings out, notes, arrows and so on, 'the relationship between the words you write now and the words you wrote earlier becomes ever more tenuous' (Mendelson, 1991: 28). Even the physical limitations of the computer screen (which, Mendelson points out, 'holds fewer words than a five-by-eight-inch note card') constrain the user to focus on the twenty lines or so which appear before him/her and discourages skimming over full pages, something more easily done when writing on paper.

From the opposing perspective, composing on a word-processor has been shown to be particularly valuable for language learners: 'Writing becomes less static and "final" since it is perceived as more changeable, and thus the students learn to perceive it as a process [...] a way of thinking; it can actually help them with ideas, with organisation, and with their thought processes' (Belisle, 1996). Little points out, with reference to a 1991 study by Legenhausen and Wolff, that in word-processing, the combination of the informality of spontaneous speech (in which learners tend to take more risks) with the formality of written language (which is less tolerant of errors) is a felicitous one for language learning (Little, 1996: 214). Furthermore, he points out, working collaboratively on the word-processor can help learners externalise and make explicit ideas and strategies.

5.4. Autonomous learning

Autonomous learning is fundamentally about accepting responsibility for one's own learning (Little, 1996: 203–4) and pro-actively taking control over one's own learning (Benson, 2001: 2). The Internet is a medium that supremely offers the potential for re-orientation towards learner autonomy. The permeation of ICT into our society and the general move in pedagogy toward more autonomous modes of learning can be no coincidence. Yet the relationship between ICT and learner autonomy is by no means uni-directional. The Internet is both an agent of autonomous learning and dependent on it: 'Flexible, autonomous lifelong learning is essential to success in the age of information [...] Language professionals who have access to an Internet computer classroom are in a position to teach students valuable lifelong learning skills and strategies for becoming autonomous learners' (Shetzer and Warschauer, 2000: 176). The autonomous learning ethos is intrinsic to the learner Web-authoring approach, in the way that the task is set in terms of its ultimate objective and not in terms of paths to achieving this. By imposing broad parameters within which learners can operate independently and collaboratively, the task-based Web-authoring approach furthers the acquisition of skills – language, technical and general learning skills. Particularly in its emphasis on creativity in an ICT context, the approach can be said to both support the development of learner autonomy and promote language learning. As Little asserts, the aspect of ICT systems that is most essential to the development of learner autonomy is their capacity to facilitate externalisation and make explicit metaprocesses, thus strengthening 'the bi-directional relationship between language learning and language use' (1996: 218).

5.5. Skills

This reciprocity of language and electronic literacy pointed out above with reference to Shetzer and Warschauer (2000: 172) can be seen to apply at the level of skills. Skills essential to language learning, such as the reading skills of skimming and scanning, are associated with some of the cognitive skills required when using the Internet, such as searching for, evaluating and processing information. Searching and evaluating Web material are 'new' skills, developed in response to the new technology: 'The tool we use to complete a task inevitably transforms the task itself' (Warschauer, 1998a: 85). Web-authoring tasks hinge on these skills; in the conception phase, for instance, where learners are viewing and evaluating other sites, in the content creation phase, where they are searching for, evaluating, and culling authentic online texts for use on the site, and so on. Searching the Web is conceptually different from accessing information from conventional sources (encyclopaedias, directories etc.), which is essentially a uni-directional process. Web searching involves development of a new set of skills that enable the user to cope with the – to many – impenetrable organisational system of the Web and to effectively 'interrelate' according to a hierarchy based on its own criteria. For NNSs of English, the complexities of searching are often compounded by the linguistic basis of the process, the use of concept-based keywords. The most time consuming aspect of Web-searching can be evaluating the results of the search. The first step in evaluation is 'eliminative evaluation'; assessing the validity and relevance of the information retrieved and disre-garding the non-relevant; users soon learn to be circumspect about the results their search query has thrown up. While evaluation is a particularly demanding task for NNSs, visual cues alone can act as useful initial criteria; is the site attractive to look at and does it seem professional? Practical/technical indicators of the sources of the results are also useful criteria for evaluation. These include the Web address (URL) itself, which can reveal the geographical source, whether the Web site is personal, educational, commercial etc., and currency, which can be checked by seeing when the Web site was last updated. Linguistic indicators of the quality of the data, such as genre and register, may be more difficult for the non-native speaker-user to discern. The next aspect of evaluation involves detailed reading to identify and select useable material and discard the 'dross'. Once the required information has been culled through these processes, material can be downloaded onto the user's PC, and synthesised into a usable form. This involves reworking the information by editing, paraphrasing and so on. The entire process of making Web material 'usable', in brief, involves a fine interplay of technical, cognitive, and linguistic skills.

Supporting these electronic literacy skills in the Web-authoring approach are interactional skills, as learners communicate in the performance of the task/s. Verbal interaction is important to language learning because 'it helps to make the "facts" of the L2 salient to the learner' (Ellis, 1994: 244). The negotiation of meaning that speakers (especially NNS interactants) engage in – requesting reformulation, manipulating output – is a crucial part of learning as it results in the 'comprehensible input' necessary for language acquisition. The actual use of these interactional skills is important in itself as, according to the skill-building hypothesis (Krashen, 1989) the language rules etc. that we learn consciously become gradually automatised through practice (Ellis, 1994: 280). Finally, that this interaction takes place within the meaningful context of the task, i.e., that it has an authentic purpose, is known to be conducive to language learning (this, of course, is the principle that underlies CLT).

It can be claimed, in conclusion, that the skills honed in Web-authoring tasks are of multiple benefit to language learners. They provide the bases for further language acquisition and for electronic literacy, they promote independent learning and, ultimately, they improve learners' employability. They are, in short, indispensable skills for functioning in the electronic age.

6. Conclusion

In this description of the task-based approach to learner Web authoring it has been shown that, as was suggested in the introduction, this type of approach implicates 'the three A's' underpinning the latter-day communicative approach:

- Autonomy, by transferring the responsibility for learning materials design from teacher to learner and through the use of autonomous modes of learning in doing this; control over one's own learning, collaboration, research and reflection.
- Authorship, which through the electronic medium 'becomes the privilege of any language user' (Kramsch *et al.*, 2000: 96).
- Authenticity, in terms of the authenticity of the task itself and of the authentic materials with which learners interact.

With Web sites today being created by everyone from individuals to global conglomerates, it would seem time for the language learner to join the fray, with the proviso that this is done within a controlled pedagogical framework such as the one proposed here. The technology is no longer an obstacle; user-friendly HTML editors and authoring facilities integrated into the word-processor make creating a Web page little harder than word-processing. The general shift in pedagogy towards more independence in learning combined with the technology to facilitate this, is empowering the language learner as never before. And what better way to assume control over one's own learning than to enter the Internet arena as an equal and open the way for a potentially global dialogue with speakers of the target language.

Notes

1. As of April 2004, there were 6,330 million Internet users in nearly 100 countries. Figures from Global Reach http://www.glreach.com/globstats/ downloaded 6 April 2004.
2. Web66, the International registry of schools' Web sites, registered over seven thousand school Web sites in the secondary sector and six in the primary sector in 1998. http://web66.coled.umn.edu/schools.html downloaded 26 February 2002.
3. However, by the year 2005 it is projected that the number of non-English-speaking users of the Internet will outnumber English-speaking users by more than 2 to 1. Figures as of 25 February 2002 from Global Reach (online).
4. An accessible introduction to copyright can be found on: http://www.utsystem.edu/OGC/IntellectualProperty/student.htm#law
5. Two accessible referencing guides can be found at: http://www.lib.monash.edu.au/vl/cite/harvex.htm http://www.wisc.edu/writing/Handbook/DocAPA.html
6. Such as *Dreamweaver, Front Page* 2002 and GoLive.
7. According to Macromedia, *Dreamweaver* currently has the largest share of the Web authoring market.
8. Action mazes are described as interactive case-studies in which the user is confronted with a situation and a number of possible actions to deal with it. The user's choice generates another set of options and so on. (From the description of the application on http://www.halfbaked-software.com/index.htm?quandary/ .)
9. Based on comments from the author's students following 1997/1998 projects.
10. Swain's (1985) comprehensible output hypothesis; Skehan and Foster (1996) provide similar evidence.

Bibliography

Amitay, E. (2000) 'Anchors in context: A corpus analysis of authoring conventions for Web pages'. In L. Pemberton and S. Shurville (eds.) *Words on the Web*, 25–35.

Arnold, J. and D. Brown (1999) 'A map of the terrain'. In J. Arnold (ed.) *Affect in Language Learning*. Cambridge: Cambridge University Press, 1–24.

Atkinson, T. (1998) *WWW - The Internet*. London: CILT (Centre for Information on Language Teaching and Research).

Baker, D. (1997) 'Using the World Wide Web as a business English resource'. *IATEFL Computer SIG/ BESIG presentation*. University of Manchester, March 1997. Available at:
http://www.iateflcompsig.org.uk/media/manchester1997.pdf

Barrows, H. (1985) *Designing a Problem-Based Curriculum for the Pre-Clinical Years*. New York: Springer Publishing Company.

Belisle, R. (1996) 'E-mail activities in the ESL writing class'. *The Internet TESL Journal*, 2.12, available at: http://iteslj.org/Articles/Belisle-Email.html

Benson, P. (2001) *Teaching and Researching Autonomy in Language Learning*. London and New York: Longman.

Bruner, J. (1960) *The Process of Education*. Cambridge, MA: Harvard University Press.

Carter, R., R. Hughes and M. McCarthy (1998) 'Telling tails: Grammar, the spoken language and materials development'. In: B. Tomlinson (ed.) *Materials Development in Language Teaching*, 67–86.

Chambers, A., and G. Davies (2001) *ICT and Language Learning: A European Perspective*. Lisse: Swets and Zeitlinger.

Chapelle, C. (2001) *Computer Applications in Second Language Acquisition*. Cambridge: Cambridge University Press.

Chun, D and J. Plass (2000) 'Networked multimedia environments for second language acquisition'. In Warschauer M. and R. Kern (eds.) *Network-based Language Teaching*, 151–70.

Conacher, J. E. and F. Royall (1998) 'An evaluation of the use of the Internet for the purposes of foreign language learning'. *Language Learning Journal*, 18, 37–41.

Corder, P. (1974) 'The significance of learners' errors'. In J. Richards, *Error Analysis: Perspectives in Second Language Acquisition*. London and New York: Longman, 19–30.

Eayrs, M. (1999) English teachers on-line – accessing e-mail and internet resources for ELT. Paper presented at *MATSDA conference*, Dublin, January 1999.

Ellis, R. (1994) *The Study of Second Language Acquisition*. Oxford: Oxford University Press.

Felix, U. (1999) 'Web-based language learning: A window to the authentic world'. In C.B. Debsky and M. Levy (eds.) *WORLDCALL: Global perspectives on Computer-Assisted Language Learning*. Lisse: Swets and Zeitlinger, 85–98.

Fox, G. (1998) 'The Internet: Making it work in the ESL classroom'. *The Internet TESL Journal*, IV.9. Available at: http://iteslj.org/Articles/Fox-Internet.html [Downloaded 19 September 2003].

Godwin-Jones, B (2000) 'Web browser trends and technologies'. *Language Learning and Technology*, 4: 1, 6–11.

Godwin-Jones, B. (1998) 'Dynamic Web page creation'. *Language Learning and Technology*, 1: 2, 7–13.

Henriquez, J. (2000) 'One-way doors, teleportation and writing without prepositions: an analysis of WWW hypertext links'. In L. Pemberton and S. Shurville (eds.) *Words on the Web*, 4–12.

Kimball, J. (1998) 'Thriving on screen: Web-authoring for L2 instruction'. *The Internet TESL Journal*, IV: 2. Available at: http://iteslj.org/Articles/Kimball-WebAuthoring.html [Downloaded 19 September 2003].

Kohonen, V. (1992) 'Experiential language learning: Second language learning as cooperative learner education' In D. Nunan (ed.) (1992) *Collaborative Language Learning and Teaching*. Cambridge: Cambridge University Press, 14–39.

Kolb, D. (1983) *Experimental Learning: Experience as the Source of Learning and Development*. New York: Prentice-Hall.

Kramsch, C, F. A'Ness and W. Lam (2000) 'Authenticity and authorship in the computer-mediated acquisition of L2 literacy'. *Language Learning and Technology*, 4. 2, 78–104.

Krashen, S. (1989) *Language Acquisition and Language Education*. Hemel Hempstead: Prentice Hall International.

Kubota, R. (1999) 'Word Processing and WWW Project in a College Japanese Language Class'. *Foreign Language Annals*, 32.2, 205–18.

Larsen-Freeman, D. and M. Long (1991) *An Introduction to Second Language Acquisition Research*. London and New York: Longman.

Laurillard, D. (1993) *Rethinking University Teaching: A Framework for the Effective Use of Educational Technology*. London/New York: Routledge.

LeLoup, J. and R. Ponterio (1995) 'Addressing the need for electronic communication in foreign language teaching'. In R. Steinfeldt (ed.) *Educational Technologies*. Monograph of the New York State Council of Educational Associations, 39–54. Available at:
http://www.cortland.edu/www/flteach/articles/nyscea.html

Little, D. (1996) 'Freedom to learn and compulsion to interact: promoting learner autonomy through the use of information systems and information technologies'. In R. Pemberton, E. Li, W. Or and H. Pierson (eds.) *Taking Control: Autonomy in Language Learning*, Hong Kong: Hong Kong University Press, 203–18.

Little, D. and D. Singleton (1990) 'Cognitive style and learning approach'. In R. Duda and P. Riley (eds.) *Learning Styles*, European Cultural Foundation, proceedings of the first European Seminar, Nancy, 26–29 April, 1987. Nancy: Presses Universitaires de Nancy, 11–19.

Little, D., S. Devitt and D. Singleton (1989) *Learning Foreign Languages from Authentic Texts: Theory and Practice*. Dublin: Authentik

McBride, N. and K. Seago (1997) 'Bridging the gap: Grammar as hypertext'.

ReCALL, 9.2, 17–25.

Mendelson, E. (1991) 'How computers can damage your prose'. *The Times Literary Supplement*, 4586, 22 February, 28.

Mills, D. (1996) 'The WWW as a project for collaboration'. In V. Hegelheimer, A. Salzmann and H. Shetzer, *WWW Activities that Work*. Presentation, TESOL 1996.

Murray, J. (1997) *Hamlet on the Holodeck: The Future of Narrative in Cyberspace.* Cambridge, MA: MIT Press.

Pemberton, L. and S. Shurville (eds.) (2000) *Words on the Web: Computer-Mediated Communication*. Exeter: Intellect Books.

Richmond, A. (2002) *A Guide to Creating Web Sites with HTML, CGI, Java, JavaScript, Graphics.* Available at: http://wdvl.internet.com/Authoring/

Riley, F and G. Davies (2000) *Module 3.3: Creating a World Wide Web site.* Available at http://www.ict4lt.org/

Schultz, J. (2000) 'Computers and collaborative writing in the foreign language curriculum'. In Warschauer M. and R. Kern (eds.) *Network-based Language Teaching*, 121–50.

Shetzer, H. and M. Warschauer (2000) 'An electronic literacy approach to network-based language teaching'. In M. Warschauer and R. Kern (eds.) *Network-Based Language Teaching*, 171–85.

Skehan, P. (1996) 'A framework for the implementation of task-based instruction'. *Applied Linguistics*, 17.1, 38–62.

Skehan, P. and P. Foster (1996) 'The influence of planning and task-type on second language performance'. *Studies in Second Language Acquisition*, 18.3, 299–324.

Swaffar, J. (1985) 'Reading authentic texts in a foreign language: A cognitive model'. *The Modern Language Journal*, 69.1, 16–32.

Swain, M. (1985) 'Communicative competence: Some roles of comprehensive input and comprehensible output in its development'. In S. Gass and C. Madden (eds.) *Input in Second Language Acquisition*. Cambridge, MA: Newbury House Publishers, 235–57.

Tomlinson, B. (ed.) (1998) *Materials Development in Language Teaching*. Cambridge: Cambridge University Press.

Tudor, I. (1996) *Learner-centredness as Language Education*. Cambridge: Cambridge University Press.

Warschauer, M. (ed.) (1995) *Virtual Connections – Online Activities and Projects for Networking Language Learners*. Honolulu, HI: Second Language Teaching and Curriculum Center: University of Hawai'i Press.

Warschauer, M. (1996) 'Motivational aspects of using computers for writing and communication'. In M. Warschauer (ed.) *Telecollaboration in Foreign Language Learning*. Honolulu, HI: Second Language Teaching and Curriculum Center:

University of Hawai'i Press, 29–46. Also available at: http://nflrc.hawaii.edu/NetWorks/NW01/

Warschauer, M. (1997) 'Computer-mediated collaborative learning: Theory and practice'. *Modern Language Journal, 81.3*, 470–81. Also available at: http://www.gse.uci.edu/markw/cmcl.html

Warschauer, M. (1998a) Online learning in sociocultural context. *Anthropology and Education Quarterly*, 29.1, 68–88. Also available at: http://www.gse.uci.edu/markw/online.html

Warschauer, M. (1998b). 'Interaction, negotiation, and computer-mediated learning'. In V. Darleguy *et al.*, (eds.) *Les Nouvelles Technologies Educatives dans l'apprentissage des langues vivantes : réflexion théorique et applications pratiques. Educational Technology in language learning: Theoretical considerations and practical applications Practical Applications of Educational Technology in Language Learning.* Lyon, France: Institut National des Sciences Appliquées. Also available at: http://www.insa-lyon.fr/Departements/CDRL/interaction.html

Warschauer, M. (1999) *Electronic Literacies : Language, Culture, and Power in Online Education.* Mahwah, NJ: Lawrence Erlbaum Associates.

Warschauer M. (2000) 'On-line learning in second language classrooms: An ethnographic study'. In M. Warschauer and R. Kern (eds.) *Network-based Language Teaching: Concepts and Practice*, 41–58.

Warschauer, M. and D. Healey (1998) 'Computers and language learning: An overview'. *Language Teaching*, 31, 57–71.

Warschauer M. and R. Kern (eds.) (2000) *Network-based Language Teaching: Concepts and Practice.* New York: Cambridge University Press.

Warschauer, M. and P. Whittaker (1997) 'The Internet for English teaching: Guidelines for teachers'. *TESL Reporter*, 30.1, 27–33. Also available at: http://www.aitech.ac.jp/~iteslj/Articles/Warschauer-Internet.html

Willis, J. (1996) *A Framework for Task-Based Learning.* London and New York; Longman.

Yano Y., M. Long and S. Ross (1994) 'The effects of simplified and elaborated texts on foreign language reading comprehension'. *Language Learning*, 44.2, 198–219.

Web sites

Copyright (introduction for students):
  http://www.utsystem.edu/OGC/IntellectualProperty/student.htm#law
Global Reach Internet statistics: http://www.glreach.com/globstats/
Hot Potatoes and *Quandary* available at: http://web.uvic.ca/hrd/halfbaked/
Information and Communications Technology for Language Teachers available at
  http://www.ict4lt.org/ (see, in particular, *Module 3.3 Creating a World Wide
  Web site*)
Intranet information at: http://www.intrack.com/intranet/index.cfm
  [Downloaded 19 September 2003].
Microsoft Solutions for intranets: http://www.microsoft.com/solutions/msi/.
PC Magazine on-line: http://www.pcmag.com/
Quia available at: http://www.quia.com/

Referencing guides for students:
http://www.lib.monash.edu.au/vl/cite/harvex.htm
The List of Internet Service Providers: http://thelist.internet.com/
Tripod-Lycos, Web account providers: http://www.tripod.lycos.com/
Yahoo: http://yahoo.com
Yale Style Manual available at:
  http://info.med.yale.edu/caim/manual/contents.html

Sites showing examples of good Web site design
http://www.ratz.com/features.html
http://www.worldbestwebsites.com/

Site showing examples of bad Web site design
http://www.webpagesthatsuck.com/

7 Intercultural e-mail exchanges in the foreign language classroom

Robert O'Dowd

1. Introduction

E-mail exchanges between language learners in different cultures is arguably one of the most well known uses of new technologies in the foreign language classroom. However, the outcome of such exchanges is often not as positive as teachers may expect. The following example is taken from a recent e-mail exchange carried out between third-level Spanish and English foreign language students. Juan, from the town of León in northern Spain, sent the following introductory message to Alice, his English partner:

> I'm going to tell you something about Llión and about my nation (situated within an area of the North-West of Spain): Llión is an ancient town of about 150,000 inhabitants. Llión and the Leónese Country ('País Llïonés' in the Astur-Leónese language) are the result of a mixture of Celtic, Roman, Germanic, Arabic, Jewish and other cultures. Because of this fact, we have monuments from different ages and cultures and our traditions are also the result of that mixture. For example in Llión there're some Romanic churches and a gothic cathedral and in some areas of the 'País Llïonés' (Leónese Country) there're buildings of pre-roman art.

In this message Juan tries to express his regional identity to Alice and show her that his homeland has little to do with the common perception which many British people have of Spain. But despite Juan's good intentions, later feedback from his partner revealed that this message had come across as boring and condescending to his partner. The partnership never recovered from this opening case of intercultural miscommunication. Alice never reacted to Juan's description of his homeland and later commented that 'his description of his area didn't particularly make me want to visit his "Lionese country"'. His own feedback at the end of the exchange reflected a lack of motivation, as well as a belief that his stereotypes about the English had been confirmed. In it he described his partner as 'not very friendly' and he believed that she continued to have an unrealistic image of Spain: 'She still thinks that a lot of commonplaces like bull-fighting and flamenco are true. It doesn't surprise me at all.'

Of course, such attitudes need not have come out of the exchange. If Juan had received more help in class on how to express himself more appropriately in English through the medium of e-mail, and if Alice had been helped in analysing the cultural background and significance of this message then perhaps this could have gone on to become a rich intercultural learning experience.

Such an example illustrates that e-mail exchanges require much more from teachers than simply organising the initial contact between classes and bringing the learners together. Maintaining motivation, developing interesting tasks, successfully developing working relationships, and helping to interpret the messages from the other culture are only some of the issues which teachers are faced with when they try to integrate e-mail exchanges into their classrooms.

In an attempt to present the challenges and potential of this potentially powerful learning activity, this chapter provides, in Section 2, the background for e-mail exchanges in the foreign language classroom as well as the principles upon which the activity is based. Section 3 presents a typology of tasks which teachers can adapt for their classes and this is then followed, in Section 4, by a reflection on both the learning opportunities and organisational problems which can arise during an exchange. Section 5 outlines some key guidelines for good practice which have been taken from the literature and my own experience, and Section 6 suggests a format which an intercultural exchange might take. Finally, Section 7 looks at some areas where action research by teachers could contribute to maximising the activity's potential.

2. Background to online e-mail exchanges

The use of e-mail exchanges as a tool for language learning has received a great deal attention from educators and researchers in recent years (Gaer, 1999; Müller-Hartmann, 2000; Warschauer, 1997). There are various practical and pedagogical reasons for the popularity of this asynchronous (i.e., not in real time) medium and these are worthy of mention.

From the simply practical point of view, e-mail accounts can, first of all, be quite easily obtained (either from local internet providers or from companies which offer free Web-based e-mail accounts) and used by both teachers and learners who have minimal technological experience. Secondly, the asynchronous nature of the technology means it can be accessed when it suits the participants, therefore it is not necessary for exchange partners to be connected, nor for a whole class to have access to computers, at the same time. Thirdly, the availability of a large number of networks and agencies online which allow teachers to find partner classes for their e-mail exchanges has meant that it is relatively easy for classes to establish contact and organise projects with distant partners.

E-mail exchanges have often received praise in the literature as they bring learners to engage in an activity which has been based on the principles of constructivist learning theory (Rüschoff and Wolff, 1999), learner autonomy (Little, 1997), and intercultural learning (Byram, 1997). Constructivist theory suggests that students learn most effectively not by being instructed, but through interacting with others, thereby testing out their own hypotheses and consequently adapting what they know and understand. Learner autonomy involves learners organising and taking control of their own learning, as well as preparing themselves for the process of lifelong learning. Finally, intercultural learning refers to the learners' ability to become more aware of their own as well as the target culture, and the ability to engage in effective intercultural interaction. Networked intercultural exchanges reflect all of these principles as they encourage learners to reflect on their writing and also involve interaction and collaboration with foreign partners which usually takes place outside of the classroom and away from the control of the teacher.

Intercultural exchanges in education have their origins in the global learning networks pioneered by Célestin Freinet in 1920s France and later by Mario Lodi in 1960s Italy (Cummins and Sayers, 1995: 119–36). Freinet made use of the technologies and modes of communication available to him to enable his classes to exchange 'cultural packages' of flowers, fossils and photos of their local area, while Lodi motivated his learners and helped to develop their critical literacy by encouraging them to create student newspapers in collaboration with distant partner classes.

It is practically impossible to assess how many foreign language classes have become involved in intercultural e-mail projects since the pioneering work in the late 1980s of the Orillas Network (Cummins and Sayers, 1995; Sayers, 1991) and the ATandT Learning Circles (Riel, 1997), but the 'Intercultural E-Mail Classroom Connections' Web site (http://www.iecc.org/) reports to have sent out over 28,000 requests from teachers for project partners since its creation in 1992, while The International Tandem Network (http://www.slf.ruhr-uni-bochum.de/) has created over 12,000 e-mail tandem partnerships. These are only two of the many Web sites which allow teachers and students to come together to form language learning exchanges. (Many more can be found in Appendix 1). The following section looks at the types of activities which classes engage in when they are brought together for a networked exchange.

3. An overview of activities

The types of tasks and activities that language learners can engage in within the framework of an e-mail exchange are varied and often are combined with other online technologies such as the WWW, videoconferencing, or online chat forums. These exchanges may take place on a one-to-one basis, where a student in one country writes directly to his/her partner in the other country about a given task or topic. Alternatively, the project may take place on a class-to-class basis, where groups of students in a class prepare and write their e-mails together and these are then answered by their partner class in the other country. Avots supports the latter format for the following reasons:

> Writing one class to another, or group to group within a class to another, allows students to interact with each other, to formulate ideas using the target language, and to practice peer editing skills.
>
> (Avots, 1991: 135)

In both formats, four principle types of activities can be found in the literature, and these will be looked at now in the hope they may serve as a guideline for introducing e-mail exchanges into foreign language classrooms.

Firstly, the most common type of activity involves connecting students virtually in order to discuss and compare opinions on topics and issues which are of interest to both groups. Bee-Lay and Yee-Ping (1991) and Gray and Stockwell (1998) organised their classes into tandem exchanges with learners from other cultures and had them describe and compare different cultural topics such as dining out, relaxation and dating in the C1 and C2. In a similar activity described by O'Dowd (2000), a class of Spanish students of EFL, working in tandem with a group of Spanish learners in the USA, watched two Spanish and American films and then exchanged reviews and reactions with their partners via e-mail and videoconferencing connections. The Spanish students were amazed at the different reactions to the films from the other group and much class time was spent discussing why certain cultural products might be more successful in some cultures rather than in others.

In a second type of activity, teachers such as Meadows (1995), Shorer (1995), and Kern (1997) have engaged their classes in cross-cultural exchanges of folklore collections as well as of accounts of their own families' life stories which they have collected from their parents and grandparents. Kern's project brought together students from the USA and France who exchanged essays on their different experiences of immigration and acculturation. Such projects involve considerable preparatory work by the students as they need to collect material on their home culture and their families from the people around them. However, it can also be a very productive and motivating activity as students are often proud to present aspects of themselves and their local identity to others.

Thirdly, teachers have attempted to prepare their students for the challenges of living and working in a multicultural society by organising projects in which two or more classes must collaborate by e-mail on a task or problem in order to achieve a common objective. Barson (1991) and Sayers (1991) report on international projects which involved classes working together via e-mail to produce student newspapers, while Vilmi (1994, 1998) describes the robot and environment projects, in which classes from various countries combined their skills in their different subject areas to design a robot or solve an environmental problem.

Finally, e-mail has also been exploited by language classes to send out surveys and questionnaires to members of other cultures in order to find out more about their lifestyle or opinions (Ady, 1995; Kendall, 1995). This form of exchange may involve relatively little interaction with the partner class but it does allow teachers and students to bring authentic raw material on foreign cultures into the classroom and to integrate this with other learning materials. The IECC surveys mailing list is specially designed for teachers who wish to send their surveys to classes around the world.

An interesting version of this activity is reported by Meskill and Ranglova (2000). In their third-level Bulgarian classes on American literature, their students used e-mail connections with students from the United States to add further interpretations on the literature to their own analyses. The input from their American partners gave the Bulgarians multiple interpretations of the literature and moved the focus away from the traditional teacher-led lectures about the literature.

Box 1 'Activities for Culture Learning via e-mail and newsgroups' offers a brief summary of the different types of activities which have been discussed here. Further examples of e-mail projects can be found on the Web sites mentioned in Appendix 2.

Box 1: Intercultural E-mail Exchanges: Types of Activities

- Comparative investigation into a cultural product (for example, a film or book) or a theme common to both cultures (for example, racism, pollution)
- Presentation and exchange of folklore collections, oral histories with partner class in C2
- Collaborative problem solving or product creation by multi-cultural teams
- Surveys / questionnaires sent to members of target culture

---

4. The opportunities and challenges of networked exchanges

Some of the pedagogical advantages of such projects and exchanges may be immediately evident, but it is nevertheless worth looking at some of the key learning opportunities and challenges which repeatedly emerge in the literature on e-mail exchanges.

Firstly, students tend to consider e-mail exchanges with native speakers as an excellent way of improving their knowledge of grammar and vocabulary in the foreign language. In the well-known 'Tandem' system of e-mail exchanges (Brammerts, 1996), students are required each time they write to include corrections of some errors from their partners' previous e-mails. This form of correction by their long-distance partner may be valued by students as they are receiving the suggestions from a peer and not from their teacher. A comment which one of my Spanish students included in an e-mail to his partner reflects her appreciation of the peer correction system:

> I'm very happy because the corrections of mistakes you send
> me are improving my English, I hope I am helping to you too.

Research by St. John and Cash (1995) showed that learners seem to further improve their communicative competence in e-mail exchanges by integrating new vocabulary which they have learned into their e-mails and also by taking the opportunity to 'try out' newly learned words and expressions on their partner. It is possible that they would not attempt using these in a normal classroom situation in case they would use them incorrectly. Writing to peers can give students more confidence and encourage them to take more risks than usual. Some examples of this which I have come across with my EFL learners include the following. In the second example the student uses a new expression ('to beat about the bush') which she had only learned days before in class. Although, in this case, it is not used in a suitable context, the student is nevertheless trying to integrate newly learned language into her mails.

> Well, that's all. Break a leg for your exams...(It's a
> desire of good luck...Isn't it??)
>   The day after Halloween we usually go to the cemetery to
> put flowers on the graves. That is supposed to be something
> devout but for most of the people is just an occasion to
> show the neighbour your new dress, car husband,...I hate
> that   and   it   happens   a   lot   in   the   villages.
> I think I am beating about the bush but I want you to know
> the truth.

Successful intercultural exchanges can also be advantageous in the foreign language classroom as they motivate learners to write more in the target language and to reflect more on the language they are producing (Tella, 1992a: 194; Tillyer, 1996: 4). An e-mail project may be the first time a language learner has an opportunity to use their foreign language in order to engage in authentic communication with a native speaker. When they take part in this type of activity, educators argue that learners are no longer writing simply for their teacher, nor are they writing in order to have their grammatical and lexical mistakes identified and corrected. Instead, they are using the foreign language to communicate with a distant peer who will be reading the messages primarily for their content and not for their grammatical correctness. Being aware of this can increase motivation and can bring them to express themselves more clearly and take more care in the grammatical correctness of their writing (Tella, 1992a). A Spanish student of mine reflected this in her feedback form at the end of an intercultural exchange:

> I really like doing this because every week we write an essay in class and sometimes you like the topic, sometimes not. But this [e-mail exchange] is different. As it is for a friend, because for me she is a friend, you make a much bigger effort.

A further benefit of e-mail exchanges is their potential for helping students to improve their intercultural awareness. The opinions and insights which students receive from their partners in the target culture can allow them to supplement the information which they have in their textbooks with real-life examples and may encourage them to avoid stereotypes and be aware of the heterogeneous nature of a modern-day society (Cummins and Sayers, 1995: 170; Kern, 1997: 75). Intercultural awareness can also be developed by the questions which students receive from their partners about their own culture. These can serve to make students aware of how others see them and it can also make them reflect on and criticise aspects of their own culture which they had, until now, taken for granted. This process of developing a greater awareness of one's own culture through questions from abroad is known as 'distancing' and Gervilliers *et al.* (1977) explain it in the following way:

> The student, because she needs to describe them, develops an awareness of the conditions of her life, of the life of her town or her neighbourhood, even of her province [...] She had been living too close to these conditions and through inter-school exchanges she distanced herself from them in order to better comprehend the condition of her life.
>
> (Gervilliers *et al.*, 1977: 31)

Finally, exchanges can help to make students more aware of the link between language and culture. Kern (1997) in his report on the American–French personal histories exchange, describes how he helped an American student to reinterpret a message which she had originally considered offensive as it had been unsuitably phrased in English by her French partner. The French student had translated the French phrase 'vous devez savoir' as 'you should know' instead of the more appropriate 'as you know' and the American student had found this condescending. He concludes:

> It is by identifying such 'hot points' in the language and exploring the responses they evoke that students and teachers begin to develop an awareness of how cultural stereotypes are formed and perpetuated.
>
> (Kern, 1997: 73)

Of course, networked exchanges should not be seen as guaranteed agents of motivation and learning in the classroom. Over the past two decades, teachers have repeatedly come up against the same stumbling blocks which have hindered the success of their students' intercultural connections. It is worthwhile looking at some of these recurring challenges or problems before going on, in the next section, to outline some guidelines for good practice which may help in the development of future exchanges.

Firstly, teachers have found that reliability can often be a problem. Students may find that after two weeks of an exchange their partners have stopped answering their messages because of study demands, technological problems or simply a lack of interest. This can be disappointing for students who have invested time and energy into preparing and sending their e-mails and it may also lead to students developing the stereotype that members of the target culture are cold, unfriendly, or rude. It is, of course, also a major organisational problem for teachers who may find that half their students are still writing to their partners while others have lost contact and are not receiving answers to their mails.

Secondly, teachers often find that after the initial 'novelty factor' of the exchange wears off, the motivating element of e-mail exchanges can quickly disappear and students may complain that they don't know what to say to their partner and that they no longer enjoy taking part in the exchange. When exchanges are not clearly goal-orientated, they can quickly lose direction and are reduced to relatively limited pen-pal type exchanges where students exchange messages but fail to gain a deeper insight into the foreign culture. This can soon become tiresome and boring for students as they find themselves searching for topics of conversation with someone they do not know, and can find little common ground to strengthen the initial link.

Finally, while examples of intercultural communication breakdown can be a great source of learning in the classroom, they can also cause the failure of an exchange. Fischer (1998: 70) points out that e-mail messages carry both informational content and emotional overtones and that students from different cultures risk misunderstanding and over-reacting to the purpose of their partners' messages. Juan and Alice's communication breakdown shown at the beginning of this paper is a good example of this.

Furthermore, Kern states that the language of e-mail often fails to take into account social status, and that messages can blur differences in social status between participants (Kern, 1997: 74). This may be particularly important in cultures where social distance and formality play an important role in both written and oral interaction. Liao (1999), for example, warns that Chinese students have a tendency in their culture to ask many personal questions when trying to get to know someone. While this may be suitable in China, students in other countries may find a barrage of questions overbearing or perhaps an intrusion on their privacy. Liao suggests the key to intercultural communication online is tolerance and an awareness that not all cultures have the same rules for interaction and communicating. Other suggestions for making exchanges more effective will be looked at in the following section. The opportunities and challenges which have been discussed here are recapitulated in Table 1.

Pedagogical Opportunities	Challenges
• Improving language skills	• Reliability of student partnerships
• Motivating learners	• Maintaining motivation and interest
• Increasing intercultural awareness	• Avoiding intercultural misunderstandings
• Highlighting link between language and culture	

Table 1: Pedagogical Opportunities and Challenges of Intercultural E-mail Exchanges

5. Effective exchanges: Identifying teacher and learner roles

Having looked at the problems which can arise during networked exchanges, it is important to define some guidelines which may help to bring about a productive learning experience. Very often the failure of an exchange can be explained by a lack of awareness on the part of teachers and students of the roles which they have to take on during the activity. As e-mail exchanges are often considered an 'extra activity' which can be carried out outside of the classroom, many teachers and students tend not to give it the attention it deserves and the partnerships are quickly finished when more pressing demands such as exams arise.

To avoid such a scenario, teachers need to be aware of their role in planning and integrating the exchange into their classes, while learners need to assume the responsibilities of being both a more autonomous language learner and an intercultural researcher.

5.1. Teachers as project planners

Any e-mail exchange will involve a great deal of preparation on the part of the organising teachers. Firstly, it is necessary to make contact with some possible partner classes through one of the various online networks (see Appendix 1). Through the exchange of several e-mails the teachers must then establish if the learning goals and levels of their classes coincide.

It is also necessary to reach agreement on the structure and content of any future exchange. Issues which need to be dealt with include short and long-term goals, their term structures (classes in some countries may last from September to June, while others may go from January to November), which tasks to set, and which languages to use. Are students asked to write about specific topics or are they required just to write to their partner discussing topics of their own choice? Are they expected to write in both their native and target languages or will just one of the languages be used in the exchange? Are they expected to correct the mistakes of their partners when they write in their target language or is the exchange to focus exclusively on content? All of these are questions which need to be cleared up in the course of the initial exchange of e-mails between the teachers.

Teachers should be wary of partners who suggest simply getting their students 'to write to each other from time to time'. Tillyer (1996) suggests that this usually result in exchanges which are short lived, disorganised, and inevitably unsatisfactory. If a teacher is unwilling to spend time preparing a project, then neither are his/her students likely to invest much time taking part.

Finally, another important part of the project organisation involves making sure that students will have access to online computers which are close-by, working, and relatively easy to use. If students find it difficult to send and receive their e-mails, then their motivation for taking part is likely to decrease. Conferring with the technological department of the home institution may be a useful step in finding out beforehand how easily students will find participating in a technology-based exchange.

5.2. Teachers as project integrators

Having found a partner class and matched students in working pairs or groups, the next task for the teachers is to make the exchange an integral part of their classes, as opposed to simply a novelty activity which will not be considered a serious part of the learning process. For many years the term 'guide on the side' has been used to describe the role for teachers in the technology enhanced classroom, where their function is seen to be that of 'a facilitator of knowledge rather than the font of wisdom' (Warschauer and Healey, 1998: 57). However, many researchers (Feldman *et al.,* 2001; Fischer, 1998) have criticised this view of the teacher's role as being too limited and have suggested that while networked exchanges may provide access to great amounts of linguistic and cultural information, the teacher needs to take on the role of expert in order to help students develop the appropriate communicative and analytic skills. For this reason, the content of their exchange must be fully integrated into their day-to-day language classes.

Bruce Roberts, one of the founders of the important e-mail exchange network IECC, explains the difference between effective and ineffective approaches to dealing with e-mail exchanges in the following way:

> There is a significant difference in educational outcome depending on whether a teacher chooses to incorporate e-mail classroom connections as:
> – an ADD-ON process, like one would include a guest speaker, or
> – an INTEGRATED process, in the way one would include a new textbook.
> The e-mail classroom connections process seems sufficiently complex and time-consuming that if there are goals beyond merely having each student send a letter to a person at a distant school, the ADD-ON approach can lead to frustration and less-than-expected academic results [...] On the other hand, when the e-mail classroom connection processes are truly integrated into the ongoing structure of homework and classroom interaction, then the results can be educationally trans-forming.
>
> (Roberts, cited in Warschauer, 1999: 100–101)

Teachers therefore need to integrate the e-mail exchange into their classes and use them as additional teaching material. They can gain access to the e-mails by asking students to 'CC' the teacher all the messages which they exchange with their partner. Alternatively, Appel and Mullen (2000) have developed an online platform which students can use for exchanging mails and which also gives teachers access to the texts which have been sent and received. In this way they can help their students to analyse and understand the data which they encounter in their exchanges. For example, teachers may be called on to provide background information about the target culture so that students could put the information they received from their partners into perspective. They may also be required to show learners how to write effective e-mails which take into account the cultural norms of communication in the target culture.

5.3. Students as more autonomous language learners

The success of an intercultural exchange also greatly depends on the ability of the learners to take on and develop responsibility for their own learning during the project. This involves various different tasks. Firstly, learners need to take on a tutor role in which they correct their partners' language errors and answer their questions on the home culture and language. According to Kleppin (1997: 82), good tandem-exchange learners should also be able to extract information about the foreign language and culture from their partners' messages, they must be able to learn from the language corrections which they receive and finally, they must be able to identify and then express to their partner what they wish to learn during the exchange. Engaging in such a way can be very demanding for students, but it can be very rewarding as well. Students need to be reminded that they are likely only to get out of the exchange what they put into it.

One Spanish student summed up how liberating this activity can be for learners when they decide to take responsibility for the learning process in their exchange:

> All these years we have been learning English, reading books, studying grammar, and listening to our teachers. Now we have the opportunity to have a teacher for ourselves and, at the same time, to be teachers.

5.4. Students as intercultural researchers

E-mail exchanges are a great opportunity for language learners to find out about the target culture by interacting with 'real people' from that country. Students working together via e-mail can discuss the stereotypes which they hold about each others' countries, they can discuss culturally sensitive issues (for example, religion, censorship, human rights) and they can challenge each other to see issues from another perspective. However, such a dialogue can only be developed in partnerships where there is a high level of trust and respect between the participants. Research into intercultural learning via e-mail by

Müller-Hartmann (2000) and Fischer (1998) has underlined the need for learners to develop a friendly relationship, which in turn will lead to an emotional stability and a willingness to take on criticism and alternative viewpoints from distant partners.

Of course, developing such friendly relationships is not easily achieved over such long distances. In my own research (O'Dowd, 2003), I have found that the following characteristics contributed to the development of good relationships between learners and consequently lead to more intensive levels of exchange and a richer learning environment:

- Students devoted time to developing a good personal relationship with their partner, as opposed to simply focusing on the activities which they had been given.
- Apart from the basic information on the topic in question, they also provided their partner with analysis and personal opinions.
- They asked questions which encouraged feedback and reflection from their partner.
- They took into account the socio-pragmatic rules of their partners' L1 when writing in that language.
- They recognised and reacted to the needs and interests of their partner, answering their questions and encouraging them to write more about the topics which interested them.

Research carried out by both Christian (1997) and Fischer (1998) has confirmed the importance of these characteristics. The following e-mail illustrates some of these elements. The message was sent by a Spanish student to her British partner, and the task was to comment on a text both classes had read about the Spanish character. It is interesting to note how the student personalises the message by writing off-task at the beginning. Furthermore, throughout the mail she constantly tries to give her own personal opinion and insight about the aspects of Spanish behaviour which are mentioned in the text, as well as asking her partner to give her opinion on the topic. Finally, she includes some corrections of her partner's previous mail followed by a compliment:

```
Hello Sarah! How are you?
I hope you have enjoyed your Christmas and you have been
in Australia. Have you already seen your sister's daughter?
I went to Portugal but we only stayed there a fortnight
more or less.
Well, now I'm going to do the next task:
I think the author of the text which is about Spaniards is
quite right. He talks about their positive things and he
says that "we" are warm-hearted, generous...but he says
```

that we are not curious and I think it's false. The eldest
people above all are quite curious and they are always
trying to "investigate" what happens with their
"neighbours" and, then, gossip begins.
It's really terrible. They criticise you , they invent
things about you... It especially occurs in little towns
like mine. Most of the people are envious. That's why it
occurs.
The fact that we're always kissing and hugging is another
true thing. Very often friends that they see each other
everyday and they kiss each other (I do it very often but
only with 4 or 5 friends). I think it's a very good thing
and you show doing this that you're really fond of those
friends. How do you find these things? Are they strange for
you?
Finally, here are some mistakes I noticed in your message:
- You put "metro" with "la" and it's masculine. The same
thing occurs with "mapa".
- In Spanish "letter" is carta and not "letera".
As you can see, they are spelling and word mistakes. You
don't have any big grammar mistake...Well done!!
Well, I have to go back class so I stop here.

Bye Anna

Writing e-mails which contribute to a relationship of trust and dialogue is not an easy task. As Tella and Mononen-Aaltonen (1998) point out, current netiquette tends to discourage long, personal e-mails and instead encourages users to write short messages, which often are no longer than one screen. Students may also find it difficult to get access to e-mail for long enough in order to compose in-depth messages. Nevertheless, my research suggests that, if online learning partnerships are to be developed successfully and if students are to gain anything more than superficial knowledge about the target culture, they need to write messages which take into account the points made above. Writing messages off-line or combining e-mails with essays and other hard copy materials are two possible solutions to this problem (Donath and Volkmer, 1997; Kern, 1997).

6. The development of an exchange

Taking into account the guidelines and observations outlined in previous sections, an intercultural e-mail exchange may take on a format similar to the following. Different exchanges will, of course, vary at certain stages from this model. The type of tasks or activities carried out and the level of teacher involvement will have particularly strong influences on how the exchange develops.

Stage One: Preparation
Do students have easy access to online computers?
Do students know how to send and receive e-mails?

Stage Two: Finding a partner class
Sending out requests for a partner class to some online class matching
networks (see Appendix 1).
The request message should contain a clear description of class size, age-
group, cultures which the partner group should come from as well as
languages to be used in the exchange.

Stage Three: Negotiating details with partner-teacher
Teachers discuss and clearly establish the following: aims and expectations,
duration of the exchange, the tasks and activities involved and the language
division.

Stage Four: Preparing and motivating students
Students are matched together either into pairs or groups. The students may
also play a role in choosing their partners by exchanging descriptions of
themselves with the other class.
Teachers explain to students why they are going to participate in the
exchange and what is expected from them (deadlines for activities etc.).
Students are prepared linguistically for the exchange: Sample e-mails and
common language mistakes are looked at in class.

Stage Five: First messages
Exchanging introductory e-mails.
Teachers receive a copy of all messages.
These might be accompanied by attached photos of the participants, their
homes and locality. Videos and text materials may also be sent by traditional
post or as an attachment via e-mail.

Stage Six: Project development
Carrying out the tasks which have been agreed on by both teachers and
students.
Each task is discussed and prepared beforehand (in class and at home).
E-mails which are to be sent to the partner class can be reviewed and
corrected by the teacher.
Received messages are looked at in class for cultural and linguistic content.

Stage Seven: Evaluation
Feedback from students on what they learned from the exchange. This may take the form of a questionnaire, interviews and/or class discussions.

Portfolios based on the information gathered during the exchange can be drawn up and handed in.

7. Conclusion

The arrival of e-mail and other communication technologies in the foreign language classroom has brought many exciting opportunities for language and intercultural learning. This chapter has shown how one type of networked learning activity – intercultural e-mail exchanges – can potentially contribute to improving learners' language skills, increasing their motivation, and further developing their intercultural awareness. Although these networked exchanges seem to be one of the most popular ways for teachers to exploit the Internet, many researchers (Warschauer, 1999; Liao, 1999) have reported that a great number of these projects fail to achieve their maximum learning potential. As was seen in Section 4, problems with organisation, student motivation, and inter-cultural misunderstandings often mean that intercultural exchanges fail to produce the desired results.

Therefore, in order to reap the potential benefits of engaging students in online intercultural interaction, this chapter has suggested that e-mail projects need to be carried out as part of an organised and well-coordinated process which makes the exchange an integral part of the everyday classroom. Students need opportunities in their classes to learn how to create e-mails for their distant partners and also how to analyse and learn from the messages which they receive. By integrating the projects at this level, and by making both teachers and learners aware of their roles in such networked activities, intercultural e-mail exchanges can have a transforming effect on how students approach the process of learning a foreign language.

However, much still remains to be learned about what and how students learn in e-mail exchanges. Much of the literature until now has focused on descriptive reports of individual projects or on general introductions as to how projects can be initiated. Exceptions to this include qualitative studies by Müller-Hartmann (2000) and Warschauer (1999) which investigated the importance of tasks and socially relevant purpose in networked exchanges. Two other studies by Meagher and Castanos (1996) and O'Dowd (2003) have looked at students' evolving attitudes to the target culture due to contact with members of that culture.

Some research questions which teachers engaging in intercultural exchanges may wish to consider for their own action research include the following:

- In what ways does e-mail contact serve to change students' attitudes and levels of motivation?
- To what extent do learners incorporate the new vocabulary and structures which they encounter in their partners' e-mails?
- How do learners' social background, gender and foreign language competence affect their performance in exchanges?
- Do e-mail exchanges make learners more sensitive to cultural differences in communication?

These questions are intended only as general pointers which teachers may care to look at when introducing e-mail into their classes. Intercultural e-mail exchanges are not a new activity, but achieving their true potential for learning still requires a genuine integration into the classroom followed by rigorous research into the outcomes.

Bibliography

Ady, J. (1995) 'Surveys across the world'. In M. Warschauer (ed.) *Virtual Connections*, 101–3.

Appel, C. and T. Mullen (2000) 'Pedagogical considerations for a web-based tandem language learning environment'. *Computers and Education*, 34.3–4, 291–308.

Avots, J. (1991) 'Linking the foreign language classroom to the world'. In J.K. Phillips (ed.) *Building Bridges and Making Connections*. Middlebury, VT: Northeast Conference on the Teaching of Foreign Languages, 122–53.

Barson, J. (1991) 'The virtual classroom is born: What now?'. In B.F. Freed (ed.) *Foreign Language Acquisition Research and the Classroom*. Lexington, MA: DC Heath, 365–83.

Bee-Lay, S. and S. Yee-Ping (1991) 'English by e-mail: Creating a global classroom via the medium of computer technology'. *ELT Journal*, 45.4, 287–92.

Brammerts, H. (1996) 'Language learning in Tandem using the Internet'. In M. Warschauer (ed.) *Telecollaboration in Foreign Language Learning*. University of Hawai'i: Second Language Teaching and Curriculum Center, 121–30.

Byram, M. (1997) *Teaching and Assessing Intercultural Competence*. Clevedon: Multilingual Matters.

Christian, S. (1997) *Exchanging Lives: Middle School Writers Online*. Urbana, Il: National Council of Teachers of English.

Cummins, J. and D. Sayers (1995) *Brave New Schools: Challenging Cultural Illiteracy Through Global Learning Networks.* New York: St Martin's Press.

Donath, R. and I. Volkmer (1997*) Das Transatlantische Klassenzimmer. Tipps und Ideen für Online-Projekte in der Schule.* Hamburg: Körber Stiftung.

Egbert, J. and E. Hanson-Smith (eds.) (1999) *Call Environments: Research, Practice and Critical Issues.* Virginia: TESOL.

Feldman, A., Konold, C., and B. Coulter (2000) *Network Science: A Decade Later. The Internet and Classroom Learning.* London: Lawrence Erlbaum Associates.

Fischer, G. (1998) *E-mail in Foreign Language Teaching.* Tübingen: Stauffenburg Medien.

Gaer, S. (1999) 'Classroom practice: An introduction to e-mail and World Wide Web projects'. In J. Egbert and E. Hanson-Smith (eds.) *Call Environments: Research, Practice, and Critical Issues.* Alexandria, VA: TESOL, 65–78.

Gervilliers, D., Bertellot, C., and J. Lemery (1977) *Las Correspondencias Escolares.* Barcelona: Editorial Laia.

Gray, R. and R. Stockwell (1998) 'Using computer-mediated communication for language and culture acquisition'. *On-Call Online, 12.3.* Available http://www.cltr.uq.edu.au/oncall/gray123.html

Kendall, C. (1995) 'What I really wanted to know was…'. In M. Warschauer (ed.) *Virtual Connections,* 97–100.

Kern, R. (1997) 'Technology, social interaction and FL literacy'. In J. Muyskens (ed.) *New Ways of Learning and Teaching: Focus on Technology and Foreign Language Education.* Boston, MA: Heinle and Heinle, 57–92.

Kleppin, K. (1997) 'Sprach- und Kulturvergleichend lernen –selbstgesteuert und ohne Lehrer?'. In Börner, W. and K. Vogel (eds.) Kulturkontraste im universitären Fremdsprachenunterricht. Bochum: AKS-Verlag, 80–95.

Liao, C. (1999) 'E-mailing to improve EFL learners' reading and writing abilities: Taiwan experience'. *The Internet TESL Journal,* 3. Available at: http://www.aitech.ac.jp/~iteslj/Articles/Liao-Emailing.html

Little, D. (1997) 'Learner autonomy in the foreign language classroom: Theoretical foundations and some essentials of pedagogical practice'. *Zeitschrift für Fremdsprachenforschung,* 8.2, 227–44.

Meadows, J. (1995) 'Global stories: Using e-mail texts in foreign language classes'. In M. Warschauer (ed.) *Virtual Connections,* 149–50.

Meagher, M. E. and F. Castanos (1996) 'Perceptions of American culture: The impact of an electronically-mediated cultural exchange program on Mexican high school students'. In S. Herring (ed.) *Computer-mediated Communication.* Amsterdam: John Benjamins Publishing Company, 187–201.

Meskill, C. and K. Ranglova (2000) 'Sociocollaborative language learning in Bulgaria'. In M. Warschauer and R. Kern (eds.) *Network-based Language Teaching: Concepts and Practice.* Cambridge: Cambridge University Press, 20–41.

Müller-Hartmann, A. (2000) 'The role of tasks in promoting intercultural learning in electronic learning networks'. *Language Learning and Technology*, 4.2, 129–47.

O'Dowd, R. (2000) 'Intercultural learning via videoconferencing: A pilot exchange project'. *ReCALL*, 12.1, 49–61.

O'Dowd, R. (2003) 'Understanding "the other side": A qualitative analysis of intercultural learning in a Spanish-English E-mail exchange'. *Language Learning and Technology*, 7.2, 118–44

Riel, M. (1997) 'Learning circles make global connections'. In R. Donath and I. Volkmer (eds.) *Das Transatlantische Klassenzimmer*, 329–57.

Rüschoff, B. and D. Wolff (1999) *Fremdsprachenlernen in der Wissensgesellschaft.* Munich: Hueber.

Sayers, D. (1991) 'Cross-cultural exchanges between students from the same culture: A portrait of an emerging relationship mediated by technology'. *The Canadian Modern Language Review*, 47, 678–96.

Shorer, E. (1995) 'Intercultural keypal oral history project'. In M. Warschauer (ed.) *Virtual Connections*, 151–2.

St. John, E. and D. Cash (1995) 'Language learning via e-mail: Demonstrable success with German'. In M. Warschauer (ed.) *Virtual Connections*, 91–7.

Tella, S. (1992a) *Talking Shop via E-mail: A Thematic and Linguistic Analysis of Electronic Mail Communication.* (Research Report No. 99). Helsinki: University of Helsinki, Department of Teacher Education.

Tella, S. (1992b) *Boys, Girls and E-mail: A Case Study in Finnish Senior Secondary Schools.* (Research Report No. 110). Helsinki: University of Helsinki, Department of Teacher Education.

Tella, S. and M. Mononen-Aaltonen (1998) *Developing Dialogic Communication Culture in Media Education: Integrating Dialogism and Technology.* Helsinki: Media Education Publications 7.

Tillyer, D. (1996) 'Tending your internet exchange: Pen pal projects need attention to thrive'. *CALL Review*, September, 1996, 4–6.

Vilmi, R. (1994) 'HUT e-mail writing project'. Available at: http://www.hut.fi/~rvilmi/Autumn94/HUT-article.html

Vilmi, R. (1998) 'Ups and downs: Creating collaborative and interactive language learning projects at Helsinki University of Technology'. Available at: http://www.insa-lyon.fr/Departements/CDRL/ups.html

Warschauer, M. (ed.) (1995) *Virtual Connections: On-line Activities and Projects for Networking Language Learners.* Honolulu: University of Hawai'i, Second Language Teaching and Curriculum Center.

Warschauer, M. (1997) 'Computer-mediated collaborative learning: Theory and practice'. *Modern Language Journal*, 81.3, 470–81.

Warschauer, M. (1999) *Electronic Literacies: Language, Culture and Power in Online*

Education. London: Lawrence Erlbaum Associates.

Warschauer, M., and D. Healey (1998) 'Computers and language learning: An overview'. *Language Teaching*, 31, 57–71.

Appendix 1: Web sites for finding partners

http://www.iecc.org/
>   IECC is a free teaching.com service to help teachers link with partners in other cultures and countries for e-mail classroom exchanges.

http://www.slf.ruhr-uni-bochum.de/index.html
>   The Tandem server matches both individual students as well as classes of language students to carry out exchanges in a variety of different languages.

http://www.epals.com/
>   Over 4 million students and teachers from 191 countries use this resource for finding cross-cultural learning partners and friends.

http://www.ruthvilmi.net/hut/Project/
>   Started in 1993, the IWE fast became a very popular collaborative writing activity, largely due to its structure. It's a flexible communicative project, with students writing to and receiving feedback from their global peers as well as their teacher.

http://www.kidlink.org/
>   Kidlink has been used by 125,000 children in 127 countries to find partners and communicate with young learners across the world.

http://mightymedia.com/keypals
>   The Key Pals Club comes from Teaching.com and offers teachers a secure service for finding intercultural partners for young learners.

Appendix 2: Examples of e-mail projects

http://www.otan.dni.us/webfarm/e-mailproject/site.htm
>   E-mail Projects Home Page

http://www.englisch.schule.de/email.htm
>   Reinhard Donath has an excellent collection (for the most part written in German) of e-mail projects which have been carried out in German schools.

http://www.tak.schule.de/welcome.htm
>   "The Transatlantic Classroom" has been developed specifically for Anglo-German exchanges.

http://www.wfi.fr/volterre/inetpro.html
>   The Volterre collection of projects includes many e-mail based exchanges.

8 Authenticity and the use of technology-enhanced authoring tools in language learning

Bernd Rüschoff

1. Introduction

Ever since the beginning of CALL and TELL (Computer-assisted and Technology-enhanced Language Learning), authoring tools have been an important aspect of the exploitation of new technologies in foreign language learning. The initial concept of authoring software was mainly to provide teachers with devices which enabled them to create interactive tutorial materials in accordance with individual learners' or groups of learners' needs. However, a number of (multimedia) authoring tools have emerged over the years, which – in addition to enabling grassroots language teachers to 'programme' their own computer-assisted exercises – allow for greater flexibility and authenticity in the preparation and exploitation of non-textbook materials in and around the language classroom. This approach is very much in line with recent considerations as to an appropriate methodological framework for language learning, as most pedagogues involved in CALL and TELL agree that one of the really innovative aspects of using new technologies in language learning lies in its potential to go beyond the limitations of traditional exercise formats and non-authentic materials.

It has often been pointed out that the advent of technology-enhanced learning materials requires a re-thinking of the methodological framework of language learning. Many assume that computer tools in particular will facilitate the implementation of a methodology for language learning that focuses more than in the past on authenticity in contents, context, and task. New technologies in the form of authoring tools may solve a large number of practical problems, particularly in the area of exploiting authentic resources. Of course, authenticity in content, task, and classroom interaction is 'a crucial issue' in language learning methodology (see, for example, van Lier, 1996: 123). It is therefore argued that authoring tools are the perfect aid to assist teachers in their 'need to broaden their scope for creative pedagogical initiatives' (Little *et al.*, 1989: I).

Consequently, this chapter will deal with aspects of authenticity and the use of authoring tools in foreign language learning from various angles. It will present:

- an overview of authoring tools for the creation of tutorial and exploratory exercises. This is the more traditional approach to authoring, allowing teachers to create standard, somewhat interactive learning materials geared specifically to the needs of their own learners;
- a description of cognitive tools and text processing tools which facilitate the exploitation of authentic texts and other materials and the preparation of texts and accompanying task- or worksheets;
- a look at authoring tools based on a concept of authenticity in language learning which goes beyond the simple idea of exploiting authentic texts or creating exercises based on authentic, real world materials, and also considers the potential of learners as 'authors', i.e., learners using such tools in the context of meaningful and productive acts of language production. As stated earlier, authenticity is not just to be considered in terms of content, but must be looked at much more with regard to the possibility of exploiting technology-enhanced tools in order to create more authentic, real-world like tasks or generate activities, which engage the learner in acts of language use not geared towards language practice in the traditional sense but real language use.

As far as authoring tools are concerned, usually the teachers are seen in a role of preparing tailor-made exercises for their classes, creating worksheets and developing tasks which permit the learners to actively and often consciously explore the target language. Such tasks and learning projects will help to develop learners' language awareness and understanding of the structure and functionality of the target language. The potential of such tools when used by the teacher is of course important and will be described here together with examples of good practice. In addition, however, and keeping the last of the above bullet-points in mind, real authenticity in tasks can only be achieved if learners are allowed to work within project-based, product-oriented learning scenarios. In order to successfully complete a project and create a product, efficient tools are needed, and this is where authoring tools of any kind can be of great help. Therefore, this chapter will also consider the possibility of placing authoring tools in the hands of the learner with the aim of enhancing the language learner's role as an experimenter and researcher in the classroom by means of authoring tasks.

For obvious reasons, many teachers are wary of using authoring tools and often prefer to integrate ready-made technology-enhanced learning materials into their curriculum. They worry about the potential complexity of 'programming' their own exercises with such tools. However, it has to be pointed out right at the outset of this chapter that innovative tools for text and data-processing, for the creation of multimedia hypertexts, and templates for creation of interactive, often exploratory exercises have now reached a level of sophistication and user-friendliness such that the didactic manipulation – as Edelhoff put it (1985: 24ff) – and adaptation of authentic materials for classroom use should soon become daily routine in grassroots teaching, comparable to the use of the blackboard or the photocopier today. In addition, a vast amount of learner relevant materials is now available in digital format, either in the format of local resources or globally accessible data on the World Wide Web.

2. Theoretical background

Our society has become a knowledge society, where information globally networked and more freely accessible than ever before needs to be processed and transformed into knowledge by those working within a technology-enriched environment. As a result, the traditional skills of information gathering and storing as well as the mere learning of facts will no longer be sufficient in order to live, work, and learn in the coming centuries. The ultimate aim of teaching and learning in this scenario will be to assist learners in their need to develop strategies for knowledge processing, i.e., strategies for knowledge retrieval, production and dissemination.

Therefore, the traditional transmission model of learning must be replaced by models which emphasise information processing and knowledge construction as acts of learning most suited for the acquisition of the kind of skills needed for the knowledge society. Education and teaching in the knowledge society can no longer be reduced to 'the act, process, or art of imparting knowledge and skill' as Roget's Thesaurus proposes, but learning must be recognised as an act in which a learner plays the role of an active constructor of knowledge. Learning must be viewed more in terms of 'an active, creative, and socially interactive process and [...] knowledge as something children must construct and less like something that can be transferred' (Harper, 1996). Criteria based on such principles need to be considered when evaluating the effectiveness and value of technology enhanced materials for language learning. For obvious reasons, an in-depth discussion of the theoretical framework referred to here is beyond the scope of this chapter. A more detailed account as to the principles of constructivist approaches to language learning can be found in a recent paper by Ritter and Rüschoff published in the CALL Journal (2001).

With regard to language learning and language acquisition, these must be regarded as interactive and dynamic processes in the sense that 'studying, learning, reviewing and recalling are not simple input – output activities any more than using language is' (DiVesta, 1974: 28). Research into language learning and acquisition processes suggests that mere training in structural (grammatical) and vocabulary knowledge will not result in real linguistic competence and language proficiency. However, apart from basic communicative competences, favoured in the communicative classroom of the 1980s, developing strategies of language processing and learning competence as much as language awareness and skills in knowledge perception, production, and knowledge construction are needed for the successful outcome of any language curriculum. Such competences, often discussed in the context of learner autonomy as well as authenticity, are of the utmost importance for language learning.

Consequently, the effectiveness of a traditional instructivist paradigm of language learning is often questioned, and the constructivist paradigm is seen as an important methodological basis for real innovation in foreign language learning. Lewis (1993: vii) is very much in line with this position by stating programmatically, '[t]he Present–Practise–Produce paradigm is rejected, in favour of a paradigm based on the Observe–Hypothesise–Experiment cycle'. A methodology based on such principles focuses on 'learner orientation, process orientation and learner autonomy' (Wolff, 1994: 407), all of which ought to be regarded as extremely important in the context of language learning and acquisition. Learning should be regarded as a process of information gathering and knowledge processing. In such a process the interaction between knowledge previously acquired and new information gathered leads to the acquisition and even to the production of new knowledge. Learning is an active process in which learners construct new ideas based upon their current and past knowledge (see, for example, Bruner, 1990).

Learning based on constructivist principles will allow learners to tap into resources and acquire knowledge rather than force them to function as recipients of instruction. Such approaches are meeting with growing approval and are regarded by many educational thinkers as a suitable theoretical framework for the learning environment of the future. This kind of approach 'perceives students as active learners who come to [...] lessons already holding ideas [...] which they use to make sense of everyday experiences. [...] Such a process is one in which learners actively make sense of the world by constructing meaning' (Scott, 1987: 4).

How then can the principle of 'learning without being taught' as proposed by Piaget (see Papert, 1980: 7) be integrated into the learning environment of the future? One might also ask, how the use of authoring tools will fit into this theoretical framework, considering that originally such tools were basically templates for the creation of rather traditional exercise materials? However, apart from such rather traditional tools, so-called cognitive tools have become available, which can be defined as follows:

Cognitive tools empower learners to design their own representations of knowledge rather than absorbing knowledge representations preconceived by others. Cognitive tools can be used to support the deep reflective thinking that is necessary for meaningful learning. Ideally, tasks or problems for the application of cognitive tools should be situated in realistic contexts with results that are personally meaningful for learners. (Jonassen and Reeves, 1996: 693)

Typical and often quoted examples of cognitive tools for language learning are concordancers and authoring tools for creating class-based learner dictionaries or similar databases. The use of word processors with appropriate add-on features, such as integrated dictionaries or style-checkers is another example. In addition, word processors with integrated templates for thought collection or brainstorming and organising ideas and vocabulary as part of text production tasks provide a further opportunity to put into practice a tools-based approach to materials design very much in line with the theoretical framework discussed above. Text-processing tools which allow teachers to create worksheets out of digital texts and thus integrate authentic texts even in paper-based formats into their language curriculum can also be defined as cognitive tools. And finally, even templates for the creation of rather traditional exercise materials could function as cognitive tools when put into the hands of language learners, providing a framework for gathering information, stimulating recall of prior knowledge, and for guiding processes of knowledge construction, for example in the form of creating grammar exercises or exercises on other language items for their peers.

Thus, it can be claimed that in order to enhance the language learner's role as an experimenter and researcher in the classroom, authoring software for the creation of tutorial and exploratory exercises as well as cognitive tools, such as the ones mentioned above, are very important. However, out of the variety of tools mentioned, only traditional authoring tools and text-processing tools will be dealt with in the remainder of this chapter. The exploitation of cognitive tools in the form of concordancing software together with ample examples for their use can be found in the following chapter dealing with corpora and concordancing.

3. Authoring tools: An overview

For obvious reasons, this chapter cannot present an extensive overview and description of the multitude of authoring tools and authoring packages available today. An impressive amount of such materials has been published over the years. As a result, this chapter will concentrate on the description of a selection of prototypical packages to exemplify the basic principles and features of this type of software. A detailed and interactive tutorial on authoring packages can be found on the ICT4LT project's excellent and resourceful Web site on Information and Communications Technology for Language Teachers in its module on authoring. The very first type of authoring tool which appeared on the CALL scene from very early on consisted of packages, which basically provide teachers with ready-made templates for most of the exercise types and interactions commonly used in computer-assisted self-study materials. These templates can then be filled with content and the authoring tool automatically 'creates' an interactive exercise using this input.

It is important to note that the creation of self-study exercises specifically geared towards a particular target group can be achieved without any knowledge of programming or script-writing, as would be the case when using programming tools such as *Toolbook* or *Macromedia Director*. The ICT4LT project on its Web site defines authoring tools or authoring packages as '[a]n *Application* which allows the author to develop learning and teaching materials with significantly less programming than if a programming language were used, or with no programming at all'. Basic computing skills are sufficient even to enable the integration of multimedia features into self-created exercises. There are quite a number of such authoring packages available, and in the following paragraphs this chapter will concentrate on a few classic examples which are representative of the type of CALL and TELL material in question.

One such classic example of an authoring tool for language learning is WIDA Software's *The Authoring Suite*, a package which will be described later on. A more recent example with additional and more flexible options for putting together complete and structured multimedia-enhanced learning packages is the *TELOS* package. Telos Language Partner (TLP Pro) is multimedia software that supports relevant language learning scenarios. Intuitive editing functions facilitate the production and customisation of multimedia language-learning content. The heart of the software is its set of multimedia templates adapted to learning activities from communicative practice (involving texts, dialogues, and video clips) to grammar and vocabulary learning. TLP Pro supports prototypical learning activities from video, dialogue, and text practice to lexical and grammatical explanations and exercises, cultural notes, and lexical look-up. As these templates can be used in a learning as well as in an editing mode, they operate as a multimedia interface between complementary tutor and learner activities. Recently, a TELOS Web-converter has been published which provides for the creation of online versions of exercises and learning packages developed with TELOS. Similarly, the *Hot Potatoes* package, another example of software which is downloadable free of charge from the Internet, allows teachers to create an interactive learning environment for self-study and to place it on the Web. A further authoring tool for off-line exercises focusing on text reception and text production skills is CAMSOFT's *Fun With Texts* or *Gap Kit* packages. Out of the examples mentioned here, WIDA's *The Authoring Suite*, CAMSOFT's *Fun with Texts*, and *Gap Kit* are often referred to as pioneer language-learning authoring routines. They have been adapted over the years as multimedia facilities have become available to computers at low cost. Their ease of use has not been compromised by these changes, and within the restricted range of exercise types on offer they still represent significant efficiency and a good ratio of developer to learner time.

As noted above, the basic principle of these materials is that teachers can create tutorial and exploratory exercises, in some cases even with multimedia-enhanced features, without any need for programming. Basic skills in handling a computer and Microsoft Windows are enough to 'write' the interactive exercises. The exercise types provided by such tools include the standard variety of formats, such as multiple choice, gap filling, matching, and open question and answer. Whenever feasible, these exercise types include the option of allowing the learner to work in either a tutorial/exploratory or in an exam or test mode. In the first instance, learners are given free access to all the text-based or multimedia help options and feedback is provided directly upon learner input, thus providing a framework for self-directed, discovery-oriented learning. The latter mode mentioned puts the learners in a test situation with feedback and help options blocked until after an exercise has been completed in full, thus giving learners a tool for self-evaluation or self-testing. Both WIDA's *Authoring Suite* and CAMSOFT's *Fun With Texts* offer an additional selection of text manipulation and text reconstruction exercises, such as total cloze or text jumbling. Such more innovative exercise formats are particularly suited to give learners tasks which challenge their mental text-processing capabilities and thus assist in strategy building rather than simple recall of facts.

A number of teachers make use of such tools to create exercises with a view to providing their learners with more effective self-study materials, for example in the form of electronic homework. However, if one intends to exploit new technologies within a more constructivist framework, such tools can also be used to engage learners in the creation of exercises for their peers. A number of colleagues have reported on their positive experiences with learner groups, where at the end of a unit dealing with a specific set of grammatical rules or lexical items, learners do not simply work through a few exercises in order to fully internalise a rule or new vocabulary, but are invited to work further on the items in a truly task-based mode, using the authoring mode of the tools discussed here. By asking learners to create an exercise dealing with what has been learned at the conclusion of a unit, one can provide them with a framework within which they have to consider the rule in more detail, think about and search for suitable examples and tasks as well as potential areas for mistakes and anticipated errors, and contemplate the necessary feedback and help options to be integrated into an exercise. In such cases, learners do work on their linguistic skills but at the same time develop what has been referred to above as language awareness and learning competence. Furthermore, using authoring tools in such a way is one possible step towards more authentic tasks, certainly more authentic than simply asking learners to work their way through the usual diet of grammar or vocabulary drills.

A further type of authoring tool that needs to be described in this chapter is text processing tools which facilitate the exploitation of authentic texts in a language curriculum, again with a view to enhancing authenticity in language learning both in content and task. In the past a major argument against the feasibility of such an approach has been that the use of authentic texts is only realistic in more advanced groups and that the adaptation of authentic texts for less advanced learners is too time-consuming and difficult. However, recently tools which provide assistance in adapting authentic texts for classroom use have become available. With such tools, texts can be adapted to the actual level of competence and knowledge of the target group. After all, the adaptation of authentic texts and the generation of exercises and worksheets based on such material is one of the areas where new technologies offer tremendous innovative potential. Textbook publishers and software developers have recognised this and are now offering the tools needed for this task. Klett's *Text Aktiv* (for French and English) is an independent word processor with text-adaptation and exercise-generation features, as is *Übungsblätter per Mausklick*, a package developed by the Goethe Institute for German as a Foreign Language and published by Hueber. Cornelson/OUP's *Toolbox* on the other hand automatically integrates such features into an existing word processor, such as *Microsoft Word*.

These tools in principle offer similar options. Firstly, they offer enhanced features of electronic text analysis, which include the creation of word lists (alphabetical or type/token based), line numbering, and searching for sample contexts, and facilitate the preparation and adaptation of texts for classroom use. In addition, these tools offer the option of identifying the kinds of linguistic aspects which can best be dealt with when using a particular text. In addition, however, these tools automatically generate paper-based worksheets based on a given text, usually in a cloze or gap format. For example, if a teacher intends to revise the use of prepositions or tenses using an authentic text, all he or she needs to do is to click on the relevant options in the exercise generator, and the program will process the text into a worksheet with all prepositions (or verbs) automatically replaced by gaps. This can be done for almost any aspect of grammar or word form. In addition to these rather traditional gap-filling exercise types with the user specifying the desired lexical or grammatical item to be deleted from a text, these tools also provide features to create more innovative worksheet formats dealing with context rather than individual gaps. Consequently, c-tests and cloze tests, jumbled text, automatically generated jumbled sentences, word-snakes, anagrams, and many other exercises of thus type can be generated, too. It must be pointed out, however, that exercises created with either tool are not interactive CALL programs but rather intended for classroom use as worksheets etc. More recently, a package called LINGOFOX has appeared which expands the features included in the above mentioned text processing tools to a much wider variety of tasks and worksheets. Altogether, 22 different types of exercise formats – grouped under four headings: gap-fill, spelling, regrouping, games – can be generated with this tool. In addition, LINGOFOX is a truly multilingual tool, as it processes texts in English, French, German, Italian, and Spanish.

A further tool, MCQ published by IMC English Training & Translation Services, is different, as in addition to printable worksheets it creates interactive exercises which can be accessed with any Internet browser and used in a online or off-line mode. Different types of exercises are produced automatically and by varying the tool's settings one can determine the degree of difficulty for each exercise. A semi-automatic mode is also available, which allows teachers to select (mark) the words to be used in a worksheet. In addition to standard multiple choice, gap-filling, and cloze exercises, MCQ also automatically creates so-called pop-up and phrase-maze exercises. i.e. essentially text reconstruction exercises where students by making choices reconstruct the text. The flexibility of MCQ (a demo is available on the website listed in the bibliography) allows the teacher to split the text up into either words, phrases or sentences so that these are presented as choices.

Such tools are in my opinion a step in the right direction when it comes to facilitating and enhancing the use of authentic texts and exercises based on such materials in the language classroom and thus are very much in line with the methodological framework outlined above. As a final note I would like to point out that teachers might want to consider the use of these tools as an aid for projects where learners are required to research and process authentic texts with relevance to a given language topic.

4. Principles of authoring and examples of use

Concerning the integration of authoring tools into a language curriculum, the first question which needs to be addressed is the choice of package. Such a decision will depend on a number of factors. Obviously, a lot depends on the infrastructure and the computing skills at a given institution. Furthermore, the pedagogical aims a language teacher or institution intends to achieve need to be considered. And thirdly, the question arises as to whether the materials developed are to be made available externally, possibly even marketed commercially, or whether a teacher simply needs a tool to provide his or her learners with additional exercises or is looking for additional options to enhance a given learning environment with more flexibility and alternative options to approach a language problem. In my opinion, based on observation and experience, a teacher or even groups of teachers very rarely use authoring packages to create publishable materials. However, if an institution intends to go in that direction, one of the more sophisticated (and more difficult to use) tools is needed. For example, a number of institutions have used TELOS Pro to create complete language courses, such as a basic English course entitled *Dublin Encounters*, and these materials are then marketed by the developers of this package via their Web site. More commonly, teachers use specific language learning tools of the kind described in the previous part of this chapter, and integrate materials developed by filling appropriate content for specific activities into the selection of templates available. Systems of courseware and courseware management as well as generic systems are usually much more flexible, but, conversely, are often harder to manage and require a significant training effort.

Further deliberations on this question can be found on the Web site of the ICT4LT project. With regard to some more general tips on authoring and preparing, their module on authoring also contains a number of very useful hints, some of which will be quoted below. Obviously, the principle that the pedagogic design should always be in charge, not technical issues, must be observed when designing the courseware. With regard to this, *ICT4LT* points out the following:

- Be prepared to reject the use of the computer for a learning outcome best handled by other media, including pencil and paper.
- Choose the authoring package which supports your needs, not vice-versa.
- Do not underestimate the time needed to author!
- Consider how the courseware you create will fit into a wider curricular design.
- Decide whether discrete exercises are what you require, or whether you need a more sophisticated structure, with conditional branching, remedial loops and so on.

Allow time and resources for the creation of the media which will be used in your courseware – the text, images, audio recordings, and video – which are known in technical jargon as assets. You need to be able to handle a variety of tools for the creation of your assets – at the very least a word-processor for editing text.

Above all, pay careful attention to the question of feedback and its relevance to your learners.

- Create courseware in small, meaningful 'chunks' – the attention span of learners on a computer is probably less than you think.
- Try to get others involved in a collaborative process once you have become familiar with your chosen tool – you are more likely to be successful if you can demonstrate a degree of confidence and show that the eventual ratio between developer and learner time offers some efficiency gains. Always treat the development of courseware within the overall needs of your curriculum.
- When creating new courseware, ensure that you trial the first drafts with at least a small number of end users to ascertain its likely success.

These and many other useful aspects of choosing authoring tools and getting ready for the use of such packages are available on the ICT4LT Web site. For the remainder of this chapter, we shall very briefly turn to a few examples of use of self-authored materials.

As far as the creation of traditional gap-fill, multiple-choice, matching, or open-question exercises are concerned, the description of examples of good practice is not really necessary, as all of us are well aware of suitable or less suitable content for such materials. With regards to exploring the tutorial function of these exercise formats, it should be noted that despite evident limitations in such traditional designs and some scepticism as to the effectiveness of formal exercises, tutorial software which complies with certain criteria as to flexibility in content, input analysis, and design might still be of some use in foreign language learning. When creating such exercises with authoring tools, the following principles should be kept in mind:

- Such exercises must permit learners to 'interact' with language data in order to modify acquired linguistic knowledge on the basis of analysis and testing. This means that the help and feedback options as well as the 'slots' for integrating reference materials into exercises, for example, additional texts, multimedia materials, visuals etc., should be used creatively.
- Consequently, the content of tutorial exercises should be designed in a way which does not put the learner simply into the role of testee, but in a manner which facilitates his/her role as an experimenter and researcher.
- Furthermore, control over what the software does or what one wants to do with the software has to be left to the learner to a much higher degree than in most examples to date.

Consequently, one should look very carefully at the templates for the integration of additional materials as well as the flexibility of interaction allowed for when selecting an authoring tool. WIDA's *TestMaster* module is a good first example, as it allows for the creation of open question activities with a tremendous variation of potential answers processed by the program. Consider the following content provided in one of the sample exercises focusing on situational dialogues. A question on the screen, such as 'You're in the office of someone you don't know well. It's hot. Ask permission to open the window.' is intended to stimulate the learner to speculate as to all the various things one could say in such a situation and test their hypotheses by entering them into the answer box. All of the following answer and variations are provided for:

> *[Can\Could\May] I open the window(please)?*
> *Would [you mind\it be all right] if I open(ed) the window(please)?*
> *I don't suppose I could open the window, could I?*
> *It's(rather\ very) hot(in here)(isn't it?)*

The brackets are part of the authoring procedure and make it easier to integrate alternative answers including variations within a given structure. Further feedback is given on each of the variants, for example 'this is a standard variety', 'this is very polite', or even 'OK, but you're overdoing it a little'. Exercises of this kind, though traditional in format, are a first step into the creation of exploratory tasks in line with the principles stated above.

A .further example of how even traditional multiple-choice exercises with integrated multimedia features can be used to provide learners with a tool for text discovery in preparation of a classroom session is one of the sample exercises provided with WIDA's *Authoring Suite*. Of course, this exercise, based on a fireman's account of how he got to be a fireman, could be simply used as a follow-up listening or text-comprehension task. The fact, however, that learners are allowed to look at background materials before starting to work on the questions and can access the dialogue and listen to the full text or access short extracts relevant to a given question together with visual help can turn this exercise into a useful while-listening activity. Such an exercise can be used by learners to prepare a text rather than simply practise at the end of a class.

A perfect example of an authoring package which provides all the flexibility required to put into practice the principles listed above is the TELOS software. The multimedia templates contained in this tool are structured in a way which permits an author to create media-enhanced dialogues and leave all relevant choices as to how a dialogue should be presented on screen to the learner, for example, with or without subtitles or additional visual and audio support. Furthermore, access to glossaries, translation, and relevant grammatical or other background information can be integrated into the transcripts by means of easily created hyperlinks. All this information as well as direct links back into a listening or viewing task are also available when working on the exercises created around a dialogue or video sequence.

How well even a simple multiple-choice format can be integrated into tasks for strategy building is best exemplified by a module of *Authoring Suite* entitled *PinPoint*. To create a *PinPoint* exercise, a teacher simply enters a minimum of six short texts together with a title or headline. The template for this game-type exercise then jumbles the headlines and presents these as choices on the screen. In a text window underneath these titles, the software reveals at random a single word of one of the texts contained in the exercise. Learners can now expand the visible text by 'buying' more words at a 'cost' of 20 points. An incorrect guess 'costs' 100 points, a correct answer is rewarded with 200 points. The basic idea of this simple exercise is that learners are encouraged to think very carefully about the bits of text available and to hypothesise about the full content by reflecting about whether the words they can see might somehow fit with the messages or information contained in the headlines or titles. In my opinion, this type of exercise is very much in line with the theoretical framework discussed at the outset of this chapter, as learners are constantly engaged in processes of thinking beyond the few words given. They literally need to read between the lines, thus building the kind of strategies needed for reading and text compre-hension. *PinPoint* can be used very well with short news items, possibly taken from Web sites of TV stations such as CNN or the BBC, or newspapers available on the Internet. Descriptive texts on regions, cities, or special features of the country of a target language are suitable content, as are texts of advertisements together with the products they are promoting. Some of these are available as sample exercises with the *Authoring Suite.*

Text reconstruction and text manipulation exercises, such as those available in this authoring tool as well as CAMSOFT's *Fun With Texts,* are also activities which stimulate learners to go through their mental lexicon and draw on any other 'linguistic' knowledge available when hypothesising about words which might fit into a total-cloze exercise. From very early on, research has shown how useful text reconstruction exercises are in terms of providing learners with a platform for activities aimed at strategy building and knowledge construction (see Legenhausen and Wolff, 1989). This type of exercise is also quite useful when a teacher wants to introduce learners to authoring as another form of language practice. In a project investigating how CALL can best be integrated into language learning at tertiary level, writing tasks related to the content of a unit in their textbook were given to teams of students. The learners were asked to enter their texts into a text reconstruction template, such as *Storyboard.* Once the texts were finished, diskettes were collected and in a kind of lottery each team was asked to draw one of them and reconstruct the text. This kind of activity was very popular with the learners, as it enabled them to revise and practise the language and content learned in a unit much more intensely and cre-atively. Similarly, we asked learners to create crossword puzzles using the templates contained in *Hot Potatoes*, and these were then distributed and solved by their peers.

The amount of creativity and intensive reflection on grammatical or lexical problems which can be encouraged when engaging learners in acts of exercise creation can best be exemplified by WIDA's *TestMaster* template. Consider language items along the lines of the example about making a request quoted earlier. If learners are asked to imagine all the possible utterances available in order to perform a given function and enter them into *TestMaster* template, a lot more reflection on language takes place than when simply reproducing sample statements in a ready-made exercise. Similar creative tasks are possible with regard to grammatical problems, for example, asking learners to produce for their peers exercises dealing with the transformation of direct statements into reported speech. Projects of this kind designed around authoring packages are a perfect way of enabling learners to develop both language awareness and language learning awareness together with factual and procedural, i.e., strategic and functional competence. At a more demanding level, learners can be encouraged to *stage* complete, multimedia-enhanced dialogues and create relevant exercises using more advanced authoring tools, such as the TELOS package. Such an approach is currently being developed as part of a LINGUA project entitled *Staging Foreign Language Learning*.

In order to put a label to this approach to the exploitation of technology-enhanced learning, the author of this chapter suggests the term *template-based learning*. As a detailed description of this concept can be found in Rüschoff and Wolff (1999) and in Ritter and Rüschoff (2001), it is only necessary to refer to this idea in general terms in this text. Such a concept goes somewhat further than just using tools as part of the learning process. Among other ideas, template-based learning entails the principle that authoring tools and similar materials can be used to provide learners with a frame to assist them in structuring and co-ordinating acts of knowledge construction. Templates can be designed in the format of advanced organisers as well as tools and tasks which encourage 'on-the-hoof' recording of thoughts and impressions whilst examining learning materials. The principal function of template-based learning is to provide a framework for gathering information, stimulating recall of prior knowledge, and for guiding processes of knowledge construction. Thus, templates (such as authoring tools in the hands of the learner) are one way of creating more authentic tasks for learning. Consequently, it can be assumed that computer tools will facilitate the implementation of the methodological framework discussed at the outset of this chapter and contribute to solving a large number of practical problems, particularly in the area of exploiting authentic resources.

As an example for putting this approach into practice, the following activity involving the use of *PinPoint* by learners themselves might serve as an illustration towards the end of this chapter. Within a WWW-project conducted around reading and analysing the novel *The Pigman* by Paul Zindel, learners not only worked towards creating a Web site and filling it with content, but also used authoring tools to produce learning materials for their peers. One such task included the writing of additional scenes, dialogues, inner monologues or whatever was considered appropriate in order to make some of the minor characters and their function in the novel more transparent. Learners selected a character and wrote such additional material using both *PinPoint* and *Storyboard* as writing tools. The result was that students on the one hand produced texts which they knew would be looked at and worked with by others, and on the other hand they did not simply read the texts written by their peers but worked with them in the context of various text-manipulation activities. *PinPoint*, for example, was a great activity stimulating learners to look at such texts more closely while trying to identify which character of the book the text fragment on the screen actually referred to. The integration of a text-production activity using an authoring tool described here is based on ideas and similar activities described in Kallenbach and Ritter (2000), where learners worked on tasks, such as 'Guess Who', writing texts describing famous people or other persons, created *PinPoint* exercises out of their texts, and subsequently worked with the resulting exercises. This type of example should make clear what is meant by authenticity in both content and task in the context of language learning and how authoring tools in a variety of forms and ways of exploiting them can be considered as a true enrichment of the learning environment.

5. Conclusion

A full presentation in greater detail of all the features of the software examples discussed here, as well as an extensive description of more examples of their use in language learning, would clearly be beyond the scope of this chapter. The intention here is to exemplify the general principles of how authoring tools can be made use of in order to a) generate more authentic materials for use in language learning, b) expose groups of learners to learning materials and exercises geared specifically at their individual needs, and c) engage learners in productive and creative tasks aimed at putting constructivist principles of learning into practice. In addition, the theoretical framework, upon which this approach to the exploitation of new technologies in foreign language learning should be based, needed to be discussed briefly. Such an approach might best be summarised by labelling it cognitive learning within the context of a constructivist rather than instructional paradigm of CALL and TELL. Such a cognitive-constructivist approach distinguishes itself from more radical concepts of constructivism by accepting that learning, however flexible and learner-oriented, still requires forms of cognitive scaffolding and activities which allow for conscious cognition. Papert's idea of constructionism, as well as concepts of template-based learning, take this into account. This is very much in line with developments over the past decade, when language learning theory has seen a shift from the highly guided to the more open learning environment, with constructivism as a new and very much learner-centred paradigm for learning.

An important feature of this paradigm of learning with multimedia resources is the fact that these do not simply confront learners with traditional exercise formats in the form of pattern practice and comprehension tests but rather with tools that allow them to prepare for and handle difficulties in language processing and production, i.e., students should be given the tools to build knowledge instead of simply consuming it. If authoring tools and resources are used in the way exemplified in this chapter, they can provide both teachers and learners with powerful utilities to handle authentic learning materials more effectively. As stated at the start of this chapter, a number of authoring tools have emerged over the years, which – in addition to enabling grassroots language teachers to 'programme' their own computer-assisted exercises – allow for greater flexibility and authenticity in the preparation and exploitation of non-textbook materials in and around the language classroom. The potential of such tools when used by the teacher was described together with examples of good practice. In addition, the possibility of placing authoring tools in the hands of the learner was considered, with the aim of enhancing the language learner's role as an experimenter and researcher in the classroom by means of authoring tasks. As has been pointed out a number of times, 'Constructionism asserts that people construct new knowledge with particular effectiveness when they are engaged in constructing personally meaningful artefacts. Authorware is a perfect tool for facilitating the constructionist approach'. (Thornton and Rule, 1997) What is needed, therefore, is a closer look at existing authoring tools with the aim of designing creative and product-oriented learning scenarios around them. In addition, one might consider integrating features specifically aimed at such an approach into the future development of such tools. To give but one example, an interesting development, based on the idea of template-based learning, might be a tool for Web-based projects which provides learners with an integrated platform consisting of project-folders and regular tools for creating a Web site, as well as templates for the creation of language-learning tasks and inter-activities.

Bibliography

Bertin, J.-C. (2001) *Des Outils pour des langues – multimédia et apprentissage.* Paris: Ellipses.

Blin, F. and R. Donohoe (2000) 'Projet TECHNE: vers un apprentissage collaboratif dans une classe virtuelle bilingue'. *Apprentissage des Langues, Systèmes d'Information et Communication (ALSIC)*, 3.1, 19–47.

Bruner, J. (1990) *Acts of Meaning.* Cambridge, MA: Harvard University Press.

Davies, G.D. (1997) 'Lessons from the past, lessons for the future...'. In *New Technologies in Language Learning and Teaching.* Strasbourg: Council of Europe, 40–42.

Di Vesta, F.J. (1974) *Language, Learning, and Cognitive Processes.* Monterey: Brooks/Cole Publishing Co.

Edelhoff, C. (1985) 'Authentizität im Fremdsprachenunterricht'. In C. Edelhoff (ed.) *Authentische Texte im Deutschunterricht.* München: Hueber, 7–30.

Harper, B.M. (1996) 'Using cognitive tools in interactive multimedia, from virtual to reality'. Apple University Conference, University of Queensland, Queensland, 24–27 September, 1996 (http://auc.uow.edu.au/conf/Conf96/Papers/Harper.html).

Jonassen, D.H. and T.C. Reeves (1996) 'Learning with technology: Using computers as cognitive tools'. In D.H. Jonassen, (ed.) *Handbook of Research on Educational Communications and Technology.* New York: Macmillan, 693–719.

Kallenbach, C. and M. Ritter (eds.) (2000) *Computer-Ideen für den Englischunterricht. Anregungen und Beispiele für den Software- und Internet-Einsatz Klassen 5–10.* Berlin: Cornelsen.

Kohn, K. (2001) 'Developing multimedia CALL: The Telos Language Partner approach'. *Computer Assisted Language Learning*, 14: 3–4, 252–67.

Legenhausen, L. and D. Wolff, (1989) 'Lernerstrategien bei der Textrekonstruktion: STORYBOARD als Übung im Fremdsprachenunterricht'. *Die Neueren Sprachen*, 88, 3–20.

Legenhausen L. And D. Wolff (1991) 'Der Micro-Computer als Hilfsmittel beim Sprachenlernen: Schreiben als Gruppenaktivität'. *Praxis des neusprachlichen Unterrichts*, 38, 346–56.

Lewis, M. (1993) *The Lexical Approach. The State of ELT and a Way Forward.* Hove: Language Teaching Publications.

Little, D., S. Devitt and D. Singleton (1989) *Learning Foreign Languages from Authentic Texts: Theory and Practice.* Dublin: Authentik.

Papert, S. (1980) *Mindstorms.* New York: Basic Books.

Piper A. (1989) 'Word processing – processing words or processing writing'. In Meara, P. (ed.) *Beyond Words.* London: Centre for Information on Language Teaching and Research, 67–78.

Ritter, M. and B. Rüschoff (2001) 'Technology-enhanced language learning: Construction of knowledge and template-based learning in the foreign language classroom'. In *Computer Assisted Language Learning*, 14.3–4, 219–32.

Scott, P. (1987) *A Constructivist View of Learning and Teaching Science. Children's Learning in Science Project.* Leeds: University of Leeds, Centre for Studies in Science and Mathematics Education.

Thornton, P. and S. Rule. (1997). 'Authorware and a Constructionist Approach to the ESOL Classroom', presented at TESOL Conference, Orlando, Florida.

van Lier, L. (1996) *Interaction in the Language Curriculum: Awareness, Autonomy and Authenticity.* London and New York: Longman.

Wolff, D. (1994) 'Der Konstruktivismus: Ein neues Paradigma in der Fremdsprachendidaktik?'. *Die Neueren Sprachen*, 93–4, 407–29.

Web sites

Information and Communications Technology for Language Teachers (Socrates-Project): http://www.ict4lt.org

IMC-English Training and Translation Services: http://www.intcom.se/

LINGOFOX: http://www.lingofox.de/

Staging Foreign Language Learning (LINGUA project): http://nibis.ni.schule.de/europa/englisch/start/

The *Hot Potatoes* suite: http://web.uvic.ca/hrd/halfbaked/

The *TELOS Pro* Partner Tools: www.linguaplan.de

9   Corpora and concordancing: Changing the paradigm in language learning and teaching?

Angela Chambers and Victoria Kelly

1. Introduction

Concordancing software has been described as 'technologically rudimentary, but very powerful as a cognitive tool' (Wolff, 1997: 22–3). This comment emphasises the potential of this tool in the rapidly changing environment of language teaching and learning. The concordancer, which is in its basic form simpler to use than word-processing software, allows the user to find occurrences of a word in a corpus of texts and to study the different ways in which it is used. To suggest that such a rudimentary tool can play a major cognitive role may initially seem an extravagant claim. However, five key features of the newly emerging environment make corpora and concordancing the technological development which arguably has the potential to make a significant contribution to the experience of language learning and teaching in the future. Firstly the increasing focus on learning rather than teaching, and more particularly on learner autonomy and self-directed learning, will favour those methodologies and tools which allow learners to make their own choices and create their own paths rather than to follow pre-determined courses. Secondly, in an increasingly multicultural world, there is an understandable focus on the use of authentic materials of relevance to the learner rather than reliance on published course books with their necessarily limited field of cultural reference. Thirdly, this multicultural emphasis goes hand in hand with an increasing acceptance of a descriptive rather than a prescriptive approach to the target language, which also makes it important to have access to real language use. Fourthly, the availability of large amounts of material in electronic form makes it easy for the autonomous learner to find authentic material – in the form of online books or newspapers, CD-ROM based material, company Web sites, discussion groups, etc., and to use this material as the basis for learning. Finally, despite the general acceptance of the need for computer literacy in the electronic age, it is unrealistic to expect that all teachers, and even all pupils, will be able to master complex tools. It is thus easy to argue that in the field of CALL, as in other technological developments, it is the simplest tool with the greatest potential which is the most likely to meet with the greatest success.

This chapter will begin by providing a definition of a text corpus, together with information on the existing large corpora and on the uses to which these corpora have been put, initially in the context of research into language use, more recently focusing on applications in the context of language learning. The creation of small corpora and their use in the language learning context will also be included, as it plays a particularly important role in an environment where access to large corpora is not yet easily available to all. An explanation of the key features of concordancing software will then be provided, together with information on the main brands that are available. This will be followed by the main part of the chapter, an examination of the possible uses of corpora in the language learning context, focusing on areas such as the learning of vocabulary and grammar, translation, Languages for Specific Purposes, literary studies, and cultural studies. The conclusion will investigate the implications of these developments not only for the language learning environment, but more particularly for the changing roles of language learner and teacher.

2. Text corpora: From research on language use to applications in language learning

Many definitions of the term 'corpus' have been advanced. For the purposes of the present chapter which concerns itself mainly with text corpora, McEnery and Wilson's (1996: 59) definition is most fitting: 'A corpus typically implies a finite body of text, sampled to be maximally representative of a particular variety of a language and which can be stored and manipulated using a computer'. It must be said, however, that a collection of machine-readable text does not constitute a corpus *per se*. A distinction must be made here between a corpus and an archive. 'Computerised archives (of which the best-known example is the Oxford Text Archive) have been collected more or less opportunistically, according to what sources of data can be made available and what chances for collection arise' (Aijmer and Altenberg, 1991: 10). A corpus, on the other hand, is not collected opportunistically but is designed or required for a particular representative function. Both written and spoken language may be included in a corpus. The simplest form of corpus consists of untagged written text, and can be created simply by copying and pasting written text which is already available in electronic form. The large, well known corpora, however, are tagged using a mark-up language such as SGML. This makes it possible to identify morphosyntactic aspects of the language, such as -ed as a marker of the past tense in English.

Today, the kinds of corpora in existence are extremely heterogeneous, ranging from corpora of the complete works of a particular author, to historical corpora, to specialised corpora on a wide variety of topics, to commercial corpora amongst others (for a detailed introduction to corpora types, see Kennedy, 1998). Up until very recently, Corpus Linguistics primarily focused on the use of corpora for research into language use, rather than on language teaching and learning. Some of the more notable corpora, which have been compiled to make generalisations about the nature of language or to clarify the finer points of grammar or usage in particular varieties of a language, include the Brown Corpus (Francis and Kucera, 1964), which consists of a wide range of texts in American English, and the LOB (Lancaster-Oslo/Bergen) Corpus (Johansson, Leech and Goodluck, 1978). It is worth noting that the vast majority of corpus-based studies carried out to date have been restricted to the English language. Quirk (1992) attributes this penchant for the compilation of English language corpora to the continuing dominance of English as a language of *exposition*, the international language of communication, which, in the past, 'was increasingly influencing scholars to make it also the almost exclusive *object of study*' (1992: 458). Whilst the scope of this chapter does not allow for anything more than a fragmentary list of what computer corpora exist in various languages, the authors can recommend the following sources for current developments in the field: the *ICAME* (*International Computer Archive of Modern English*) journal which distributes information on electronically available English language materials and on linguistic research involving these materials; the Georgetown University *Catalogue of Projects in Electronic Text* (*CPET*) which has access to over 312 electronic corpus projects in 27 countries and is continually updated; and the Oxford Text Archive (OTA), which is one of the largest archives of machine-readable texts consisting of over 450 separate text collections in more than 30 languages. In recent years there has been an increasing interest in the use of parallel corpora, consisting of texts and their translations, as a resource for language learning and teaching, but as monolingual corpora and concordancing is already a very broad area, the authors have decided that parallel corpora are beyond the scope of this chapter. Consequently this area will only be briefly mentioned where it appears particularly appropriate.

Within corpus linguistics the development from research on language use to research focusing on applications in language teaching and learning is quite a recent phenomenon. The 'trickle down' from research to teaching, to paraphrase Geoffrey Leech, a pioneering corpus linguist who began using corpora for language learning purposes as early as 1976, is inextricably linked with techno-logical developments:

> While computers were limited to large mainframes available to the initiated few, computer corpora were largely restricted to research use. But as computers have grown smaller, cheaper, and massively more powerful, their use in teaching has grown immeasurably. It is natural that the movement from research to teaching has taken place in this way, as the information revolution in the use of computers has more and more extended itself from the laboratory to the classroom.
>
> (Leech, 1997: 2)

This expansion is also largely due to a dominant trend in language teaching theory over the last twenty years which involved a shift, from what Laurillard (1993) has termed 'teaching as imparting knowledge' to 'teaching as mediating learning' (1993: 14). In the particular case of the use of corpora in teaching, this student-centred model has been largely expounded by one leading figure, Tim Johns, who was among the first to advocate and to explore the use of corpora and concordancing in teaching. Nowadays it is commonplace to see titles such as 'Small and large corpora in language learning' (Aston, 1997); 'Improvising corpora for ELT: quick-and-dirty ways of developing corpora for language teaching' (Tribble 1997); 'Concordancing with Language Learners: Why? When? What?' (Stevens, 1995) appearing in various language journals and books. 'The corpus is no longer the sole preserve of the university or commercial research team. Teachers and students are beginning to have access to corpus resources and are beginning to work with them in interesting and creative ways' (Tribble, 1997: 116).

While increasingly vast corpora are invaluable for large research projects in linguistics, the role of the small corpus, particularly in the area of language teaching and learning, cannot be overestimated. With a little practice, a person with a reasonably good command of word-processing skills can easily create a small untagged corpus of between 10,000 and 20,000 words in 20 or 30 minutes, and well known researchers in the area such as Tribble emphasise that 'small, informally produced corpora can be a useful resource in the language learning/teaching project' (Tribble, 1997: 106). Aston (1997), defining a small corpus as being typically between 20,000 and 200,000 words, underlines that using a small corpus has many advantages for those without the training to enable them to work with large corpora, even if access to the larger collections of texts were easily available. He notes the following advantages over their much larger counterparts: they are easier to manage; easier to become familiar with; easier to interpret; easier to construct; easier to reconstruct; more clearly patterned; and their limits are clearer. He concludes:

> To sum up, I would suggest that work with small specialised corpora can be not only a valuable activity in its own right, as a means of discovering the characteristics of a particular area of language use, but also an instrument to help and train learners to use larger ones appropriately.
>
> (Aston, 1997: 61)

Thus a language teacher could create a corpus using newspaper articles in electronic form, or e-mails or other texts produced by native speakers of the target language. As we shall see presently, these can then be used in either of two ways. On the one hand they provide an invaluable resource for the teacher to check on native speaker language use and to create examples and exercises based on authentic texts. On the other hand, if the learners themselves have access to PCs and (inexpensive) concordancing software, they can be encouraged to consult the corpora directly to construct their own learning, and perhaps even to use this direct access to the data to call into question the authority of the teacher.

It is of course important to note that the electronic texts, which form such excellent raw material for text corpora, are subject to copyright, with the result that teachers creating corpora and making them available to their students must ensure that they have the appropriate permission. A simple authorisation form signed by native speakers participating in an e-mail exchange could enable a teacher to produce an extremely useful corpus of authentic language by people of the same age and with the same interests as their counterparts learning the language. Furthermore, many editors of newspapers will grant permission for their texts to be used, although they might become less enthusiastic if flooded by letters of request from thousands of individual language teachers. This is an area where a concerted action by a broad-based association supporting teachers of a particular language could be very successful in ensuring that teachers have access to material in electronic form with permission from those who own the copyright.

3. Concordancing software

The primary tool in all corpus study is the concordancer, a user-friendly software package designed to enable the user to discover patterns that exist in the corpus under investigation by grouping text in such a way that the patterns are clearly visible, thus making it possible to go straight to the primary source – the language actually in use. The output produced by the concordancer is known as a concordance:

> A concordance is a list of occurrences of a particular word, part of a word or combination of words, in its contexts drawn from a text corpus. The most common way of displaying a concordance on screen or as print-out is by a series of lines with the keyword in context (KWIC-format).
>
> (Botley *et al.*, 1996: 6)

For example, this concordance of 'learner' in a draft of this chapter, has been produced in a few minutes using *Monoconc*.

...than teaching, and more particularly on	[[learner]]	autonomy and self-directed learning, wi...
...authentic materials of relevance to the	[[learner]]	rather than reliance on published cours...
...c form makes it easy for the autonomous	[[learner]]	to find authentic material - in the for...
...arly for the changing roles of language	[[learner]]	and teacher. Text corpora: fro...
...onable authority to something which the	[[learner]]	can question, explore and hopefully com...
...arner's questions. It is then up to the	[[learner]]	to find the answers. Various types of c...
..radigm in language learning focusing on	[[learner]]	autonomy, namely encouragement of
...al dictionary and grammar, enabling the	[[learner]]	to find relevant examples of authentic...
...exercises such as comparing 'samples of	[[learner]]	writing with native speaker text ...

Concordances are not a new phenomenon. They have been in use since the Middle Ages. Originally concordancing was a paper-based method of analysing valuable texts such as the Bible or the works of Shakespeare. The simple reason for this restriction is that the work involved in compiling a complete concordance for any large text by hand is so huge that only texts which were studied repeatedly were chosen. In more recent times, concordancing has been used by language teachers and learners, encouraged by the work of Tim Johns. For Johns and a growing number of language teachers using ICT in the language classroom, concordancing and corpus-based exercises are useful because they 'favour learning by discovery – the study of grammar (or vocabulary, or discourse, or style) takes on the character of research, rather than spoonfeeding' (Tribble and Jones, 1990: 12). The concordancer challenges the role of a set text in the learning process. The text changes from being an unquestionable authority to something which the learner can question, explore, and hopefully come to understand. Essentially, what the corpus and the concordancer do is provide the evidence needed to answer the learner's questions. It is then up to the learner to find the answers. Various types of concordancers are now widely available to language researchers and teachers alike, some of which are available as freeware from the Internet. *MonoConc* is a simple user-friendly concordance package especially suited to pedagogic applications. The program's basic outputs are KWIC concordances, such as that given above, and frequency lists, but it also has a facility allowing the user to blank out the search-word allowing for a wide range of language exercises to be generated. A free version of this program is available for the Macintosh user. For PC users, a license fee is required. A more sophisticated package for more detailed analyses with proficient language learners is *Wordsmith Tools*. This set of tools, developed by Mike Scott, not only allow the user to produce wordlists and KWIC concordances but also to compare wordlists, to identify and extract collocations and word clusters, to produce graphs of the distribution of words through a text or corpus amongst other things. A more detailed glossary of concordancers with information on where to get them is available in McEnery and Wilson (2001).

4. Using corpora in language learning

It is in the area of teaching and learning vocabulary and grammar that the concordancer has had the greatest impact. In the mid 1980s it was first described as the 'language learner's research tool' (Johns, 1986: 151), the basis for what has become known as 'data-driven learning' (DDL), in which 'the learner's own discovery of grammar-based on evidence from authentic language use becomes central to the learning process' (Stevens, 1995: 3). Johns's examples include the use of concordance printouts by the teacher to create exercises, for example on the use of prepositions in English (1986: 160) or on the presence or absence of the definite article in English, which he describes as a notoriously difficult area for learners (Tim Johns's Virtual DDL Library). Learners are given concordance printouts of examples of the definite article and zero article and are then given the following exercise, in which they must decide if the definite article should be included or omitted.

1.   they would all get jobs in _____ British industry, Still more alarmist about the flow of ski
2.   ne lead-free fuel. And _____ British car industry, in the face of mounting environmental and
3.   ith the huge expansion in _____ chemical industry that took place after the Second World War
4.   and on Hunt's knowledge of _____ modern industry, It is lavishly illustrated [sic], partly in colo
5.   research on new ideas in _____ European industry. One of the major aims of the shake-up is
6.   for storage heaters). _____ electricity industry does not intend to make a habit of cutting
7.   to seek firm proposals from _____ private industry to take over the government's remote-sensi

8. olic work. Glucose is used by _____ food industry mainly in the manu-
   facture of confectionary
9. rea used to be the centre of _____ heavy industry. For 100 years after 1830,
   when the Cathol
10. ical profession and _____ pharmaceutical industry has tottered from crisis
    to crisis now for
11. management, such as _____ manufacturing industry, local authorities,
    reclamation and recycl
12. left _____ French information-technology industry in a mess - at least
    compared with America

Rather than simply being presented with a set of rules, the learners infer the rules from the examples and then apply their knowledge in exercises created from authentic texts. It is easy for a teacher of any language to create a corpus which can then be used as a source of exercises. The authors of this chapter have used concordance printouts on the use of 'ce qui' and 'ce que' in French, for example, and colleagues in German have produced printouts suitable for beginners on the distinction between 'sondern' and 'aber'. A variety of examples of exercises is provided in the section on corpora and concordancing in the Web site of the LINGUA ICT4LT project . More recently Johns, Rézeau and others use parallel corpora to create exercises which can be used in more than one language, and examples of these are available on the World Wide Web (see, for example, Tim Johns's Virtual DDL Library and Joseph Rézeau's homepage).

Another early recommendation of Johns is even more in keeping with the new paradigm in language learning focusing on learner autonomy, namely encouragement of learners to use the concordancer on their own initiative as a language learning resource.

> One possibility with which we have experimented is its use in helping students to correct their written work, some mistakes being underlined and a 'C' placed in the margin signifying 'You have used this word in a way which is different from how an English person would use it: if you get a concordance of the word you should be able to work out a suitable correction for yourself.
>
> (Johns, 1986: 161)

In this scenario the corpus and the concordancer provide a much richer resource than the conventional dictionary and grammar, enabling the learner to find relevant examples of authentic language in use. Needless to say, all this pre-supposes that the learners have access to corpora of suitable texts to consult in the target language, or that they are capable of creating corpora to meet their needs. This type of activity opens up a vision in which advanced learners can effectively create their own customised language learning materials, and improve their language skills by consulting examples of authentic use.

Despite the increasing popularity of the concordancer as a language learning tool, and the claims concerning its potential made by several researchers, there has been relatively little empirical research attempting to quantify the benefits to learners of using the concordancer. A notable exception is Cobb's study of the role of the concordancer in vocabulary acquisition, which revealed that learners using a concordancer had measurably better results than the control group (Cobb, 1997). More recently, Kennedy and Miceli evaluate intermediate students' use of a corpus of their own compilation, Contemporary Written Italian Corpus (CWIC), reporting on how they guide students in the use of the corpus for both problem-solving and what they call 'treasure-hunting' or 'finding models of ways to express things' (2001: 79). They conclude that there is a need for 'the development of appropriate research habits – incorporating observation and logical reasoning as well as techniques in corpus searching' (2001: 88). Despite research such as this, which provides a sound basis for the development of new literacies in language studies, the fact remains that there is still a need for substantial empirical studies in this area.

5. Translation and LSP

As it is increasingly accepted that consulting a corpus with the help of a concordancer is an effective way of acquiring vocabulary and discovering how native speakers use it, it is not surprising that specialised corpora have come to be regarded as a useful resource for those wishing to acquire knowledge of specialised language use, either as translators or as students or specialists in the field. In recent years a considerable amount of research has focused on the development and use of parallel corpora as a resource in the teaching of translation (see, for example, Botley, McEnery and Wilson, 2000). In addition Bowker (1998) has evaluated the use of a specialised monolingual native-language corpus in the teaching of translation into the native language, concluding that the corpus is a more useful resource than conventional resources used by translators:

> The general trend shows that for the categories of subject comprehension, term choice, and non-idiomatic expression, students using the corpus made significantly fewer errors than students using conventional resources. For the remaining two categories, namely grammatical errors and register, students using the corpus performed only marginally better than students using conventional resources.
>
> (Bowker, 1998: 645)

Examples of successful translations done by all the students using the concordancer include 'flatbed scanner' for 'scanner à plat', whereas almost half of the control group mistranslated this as 'flat scanner'. Bowker's method can easily be applied by teachers of translation, creating a small corpus to serve as a resource for their students in addition to conventional dictionaries. In one such exercise at the University of Limerick, some students translating a text about the closure of a nuclear reactor from French to English were able to create and consult a small corpus of texts written in English on the same subject. The corpus was easily compiled from articles found through an Internet search, using the name of the reactor as the search word. Those students who consulted the corpus showed greater command of the relevant terminology than those who did not, for example referring to the 'decommissioning' of the reactor rather than simply its closure. Interestingly, Bowker comments that some students in her pilot study were uneasy with the corpus tools and concludes, like Kennedy and Miceli (2001), that there is a need for training in the use of the corpus analysis tool.

It is in the area of Languages for Specific Purposes (LSP) that the earliest known use of corpora in language teaching is to be found; McEnery and Wilson (1997: 6) name Peter Roe's use of specialist corpora in 1969 as the first example. The advantages of having access to authentic language use in a specialised area are obvious in a situation where neither the teacher not the learners may have a high level of expertise in the area being studied. Tribble and Jones (1990: 66) suggest exercises such as comparing 'samples of learner writing with native speaker text. [...] Learners are initially asked if they can distinguish the non-native speaker text from the native speaker. Once they have worked this out they are asked to say if they can find any language items that are common to both sets of text but which are used differently'. The concordancer is then used to examine the native speaker text in more detail. One also finds several instances of spoken corpora being used as the basis for materials design in LSP. Adamson (1996) analyses deictic features in a corpus of science lectures to discover what aspects should be emphasised when training non-native students to understand this type of discourse. McEnery and Wilson (1997: 8) comment that LSP teaching is becoming corpus dominated in an increasing number of universities and note that large balanced corpora tend to contain sections of technical texts which can be extracted to form a separate specialised corpus. The example which they cite, the doctor-patient interaction section of the British National Corpus, does, however, also illustrate the fact that existing corpora are dominated by the English language, although this situation is now changing (see for example Barlow's Web site, http://www.ruf.rice.edu/%7Ebarlow/corpus.html, which provides links to electronic text corpora in different languages).

6. Literary studies

A dinner speech given by Professor Nelson Francis, the co-compiler of the Brown Corpus, the first computerised corpus, contained the following anecdote to explain why he was wearing a tie clip in the shape of a monkey wrench: 'One of my colleagues, a specialist in modern Irish literature was heard to remark that anyone who would use a computer on good literature was nothing but a plumber. Some of my students responded by forming a linguistic plumber's union, the symbol of which was, of course, a monkey wrench' (Thomas and Short, 1996: 6). The aversion of Professor Nelson's colleague to the use of computers on works of literature is not uncommon amongst literary scholars and is echoed by Dodd in his report on the relevance of corpora to German studies: 'colleagues in literary studies may be unaware of, indifferent to, or indeed hostile to the application of corpus-based techniques within their specialism' (2000: 13). However, the benefits to be gained from corpus-based analyses of literary studies have been well-documented by scholars such as Tribble and Jones (1990), Kettemann (1995), Dodd (2000), and McEnery and Wilson (2001) amongst others. 'The application of concordancing to the teaching of literature is a particularly fruitful area for classroom research and teaching/learning.' (Tribble and Jones, 1990: 72). 'Collocation and frequency are also likely to be instrumental in illuminating the particular qualities of texts, by enhancing our understanding of the ways in which language is employed in literary texts' (Dodd, 2000: 13). The concordancer can be used in a stylistic approach to literature giving learners 'basic insights into the structure of literary writing, while at the same time providing a motivation for reading and raising language awareness and enhancing linguistic and stylistic competence' (Kettemann, 1995: 316). These are just some of the benefits of using a concordancer on a corpus of literary texts. Let us now look at some examples.

Kettemann (1995) chose the different characterisation of men and women in an early emancipatory American short story, 'The Revolt of Mother' by Mary Freeman Wilkins (1890) to use with his learners as an experiment to prove that 'the use of concordancing in the teaching of a linguistic approach to literary analysis is motivating and rewarding' (1995: 307). Kettemann first asked his students to study the frequency list for 'The Revolt of Mother'. This is a simple command carried out by the concordancer which tells the computer to count up the occurrence of each word form and list all words in descending or ascending order of frequency, or alphabetically. This helps form an idea of what the story is about. The frequency list reveals that the story is about a farming family. From this the students can then search for farm-related or home-keeping-related vocabulary, bearing in mind that this story was written at the end of the nineteenth century. This will then lead the students to study how women and men are portrayed in the story and what roles each of them play. This is where the real role of the concordancer comes into play.

A concordance of 'she' shows some actions performed by women in the story as can be clearly seen from the extract below:

Better than any other kind.	*She*	baked twice a week. Adoniram
nny and Sammy watched.	*She*	brought out two cups and saucers,
down with her needlework.	*She*	had taken down her curlpaper
aside. 'You wipe 'em', said	*she*,	'I'll wash. There's a good power.

'She' collocates with traditional home-keeping verbs like baking, cooking, cleaning, sewing, etc. These are actions that we would expect to appear in a late nineteenth century story about a farming family. 'He', on the other hand, clearly collocates with a different class of verbs as can be seen from the example below:

Adoniram Penn's barn, while	*he*	designed it for the comfort of
her did one good thing when	*he*	fixed that stovepipe out there
except on extra occasions.	*He*	held his head high, with a
man said not another word.	*He*	hurried the horse into the farm
on Wednesday; on Tuesday	*he*	received a letter which changed

'He' works with the farm animals, 'he' designs, fixes, etc. However, a deeper probing of the search words 'he' and 'she' by the students revealed a very striking pattern. In the first half of the story 'she' was noticeably collocated with stereo-typical female duties such as cleaning and cooking but in the second half of the story there is a reversal of roles. 'She' is clearly collocated with more active verbs, which signals a change in the course of events. The structure of the story becomes more obvious. The author clearly breaks away from categorising her characters into traditional male/female roles. Whilst the human eye would probably be able to detect this change in roles as the story itself is not very long, the concordancer enabled the students to see patterns that might not have been obvious, by allowing them to interact with the text and to see the search word highlighted in the middle of the screen. Aside from stylistic analyses, corpora and concordancing can also be used to study the relationships between literary texts and dominant discourses of their time; to settle questions of disputed authorship by comparing linguistic features of the disputed text with those of texts known to be by particular authors; to carry out work on semantic fields and imagery and to isolate subtle textual features within an unconventional piece of writing (Wray, Trott and Bloomer, 1998: 221).

7. Cultural studies

It is notable that the potential of corpora in cultural studies has only recently begun to be explored (McEnery and Wilson, 2001). The only studies, which the authors are currently aware of, that exploit corpora for the study of culture, relate not to research focusing on applications in language learning but to research on language use. Leech and Fallon (1992) analysed the results of frequency comparisons of the Brown and LOB corpora to study the ways in which words were being used. Some of their results revealed cultural differences, for example, words relating to crime and the military were much more prevalent in the American Brown Corpus than in the British LOB Corpus (see Leech and Fallon, 1992, for more details). Stubbs (1996) carried out an analysis of some twenty words central to contemporary British culture to show how corpus data can be used 'to study the cultural connotations of words [...] which signal some central British cultural preoccupations' (1996: 157). Amongst the examples were the analysis of statements by British public figures about language in education, for example. McEnery and Wilson (2001) conclude their synopsis of 'Corpora and Cultural Studies' with this observation:

> Although such work is still in its infancy and requires methodological refinement, it seems an interesting and promising line which, peda-gogically, could also more closely integrate work in language learning with that in national cultural studies.
>
> (2001: 129)

The authors of this chapter have introduced training in corpus analysis skills for the purpose of text analysis at undergraduate level in the University of Limerick. In a module entitled Language and Technology students of French, German, Spanish, and Irish, together with ERASMUS students, choose an area of interest, and each student creates and analyses a corpus of approximately 20,000 words. The subjects range from literary texts, often short stories, to topical subjects covered in newspaper articles. Studies of the presentation of one or more political figures in newspapers with differing political tendencies are common, as are areas covered in other parts of the students' programmes of study. For example, one student analysed the defensive position adopted by the French in relation to their language. She gathered 28 articles from the French newspaper *Le Monde* which focused on defending the French language. After reading some of the articles and looking at the frequency list for her corpus, she chose to focus on three keywords which she felt revealed the most interesting results and she analysed them in detail. Her first search word was the word 'langue'. This search resulted in 172 matches. From these the student was provided with obvious and emphatic evidence that France has adopted a defensive strategy as regards the preservation and safeguarding of its language. She discovered that the pride and delight of the French concerning their language was emphasised by words such as 'amour', 'vitalité', and 'respect', and that this pride and delight was often accompanied by an underlying sense of duty, with the word 'défense' appearing quite frequently as well as other words with defensive connotations such as 'police de la langue' and 'gendarmes'. Another interesting discovery concerned the word 'avenir'. While it only occurred 6 times, on 3 of these occasions the word 'défense' appeared on the same line. In the student's own words, *'To many French people the future of the language is clearly entwined with a defensive and protective strategy'*. Other subjects chosen by students include a comparative analysis of attitudes to racism in France and Ireland; a comparative analysis of attitudes to religion in France and Ireland; a textual analysis of the presentation of two French political figures in newspapers of various persuasions; an analysis of the presentation of the abortion issue in the Irish press.

8. Conclusion

Since this chapter has presented a very positive picture of the wide variety of uses of corpora and concordancing software in language learning and teaching, the reader may wonder why their use is still limited to enthusiasts and researchers in the area and has not spread to language learners and teachers in general. It is as if the use of dictionaries was mainly confined to lexicographers. McEnery and Wilson note that often 'teachers whose main interest is not in the use of corpora *per se*, but who would like to use corpus data in teaching, may be ill-equipped to house gigantic text collections, and are justifiably ill-disposed to learning SGML or whatever other markup language is necessary to exploit a corpus effectively' (1997: 9). The acquisition of the important new literacy of corpus creation, management and analysis, thus remains the major obstacle to the integration of corpora and concordancing into language learning and teaching in general. Even efforts at popularising the use of small untagged corpora (see, for example, Aston, 1997, and Tribble, 1997) do not appear to have succeeded in overcoming this obstacle. It is, after all, easy to look up a dictionary, even if a substantial number of language learners have somewhat limited skills in dictionary consultation. So in conclusion we can see two possible future scenarios. Either the acquisition of new literacies such as this will be integrated into educational structures, thus creating an environment in which corpora and concordancing will be able to fulfil their potential. Or a popularised, uncomplicated version of corpora and concordancing, involving perhaps the consultation of small or medium-sized untagged corpora, will become the norm. The corpus, as a type of dictionary of language in use, will then be able to alter the roles of learners and teachers by giving both the role of researchers working alongside each other with access to examples of real language use in a variety of areas.

Bibliography

Adamson, R. (1996) 'Science French: The language and structure of *cours magistraux*'. In F. Royall and J.E. Conacher (eds.) *Issues in Languages for Specific Purposes: Theoretical Approaches and Practical Applications.* Limerick: University of Limerick Press, 89–104.

Aijmer, K., and B. Altenberg (1991) *English Corpus Linguistics: Studies in Honour of Jan Svartvik.* London and New York: Longman.

Aston, G. (1997) 'Small and large corpora in language learning'. In B. Lewandowska-Tomaszczyk and J.P. Melia (eds.) *Practical Applications in Language Corpora*, 51–62.

Barlow, M. (1996) *MonoConc for Windows.* Houston, Texas: Athelstan.

Botley, S., Glass, J., McEnery, T. and A. Wilson (eds.) (1996) *Proceedings of Teaching and Language Corpora 1996.* Lancaster: University Centre for Computer Corpus Research on Language (UCREL) Technical Papers.

Botley, S., McEnery A. and A. Wilson (2000) *Multilingual Corpora in Teaching and Research.* Amsterdam: Rodopi.

Bowker, L. (1998) 'Using specialized monolingual native-language corpora as a translation resource: A pilot study'. *Meta*, 43.4, 631–51.

Cobb, T. (1997) 'Is there any measurable learning from hands-on concordancing?'. *System*, 25.3, 301–15.

Dodd, B. (2000) 'The relevance of corpora to German Studies'. In B. Dodd (ed.) *Working with German Corpora.* Birmingham: University of Birmingham Press, 1–39.

Francis, W.N. and H. Kucera (1964, revised 1970) *Manual of Information to Accompany 'A Standard Sample of Present-Day Edited American English, for Use with Digital Computers'.* Providence, RI: Department of Linguistics, Brown University.

Johansson, S., Leech, G. and H. Goodluck (1978) *Manual of Information to Accompany the Lancaster-Oslo-Bergen Corpus of British English, for Use with Digital Computers.* Oslo: Department of English, Oslo University.

Johns, T. (1986) 'Micro-Concord: A language learner's research tool'. *System*, 14.2, 151–62.

Johns, T. (1991) 'Should you be persuaded: Two examples of data driven learning'. In T. Johns and P. King (eds.) (1991) *Classroom Concordancing. ELR Journal*, 4, 1–16.

Kennedy, G. (1998) *An Introduction to Corpus Linguistics*. London and New York: Longman.

Kennedy, C. and T. Miceli (2001) 'An evaluation of intermediate students' approaches to corpus investigation'. *Language Learning and Technology*, 5.3, 77–90.

Kettemann, B. (1995) 'Concordancing in stylistics teaching'. In W. Grosser, Hogg, J. and K. Hubmeyer (eds.) *Style: Literary and Non-Literary. Contemporary Trends in Cultural Stylistics*. New York: The Edwin Mellen Press, 307–18.

Laurillard, D. (1993) *Re-thinking University Teaching: A Framework for the Effective Use of Educational Technology*. London; New York: Routledge.

Leech, G. (1997) 'Teaching and language corpora: a convergence'. In A. Wichmann, S. Fligelstone, T. McEnery and G. Knowles (eds.) (1997) *Teaching and Language Corpora*, 1–23.

Leech, G. and R. Fallon (1992) 'Computer corpora – what do they tell us about culture?' *ICAME Journal*, 16, 29–50.

Lewandowska-Tomaszczyk, B. and J.P. Melia (eds.) (1997) *Practical Applications in Language Corpora*. Lodz: Lodz University Press.

McEnery, T. and A. Wilson (eds.) (1996) *Corpus Linguistics*. Edinburgh: Edinburgh University Press.

McEnery, T. and A. Wilson (1997) 'Teaching and language corpora'. *ReCALL*, 9.1, 5–14.

McEnery, T. and A. Wilson (eds.) (2001) *Corpus Linguistics*. (2nd edn) Edinburgh: Edinburgh University Press.

Quirk, R. (1992) 'On corpus principles and design'. In J. Svartik (ed.) *Directions in Corpus Linguistics: Proceedings of Nobel Symposium 82*. Berlin: Mouton de Gruyter, 457–69.

Rundell, M. (1996) 'The corpus of the future and the future of the corpus'. Paper delivered at a conference on New Trends in Reference Science, University of Exeter. http://www.ruf.rice.edu/~barlow/futcrp.html

Sinclair, J. (1991) *Corpus, Concordance, Collocation*. Oxford: Oxford University Press.

Scott, M. and T. Johns (1993) *MicroConcord*. Oxford: Oxford University Press.

Scott, M. (1996) *Wordsmith Tools*. Oxford: Oxford University Press.

Stevens, V. (1995) 'Concordancing with language learners: Why? When? What?'. *CAELL Journal*, 6.2, 2–10. Also available at: http://www.ruf.rice.edu/~barlow/stevens.html

Stubbs, M. (1996) *Text and Corpus Analysis: Computer-assisted Studies of Language and Culture*. Oxford: Blackwell.

Thomas, J., and M. Short (1996) *Using Corpora for Language Research: Studies in Honour of Geoffrey Leech*. London and New York: Longman.

Tribble, C. (1997) 'Improvising corpora for ELT: Quick-and-dirty ways of developing corpora for language teaching' in B. Lewandowska-Tomaszczyk and J.P. Melia (eds.) *Practical Applications in Language Corpora*, 106–17.

Tribble, C. and G. Jones (1990) *Concordances in the Classroom*. London and New York: Longman.

Wichmann, A., Fligelstone, S., McEnery, T. and G. Knowles (eds.) (1997) *Teaching and Language Corpora*. London and New York: Longman.

Wolff, D. (1997) 'Computers as cognitive tools in the language classroom'. In A.-K. Korsvold and B. Rüschoff (eds.) *New Technologies in Language Learning and Teaching*. Strasbourg: Council of Europe Publishing, 17–26.

Wray, A., Trott, K. and Bloomer, A. (1998) *Projects in Linguistics: A Practical Guide to Researching Language*. London: Arnold.

Web sites

http://web.bham.ac.uk/johnstf/timconc.htm

This is the Web site of Tim Johns, one of the pioneers of concordance-based research and teaching. This 'data-driven learning page' contains an excellent Virtual DDL Bibliography of work in concordancing and brings together references to the direct use of data from linguistic corpora for language teaching and language learning. It also contains information on and demos of many concordance programs and provides a set of links to many other useful Web sites on concordancing.

http://www.georgetown.edu/cball/corpora/tutorial.html

This tutorial surveys free and commercial sources for electronic text corpora, and provides a critical review of concordancers as tools for discovering facts about language. The tutorial includes a demonstration of a popular scanner (HP Scanjet IIp) and OCR package (TypeReader) for creating electronic text, and uses Internet resources to find and retrieve free texts in various languages.

http://www.tsrali.com

TransSearch is an online bilingual concordancing program which allows for searches of the parallel bilingual English-French Canadian Hansard corpus and a corpus composed of documents drawn from the collected decisions of the Supreme Court of Canada, the Federal Court of Canada and the Tax Court of Canada. The documents selected range in date from 1986 to the present. There is a fee for using this parallel concordancer.

http://www.ruf.rice.edu/%7Ebarlow/corpus.html

This Web site is maintained by Michael Barlow at Rice University. It provides links to electronic text corpora in different languages, allows you to carry out searches on various corpora, presents a number of different concordancers and taggers and boasts an extensive bibliography and links to other corpus linguistics and concordancing Web sites.

http://info.ox.ac.uk/bnc/corpora.html
This page lists centres and projects from which language corpora (chiefly English language) are readily available. It also includes excellent links to resources of general interest for those working on corpus linguistics.

http://www.hit.uib.no/text.htm
This Web site is maintained by ICAME (International Computer Archive of Modern and Medieval English). This link provides information on texts, text centres, resources, and concordance programs on the Web amongst other things.

http://cedric.cnam.fr/ABU/
This Web site hosted by the Association des Bibliophiles Universels (ABU) contains a huge database of French literary works ranging from Balzac to Stendhal to Zola. There is an online concordancer which allows users to carry out concordances on the complete database of literary texts.

http://www.ruf.rice.edu/~barlow/stevens.html
Michael Barlow's Web site includes an article entitled, 'Concordancing with language learners. Why? When? What?'. Written by Vance Stevens, it begins with a brief introduction to the history of concordancing. It then focuses on the use of concordancing as a tool for language learning and finally argues for the use of concordancing in the classroom.

http://www.dundee.ac.uk/english/wics/wics.htm
This Web site offers Web concordances on the poetry of Shelley, Coleridge, Blake, Keats, and Hopkins amongst others and even workbooks and study guides to be used alongside the Web concordances.

http://www.sussex.ac.uk/langc/CALL.html
The Virtual CALL Library aims to be a central point of access to the diverse collection of Computer Assisted Language Learning (CALL) software scattered across the Internet and available for downloading.

http://www.uhb.fr/campus/joseph.rezeau/concord.htm

Joseph Rézeau's homepage contains several examples of exercises in French and English, created using a parallel corpus.

http://www.ict4lt.org/en/index.htm

The ICT4LT Web site, dedicated to Information and Communications Technology for Language Teachers, contains a broad range of training materials that are freely available in four languages: English, Italian, Finnish, and Swedish. Modules of relevance to the content of this chapter include: 'Using concordance programs in the modern foreign languages classroom', by M.-N. Lamy and H. J. Klarskov Mortensen, with an introduction by G. Davies; and 'Corpus linguistics', by T. McEnery and A. Wilson.

10 Speech in action: Teaching listening with the help of ICT

Richard Cauldwell

1. Introduction

listening

The benefits of ICT are often spoken of in terms of learner autonomy and methodology, and much of the literature on the teaching and learning of listening is similarly concerned with learner strategies and methodology. This paper argues that ICT can not only provide a new pedagogic relationship between teacher, mode of delivery, and student, but can also provide a new and refreshing perspective on the content of language teaching. By 'content' is meant the knowledge, the syllabus for teaching – the material that teachers deliver to students. ICT can provide insights into the forms of everyday spontaneous speech. With such insights, and the technology which enables them, we can tame everyday spontaneous speech and make it learner and teacher-friendly. ICT can *context* do this by helping with the design of listening comprehension exercises which focus both on the interpretation of meaning and on the forms of speech which gives substance to these meanings. ICT provides a number of different ways of dividing up and annotating the stream of speech which make it possible to observe and internalise the features of natural fast spontaneous speech.

Despite the extensive use of natural recordings of everyday spontaneous speech in the tapes accompanying main-course textbooks, listening remains the skill that lags behind the others: speaking, reading, and writing. There are number of reasons for this. First, in everyday listening, language is at its least controllable as far as the recipient is concerned. The control lies with the person producing the language: accent, speed, vocabulary, and volume are all speaker-determined features of speech. Second, listening is, in the main, a once-only experience. Although it is possible to get repeats of what was said, you cannot do it all the time without alienating the speaker. Third, listening is not as amenable to pedagogic exhortation: there is no listening equivalent to pronunciation's 'put your tongue on that ridge behind your upper teeth'. The metalanguage for teaching listening tends to focus on strategies and methodology. 'When you hear a word for the first time, ignore it' (Helgesen and Brown, 1994: ix) rather than on the forms of the incoming signal. Fourth, there is no syllabus for listening – there is no set of items to be covered in the same way that there is a pronunciation syllabus, there is little that can be identified as unique to listening. Only the first eight of Richards's (1985: 198–9) lists of 51 microskills for conversational and academic listening could truly said to be unique to listening. Fifth, listening is often done as an activity in pursuit of goals other than listening.

This paper argues that the traditional association of reading and listening, as two components of the receptive skill, has hampered the development of the pedagogy of listening (Section 2). There are advantages in thinking of listening as more associated with speaking. Traditional phonology – concerned as it has been with explaining the role and status of citation forms – has not provided the guidance that the effective teaching of listening requires (Section 3). ICT, in the hands of teachers, can help in this situation: it provides a way of observing the stream of speech which preserves its essential nature as a real-time infinitely variable stream, and permits the teaching of listening in the classroom to levels which are normally thought to require immersion in the target language environment.

Listening comprehension exercises in the classroom typically confuse activities with goals, there are very few moments in which students are taught, or have the opportunity to learn about the stream of speech (Section 4). There are patterns in the stream of speech ('speech units') which are typically multi-word units in which the sound-shapes of the words varies to a great extent according to their positions in the speech unit. ICT allows the inspection of the fate of such words, thus allowing students and teachers to see how the variety of soundshapes relate to the dictionary (citation) form of the words Section 5). A goal for listening comprehension activities is suggested. ICT, with its capacity to isolate key moments in a recording, allows immediate and repeated playback of these moments, and is therefore an important tool in transforming listening activities into true listening-goal-directed pedagogical experiences (Section 6). ICT can also provide solutions for the problem of the methodological gap in the teaching of listening, it can provide direct encounters (Cauldwell, 1996) with the essential nature of speech (its real-time acoustic substance) which can take students from (a perhaps frustrated) incomprehension to both perceptual and interpretive success (Section 7). There is then a demonstration, as far as it is possible to give one in print, of how a listening comprehension exercise would go, if it were to follow the principles outlined in the earlier sections (Section 8). The software is described and some teacher pre-requisites and needs are outlined (Sections 9–10).

2. The four skills

Traditionally, the four skills have been viewed as divided into two categories, Productive and Receptive, as shown in Table 1.

Productive	*Speaking*	*Writing*
Receptive	*Listening*	*Reading*

Table 1: Productive and receptive skills.

This table shows speaking and writing belonging together in the same category, they are twinned as being the two skills related to the task of producing language. Similarly, reading and listening are twinned as being the two components related to the task of receiving language. This method of twinning has been useful in that it has given a framework for conceptualising the four skills in a way which provided *methodological* solutions to the problems of teaching listening. From reading methodology, listening methodology has borrowed the concepts of gist/skimming/scanning perception and comprehension strategies.

The problem with this borrowing is that work on listening-skills has been dominated by approaches to the teaching and testing of reading. This is generally justified by assertions that there is a general ability for language comprehension which underlies listening and reading: but because it is easier to handle written texts than spoken texts, comprehension work, though it may start with a listening, often ends up being a reading activity. Harmer's (1991) otherwise excellent teacher training textbook exemplifies this point: his treatment of listening, in the chapter on receptive skills (Chapter 10) contains examples of listening comprehension activities, almost all of which are aimed at improving the level of general comprehension without teaching the students how to cope with the essential characteristics of speech. It is worthwhile paying some attention to what Harmer writes, as it reflects so well current assumptions and practices which underlie the teaching of listening. After a brief discussion and illustration of the differences between norms of correctness for the written and the spoken language Harmer writes, 'It is our job when training students in listening skills to help them to disregard [... hesitation, reformulation, and topic change ...] and to concentrate instead on the main message of what is being said' (1991: 212). Now there is a logical problem here: you can only disregard something that you have already noticed. You need to have noticed what you are going to disregard in order to distinguish it from those stretches of speech that you need to 'concentrate on'. This may seem to be a quibble on my part, but it is not, it is a serious point. Students have to be able to understand the bits they are going to disregard in order that they can make appropriate choices of what to disregard.

In being expected to disregard speech phenomena that are not part of the 'main message' the student is being urged to adopt native-speaker comprehension strategies. Although they may well use these strategies in their own first language, it is unreasonable to expect students to do this – untaught – in a second language. Students are expected, exhorted, to employ listening strategies without being taught a major prerequisite for their effective use. The prerequisite is the ability to attend to and perceive accurately as much of the acoustic blur of speech as is necessary for their communicative purposes. The reason why textbooks and teacher trainers recommend such practices is because of a lack of adequate descriptions of what happens in the stream of everyday spontaneous speech, and the lack of a classroom methodology for helping students become familiar and comfortable with the stream of speech: 'Ignore what you don't understand' becomes the unhelpful cry.

It is important to un-twin the reading/listening and speaking/writing pairs and to recombine them so that we can think in new ways about the teaching of listening. Table 2 re-categorises the four skills so that speaking and listening are seen as twinned components of the spoken language – as two sides of the same coin.

| Spoken Language | *Speaking* | *Listening* |
| Written Language | *Writing* | *Reading* |

Table 2: Spoken and written language.

Table 2 also encourages viewing the spoken and written languages as different entities requiring different descriptions and pedagogical treatments. This kind of assertion is not uncommon (see, for example, McCarthy, 1998), but it is possible to exaggerate the difference – assertions are often underjustified by the evidence – but there is a crucial difference which (strange as it may seem) is often ignored by native-speaker teachers, teacher-trainers, and academics. The crucial difference is that speech is streamlike in its infinite variability: as a consequence words in the stream of speech have an incredible variety of soundshapes. There will be more on this point in the sections below. Before leaving Table 2, it is worth making one further point. Viewing speaking and listening as two sides of the same coin leads to consideration of the extent to which our teaching of pronunciation and listening present a consistent view of the spoken language. It is my contention that traditional pronunciation exercises, focusing as they do on the clear pronunciation of segments and citation forms of words, actually misrepresent the essential real-time nature of the stream of speech.

3. Deficiencies in phonology

One troubling issue is the unquestioning attitude we have to the content of the training that teachers and learners get in phonology for language teaching. Content such as the inventory of phonemes, syllable structure, sentence stress, and question intonation are assumed to represent some central, essential-to-be-taught, truth. This content is derived from the phonology and phonetics departments of universities – and is thus handed down in textbooks, and teacher-training manuals.

Of course, this content has helped us: the inventory of phonemes has helped with the creation of pronunciation exercises; contrastive analysis of the target language and the first language has enabled people to devise pronunciation exercises which help specific groups of language learners. However, this type of work has depended on a stable norm for pronunciation, Received Pronunciation for British English and General American for the USA, and these stable norms are now under attack (Jenkins, 2000). It has also been dependent on the articulatory description of how speakers produce citation forms in isolation or sequence. It has had implications for pronunciation – where it is possible to focus on most of the small movements of the vocal organs at slow speeds, which suit the learner's own speed of learning. However, it has had little to contribute to the teaching of listening – where the speed of the language is not under the learner's control, and where there is little or nothing to do in terms of physical encouragement from the teacher or physical movement on the part of the student.

4. Listening activities

One of the problems with contemporary approaches to listening in the classroom, particularly with Communicative Language Teaching, is that the focus is on listening-as-an-activity rather than listening-as-a-goal. White (1987) asked a range of teachers of differing nationalities why they valued listening materials. The left-hand column of Table 3 lists the replies as published in Anderson and Lynch (1988: 66) and the right-hand column (added by myself) relates these activities to their apparent goals.

None of the reasons listed in the left-hand column relate directly to the listening skill. In my view, these reasons imply a focus on the goals listed in the right-hand column: so that (for example) a listening activity which is 'good for starting discussions' is serving a speaking goal. Listening is thus relegated to the status of a servant with speaking as the master. The only item on the list which might be directly linkable to the skill of listening is 'practises guessing from

Reason	Implied Goal
good for starting discussions	speaking skills
can be used for self-access learning	learner autonomy
contains a variety of tasks	motivation
entertaining	motivation
easy to use	teachability
practises guessing from context	general comprehension
amusing	motivation
uses authentic material	relevance
consolidates language	revision of vocab and structure

Table 3: Reasons for valuing listening materials and their apparent goals

context' which in my view is an example of linking reading and listening, which, as indicated above, is something we need to move away from.

The following sections give some indication of what needs to be taught, and what can be taught, which is unique to the listening skill, and which relates listening activities more closely to listening goals.

5. The fate of words in the stream of speech

As mentioned above, the crucial, essential feature of the stream of speech is that the sound shapes of even the most familiar words change in a wide variety of ways – often beyond the capacity of the student to perceive them. Goh (1997: 366) reports on one of her learner's (Ying's) comments on her listening problems:

> I believe I need to learn what the words sound like when it is used in the sentence. Because sometimes when a familiar word is used in a sentence, I couldn't catch it. Maybe it changes somewhere when it is used in a sentence.

To illustrate Ying's dilemma, we will focus on the fate of the word 'where' in a scripted recording taken from Brazil (1994) 'In a strange town'. A dictionary, or a pronunciation key in a dictionary will give the citation form of the pronunciation. There are four occurrences of *where* in the recording. Table 4 shows the speech units in which they occur: the speech units are shown in the left-hand column. Syllables in lower case letters are non-prominent, syllables with upper-case letters are prominent, syllables with upper-case letters and underlining are both prominent and tonic (i.e., they are the location of the tone of the speech unit).

	Speech Unit	Duration of 'where'	Intonation choice on 'where'
1	// where there were STREET LIGHTS //	0.1	non-prominent
2	// where she'd <u>SAID</u> //	0.1	non-prominent
3	// WHERE <u>MAR</u>ket street was //	0.2	prominent
4	// but i WASn't sure <u>WHERE</u> //	0.3	tonic

Table 4: The fate of 'where' in the stream of speech

In both speech units 1 and 2, *where* is non-prominent, and lasts about one tenth of a second, sounds like an abrupt truncated bleat of a lamb, and is spoken at a speed of 600 words per minute (wpm). In speech unit 3 *where* is prominent, lasts twice as long (therefore spoken at a speed of 300 wpm), and begins to resemble the citation form but is still truncated. Only in speech unit 4, in which *where* occurs before a pause does the citation form occur, at a speed of 200 wpm.

In playing these speech units to groups of learners I had not expected them to have any problems in matching what they heard with the transcripts of the speech units. In fact, they initially said that they could not hear the word *where* in speech units 1 and 2. When the non-prominent sections *where there were* and *where she'd* were isolated, they still had difficulty reconciling hearing the short sharp bleat of a sheep with their knowledge of the citation form. These learners were themselves teachers of English but their perceptual abilities were in fact being hampered by their knowledge of the citation form. The citation form was proving to be a block to improvement of their listening skills. This was astonishing for me. How could knowledge of the citation form be an obstacle to learning to listen? I now think that this was not the fault of the citation form itself, it was rather a natural consequence of the way in which the spoken language is represented and taught in language teaching. The spoken language is represented as a set of citation forms (a line of discrete segments) in the dictionary and in the pronunciation component of vocabulary lists. In natural language use, the words are streamed: the citation form (as can be seen from our examples above) only occurs under special conditions (tonic prominence before a pause). The citation form does occur, but it is a rare beast: it is a useful reference point, a useful starting point, but it is misrepresentation of speech. One of the difficulties that students have is that they expect to hear citation forms in speech, and when they fail to hear them, they attribute their failure to a lack of ability on their part, they blame themselves.

The truth is that the failure does not reside with the student, it resides with (a) the way in which the spoken language is represented (or rather misrepresented) in dictionaries and vocabulary lists and (b) the gaps in methodology. Citation forms, being brick-like, are a misrepresentation of the stream-like features of the spoken language. Listening activities, serving non-listening goals, do not teach what is vitally important to the listening skill – the ways in which the sound shapes of words vary in the stream of speech. A common argument at this point is 'It is impossible to do what you suggest as there are too many ways in which a word can vary in the stream of speech'. Rost, for example, states, '[i]t is doubtful that "fast speech rules" can be learned deductively and consciously applied in real time whenever one encounters an unfamiliar blur of sound' (1990: 57), and goes on to argue that only immersion in 'contexts of actual use' will allow learners to develop 'gradually a phonological sensitivity to the new language', leading to the adoption of 'language specific principles in decoding speech' (1990: 57). Rost's pessimism is widely felt, and is representative of the view that listening can only be learned by osmosis – by extensive exposure. It is my contention, on the contrary, that ICT offers us a means of seeing general patterns – Rost's 'fast speech rules' – in the stream of speech and to do far better with pedagogic techniques than we have done up to now. Osmosis is not a pedagogic technique – any appeal to it means that we have conceded that teaching is ineffective.

6. A goal for listening work

To improve the teaching of listening we need to readjust and refocus the teaching of listening: listening activities need to serve listening skill goals, and – methodologically – we need to do more than place our trust in osmosis. We thus need a goal for listening work. The goal of listening work should be: *to make students familiar and comfortable with the real-time acoustic blur of the stream of speech, and the way in which this stream is shaped by speakers to communicate meanings in all contexts.* This goal has a number of features worth highlighting. *First, make [...] familiar and comfortable* means that teachers have to devote time to helping students with those parts of the stream of speech that are most likely to seem strange, difficult, and frustrating. Second, by *acoustic blur* is meant the normal stream-like state of everyday spontaneous speech, where the boundaries of words are blurred together and the sound-shape of the word-bodies are altered by speaker decisions (as with *where* above) and speaker characteristics (such as gender, accent, and voice quality). Third, there is mention of the *real-time* status of speech – that it typically occurs once, quickly, and is unavailable for inspection other than in the short/medium term memory. Crucially it is unsupported by written transcription. Fourth, there is mention of both the form (*shaping the stream*) and meaning of speech: all work relating to this goal should relate to both the perception, and the interpretation of speech. Lastly there is mention of *contexts*: most of the textbook rules relating to pronunciation and listening come from an examination of decontextualised scripted language – most recordings for listening are done in studio surroundings, producing ideal, clear speech. This has resulted in students being led into false expectations concerning the acoustic clarity of what they will hear.

7. A methodological gap in listening pedagogy

It is a common criticism of listening activities that they are testing, not teaching activities: the learners are presented with questions, they hear the recording, they fill in their answer sheet, they are told what the right answers to the questions are, and then they move on to another activity (listening as servant). Most teachers are keen on this type of extensive listening (for the reasons touched on in Section 4 above) but in my view it amounts to nothing more than a classroom-based osmosis. Although there is engagement at the level of meaning, there is no serious pedagogic engagement with the essential nature (the real-time, stream-like acoustic blur) of speech.

Harmer's (1991: 228–30) chapter on listening comprehension presents three activities which show how 'detail can be accessed'. The first activity involves listening to an interview with an author, but all that Harmer recommends for accessing detail is a list of six comprehension questions (for example, 'When does John Mortimer do his writings?') which would not be out of place in a test of reading comprehension. There is no recommendation as to what to do if the students do not get the answers. The second activity 'script dictation' requires the students to fill in gaps in the script by listening to the recording: this in itself is potentially a useful activity, but unfortunately it is possible to predict the words from the written language alone, and again there is no recommendation as to what to do if students do not get the right answers. Given the limitations of audio-cassette technology, with the difficulties of rewind-inaccuracies, or the screeching of the playback heads, the easiest remedy would be to discuss the answers in terms of vocabulary learning, and/or grammatical patterns rather than in speech-unit terms. The third activity involves looking at a transcription of spontaneous speech to a recording (after having heard it twice), and students are expected to notice hesitation (thinking time) phenomena such as 'um', 'you know', and 'I mean'. The interesting thing about this activity is that it becomes a reading activity in the service of a listening goal: students are learning about real-time spontaneous speech phenomena. However, there is no direct encounter with the detail of the sound substance of these moments.

What is lacking in all these activities is a direct encounter with the sound substance of recordings at the phase in the activity when students are most ready to learn – that is when they have just completed a task set by the teacher in relation to a recording, and they know the extent to which they have been successful. The goal for listening requires that time is spent, after reviewing the answers to the task, investigating the nature of those sections of the stream of speech which were the focus of the task. This is where ICT can play its part.

8. The role of ICT in teaching listening

In this section, I illustrate the improvements that are possible for committed individuals to achieve with current technology. It is not yet possible (as far as I am aware) to buy software materials in bookshops which can do all that I describe in this section. However, in Section 9, I describe in some detail software that has been developed and used to make possible the activities described in this section.

ICT has a role in all stages of the construction and teaching of listening comprehension exercises. As far as construction is concerned it can help (a) identify those parts of a recording which are likely to challenge the students, both in terms of meaning, and in terms of perception. In other words, the issues of perception and interpretation are as inextricably linked in the exercises as they are in real life. The way in which I accomplish this is by using software (*Motormouth*) which makes it easy to identify the fastest, meaning-bearing moments in a recording. *Motormouth* aids this identification by simply counting the words in a given stretch of speech, and calculating the time between the start point and the end point, with these two figures it computes the speed in words per minute.

Motormouth helped me identify two units of speech in a recording of a colleague (Cauldwell, 1997) talking about her employment history. One feature of this recording was that the colleague spoke fastest when she spoke about money – thus making the issue of money a good candidate for incorporation into comprehension questions. There was thus the possibility of both (a) creating comprehension questions relating to the interpretation of the central issues of meaning in the recording and (b) observing how the stream of speech is patterned/structured at the highest speeds used by this speaker.

The two crucial speech units (the first referring to running a snackbar, the second referring to a textile business) were both spoken at a speed of 330 words per minute:

1   // MADE quite a bit of <u>MO</u>ney //
2   // i i didn't MAKE an awful lot of <u>MO</u>ney //

The comprehension questions relating to these speech units were:

Did Mary make a profit running a snackbar? [Answer: 'Yes']
Did Mary make a lot of money in her textile business? [Answer: 'No']

It is possible, after listening to the recording, for students to arrive at the answers to these questions in a number of ways. They may have perceived and understood everything; they may, without having perceived everything, have grasped the key meanings from these specific and neighbouring speech units; they may have inferred these answers from other points in the recording where Mary talks about her changes in job, or they may have guessed the answers. These different ways of arriving at the answers involve different levels of success in listening. And it is important for the teacher to investigate at this point the students' level of success.

Therefore the teacher should always follow up the answers by asking questions such as 'Why do you believe that is the answer?' or 'What evidence is there on the recording to justify this answer' or 'What did she say which led you to this answer?' Students should work on answering these questions without looking at the transcript – they should use their recall of what they heard by inspecting their medium-term memory. Working in this way, without the transcript, is one way of respecting the real-time nature of speech, and not transferring the task to the written medium which would run the risk of making the goal of the activity a reading goal. Where students have problems recalling the speech-units which provide the evidence for the answer, it is then important to focus on them. This is the point in the listening comprehension lesson where explicit teaching and learning about the nature of the stream of speech can take place: the point at which students can be made familiar and comfortable with the acoustic blur of speech. It is at this point that ICT comes to our aid. ICT enables us to identify and isolate short sections of the stream of speech so that they can be inspected, savoured, and learned from. These sections are so short (typically less than 2.5 seconds) that trying to access them on audio-cassette is an extremely aggravating procedure. Fortunately there are now many ways in which one can associate sound-files with text, so that merely by clicking on text, one can hear it.

As mentioned above, it is not possible, with listening (as we can do in pronunciation), to give the equivalent of 'put your tongue behind your teeth': the instruction 'incline your head to the left, and prick your ears and you will hear the correct sounds' will not work. However, there are recommendations in the teacher-training literature to get students to do something physical as they listen: to tap the desk when they hear words, and/or to watch the teacher point to the words (on the blackboard) as they occur on the tape. But these activities – though they might be helpful – are extraneous to listening: they are publicly observable physical movements which are external to the private processes of speech perception. While they may be part of a pedagogy of learning, or a motivational device, these movements are not solutions to a problem that actually requires direct engagement with the acoustic blur of speech. For a direct engagement to happen, learners need to manipulate the substance of the stream of speech – this acoustic blur – in a way which retains those characteristics of speech which distinguish it from writing. This may seem an impossible task, but the solution is in fact quite simple.

The solution is to get the students to mimic, or recreate, the features of the stream of speech in their own pronunciation. They should attempt to mouth the features of the acoustic blur that they can hear, that they have noticed, or had pointed out to them. They should, in other words, savour the acoustic blur of speech with their own physical mechanisms. They should do this not with the goal of being able to mimic the acoustic blur in their own everyday speech (though this could be a goal if they so wish) but with the goal of becoming *familiar and comfortable* with the acoustic blur of normal everyday spontaneous speech of other people. Unfortunately you are now reading a printed book, for which click-and-hear technology is not yet available. So we have to resort to the use of symbols to represent what happens in the classroom (this is, again, aggravating). Table 5 shows three ways of representing the speech-unit 'Made quite a bit of money'. The job of the teacher to demonstrate the relationships between the orthography (Row 1), the sequence of citation forms is heard with a pause between each word (Row 2), and the original speech unit (Row 3) which occurred as a continuous flow of speech (because of the blurring effects of the stream of speech on word boundaries, it is not possible to derive the Row 2 recording from the original, so it has to be separately recorded).

1	Words	made quite a bit of money
2	citation speech	meɪd kwaɪt ə bɪt ɒv mʌnɪ
3	normal speech	meikwaɪtəbɪtəvmʌnɪ

Table 5: 'Made quite a bit of money'

The teacher plays the recording of Row 2 and gets students to repeat this citation form speech (with pauses) as accurately as they can manage, respecting all the segments represented in the transcription, especially the final consonants of *made, quite, bit,* and *of.* This should preferably be done without the students seeing Table 5, or any equivalent transcription. It is shown here simply because I need a means of communicating to you as a reader in the absence of soundfiles what the relationship between the original recording and citation speech is. Thus students should do this kind of work, to begin with at least, in the absence of support from written transcription, to promote, as far as it is possible to do so, the ability to process and manipulate the stream of speech without recourse to the prop of the written medium.

The teacher should then play the original recording, here represented by Row 3, and demonstrate, either in his/her own voice, or with the use of the recordings, the relationship between the citation form version and the normal speech version of speech. This is in fact best done by the teacher, because the teacher can put in intermediate stages of blurring between the extremes of slow speech and the normal speech, by gradually increasing speed, removing pausing, increasing the extent of the deletion, and linking of sounds. But it is important to have continual reminders of the original recording, because it may have features of pitch height and tonic movements – natural features of the stream of speech – which are also worth savouring. It is also vitally important that the students mimic this process of incremental blurring and speeding up as it is their abilities in listening that we are trying to improve.

An important point to realise here relates to the earlier discussion of goals. The goal is related to the improvement of listening skills, the activity – mouthing, savouring the words – is a pronunciation activity which is serving the goal of listening. Now, it is very likely that the student's pronunciation would improve as a result of using the procedure: it is likely to provide the facility to go faster, and to mimic the 'economy features' of fast speech, to sound more fluent. However, it is not necessarily the case that the student would, however, aspire to mimic such speech. Students might be resistant to using such 'sloppy' speech as their normal way of speaking. But such practice would give them a faster gear to slip into should they find that circumstances require them to do so.

The means by which these things can be done have been developed and used in software at the University of Birmingham. It is to the description of this software that we now turn.

9. *Motormouth*

This section describes the software that I have used both to prepare and deliver listening comprehension lessons of the type described above. This software is not commercially available. The description is offered as an example of what it is possible to create given appropriate help in ICT design and implementation. In my case the help was provided by Trevor Batchelor of the University of Birmingham's Information Services, who implemented my ideas in Multimedia Toolbook 4 (Asymetrix, 1990–96).

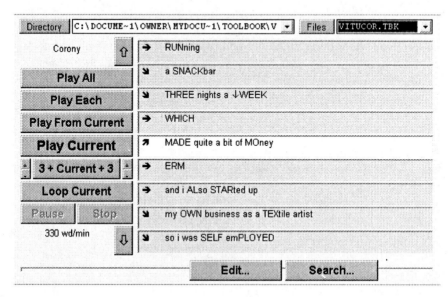

Figure 1

Figure 1 shows the main window of Motormouth. It consists of buttons down the left-hand side which control access to the sound-files which are on a Compact Disc containing audio files of the same type that you would get on a CD from your local music shop – except that they contain speech, not music. The main part of the window consists of a sequence of speech units, from 'running' to 'so i was self employed'. This window scrolls so that the speech unit which is at the centre of the window – in this case 'made quite a bit of money' – is the one which corresponds to those words being spoken on the CD. Thus Motormouth is, in essence, a CD-player with the addition of a scrolling window which shows text in time with the recording – you could use it to display the words of your favourite Beatles song in time to the music.

The CD control buttons down the left-hand side provide a variety of options for the user. The 'Play All' button plays the whole track from beginning to end, and scrolls through the whole text as described above. 'Play Each' does the same, but inserts a small pause between each speech unit; 'Play from Current' plays the track from the currently centred speech-unit; 'Play Current' plays the currently centred speech-unit only – clicking this button repeatedly provides as many repeats as the user wants. The next button, shown in Figure 1 as '1 + Current + 1' plays the centred speech-unit, plus the preceding and following units. The user can change the number of preceding and following speech-units played by clicking on the appropriate '+' and '-' buttons. Once clicked, the recording will loop through the number of speech-units selected until the 'stop' button is clicked. 'Loop Current' simply plays the currently centred speech-unit repeatedly until the stop button is clicked. Note also that just above these buttons there is the name of the speaker of the current speech-unit – Corony – and just below is the speed of the current speech-unit in words per minute – 330.

The questions arise of how the text gets into the scrolling window, and how the association is made between text and CD. The first thing to say is that this is not done automatically – it is done manually by entering text, symbols, and timings in an editing window which is accessed by clicking on the 'Edit' button below the scrolling window. Doing so brings up the window shown in Figure 2.

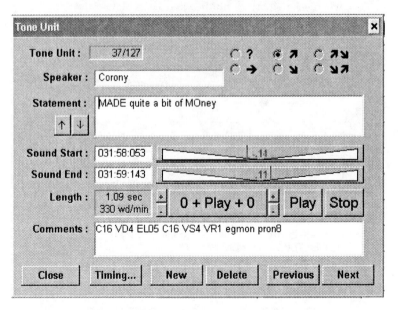

Figure 2

Figure 2 shows the editing window. I shall not give a full description of every element, I shall only describe those essential to understanding the process of creation of a *Motormouth* file. The topmost field contains the numbers 37/127 which indicates that this speech-unit ('tone-unit' is an equivalent term) is number 37 of 127; the 'Speaker' field shows that the speaker of the current speech-unit is Corony; the 'Statement' field contains the text of the current speech-unit which is entered manually according to the conventions of Discourse Intonation (Brazil, 1997); the arrow symbols below the 'Statement' field, and at the top right of the window, are also there to aid the inputting of text according to the same conventions.

The next two fields, 'Sound Start' and 'Sound End' are crucial. They are the ones that associate text and sound on the CD. The figures in these windows instruct the software as follows: 'as you play the CD and you reach minute 31, second 58, millisecond 53, make the statement *made quite a bit of money* the currently centred speech unit; and when (1.09 seconds later) you reach minute 31, second 59, millisecond 143 move to the next speech unit'. There is some automation (which I will not describe here) to help arrive at these timings, so that they do not have to be entered entirely manually. The 'Length' field gives the duration of the speech-unit, and speed of the speech-unit in words per minute. The comments field shows some codes that are there to aid searching the text.

You will recall from Figure 1 that, next to the 'Edit' button there is a 'Search' button. This, when clicked, brings up the window in Figure 3.

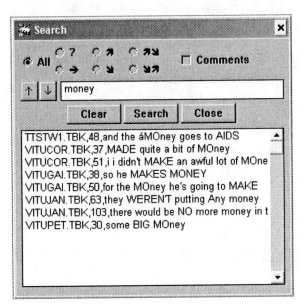

Figure 3

Once you have created a file, or a series of files, in *Motormouth* it is easy to use standard techniques to search the text, and for the results of the search to contain immediate (one click) access to both the context in which the examples occurred and (one further click) immediate access to the recording. Figure 3 shows the results for searching for speech units containing the word 'money'.

The search returned six results, from 'made quite a bit of money' to 'the money from the bananas' preceded by codes relating to files from which they came. Clicking on any one of these lines will take you to the main window for the relevant file, and one further click on the 'Play Current' button will play the relevant section of the CD. The facilities of software such as *Motormouth* to provide sound and text in immediate searchable association would, if employed appropriately, greatly improve the teaching of listening. But simply introducing the software, or products derived from it, though necessary, will not be sufficient.

10. Some pre-requisites

The previous section described the ICT contribution to a change in teaching procedures for listening comprehension, and it is clear that having access to such software and materials generated by it, would be an essential pre-requisite to effecting the changes that have been argued for. However, there also are five other, non-ICT, pre-requisites worth mentioning.

First, teachers should be sufficiently well-trained that they can themselves adequately mimic the features of the acoustic blur of speech. This requires teachers themselves to be familiar and comfortable with this acoustic blur. For this to happen, they need education in a new phonology for language teachers: one that takes the goal of listening as central. Second, traditional citation-form phonology deals with speech 'as it ought to be' or 'as it must be at some level of representation in the brain' and centres its work on the certainties of the citation form. This type of phonology will no longer do. We have reached the limits of the benefits of its assumptions and methodologies. There needs to be a new phonology with which to train teachers for listening, which takes as normal (not deviant) the infinite variability of speech.

Third, this training needs to be backed up by a technological implementation of the ideas and procedures presented in Section 8. The technology exists for this to be done, but it has not yet been implemented in such a way that it can impact widely on classroom practice.

Fourth, there needs to be a willingness on the part of teachers and students to tolerate degrees of uncertainty. Students desire to know precisely what is happening, and teachers naturally want to give precise answers as to the truth of what happens in the stream of speech. It is important however to realise that, very often, describing what has happened in a particular stretch of the stream of speech is difficult, and the honest teacher, indeed researcher, has to be prepared to say 'I don't know precisely what is happening here' or 'It's not clear what is happening here'.

Fifth, it is also important for teachers not to ignore those moments in a listening comprehension lesson in which students experience discomfort or frustration. These periods of frustration often either accompany or follow moments of incomprehension of the recording. If this frustration is not confronted and in some way dealt with, the student will leave the listening comprehension lesson with a negative assessment of their listening abilities, thus providing an obstacle (in the form of a lowered level of confidence) to future progress in listening. It is important to acknowledge that this level of frustration is a normal, and therefore acceptable, feeling. It is also vital however to use the techniques described above to help students move away from frustration towards familiarity and comfort.

11. Conclusion

We should claim for pedagogy those parts of listening that we have hitherto ignored or avoided. ICT allows us to abandon our pessimism and reliance on osmosis improve our teaching of listening immeasurably. We can bring everyday speech into the classroom, tame it and learn from it without de-contextualising it, and while preserving those characteristics which most distinguish it from the written language. ICT also allows us to observe facts about everyday speech that most traditional phonology does not care to recognise, and most traditional phonetics does not see as being its responsibility to explain. ICT enables teachers to pre-empt academia, to offer direct engagement with the infinite variety of everyday speech which the teaching and learning of listening has for so long been denied.

Bibliography

Anderson, A. and T. Lynch (1988) *Listening*. Oxford: Oxford University Press.

Brazil, D. (1994) *Pronunciation for Advanced Learners of English*. Cambridge: Cambridge University Press.

Brazil, D. (1997) *The Communicative Value of Intonation in English*. (2nd edn) Cambridge: Cambridge University Press.

Brown, G. (1990) *Listening to Spoken English*. (2nd edn) London and New York: Longman.

Cauldwell, R.T. (1996) 'Direct encounters with fast speech on CD Audio to teach listening'. *System*, 24.4, 521–8.

Cauldwell, R.T. (1997) *Voices in the University.* [Cassette and booklet]. Birmingham: The University of Birmingham.

Goh, C. (1997) 'Metacognitive awareness and second language listeners'. *ELT Journal*, 51.4, 361–9.

Harmer, J. (1991) *The Practice of English Language Teaching.* (2nd edn) London and New York: Longman.

Helgesen, M. and S. Brown (1994) *Active Listening: Building.* Cambridge: Cambridge University Press.

Jenkins, J. (2001) *The Phonology of English as an International Language.* Oxford: Oxford University Press.

McCarthy, M. (1998) *Spoken Language and Applied Linguistics.* Cambridge: Cambridge University Press.

Richards, J.C. (1985) *The Context of Language Teaching.* Cambridge: Cambridge University Press.

Rost, M. (1990) *Listening in Language Learning.* London and New York: Longman.

White, G. (1987) 'The teaching of listening comprehension to learners of English as a Foreign Language: A survey'. M. Litt. dissertation, University of Edinburgh.

Index

Printed in the United Kingdom
by Lightning Source UK Ltd.
101526UKS00001B/130-330